Q & A SERIES
EVIDENCE

FIFTH EDITION

Cavendish
Publishing
Limited

London • Sydney • Portland, Oregon

Q & A SERIES
EVIDENCE

FIFTH EDITION

Christopher Allen, LLM, PhD
Barrister, Senior Lecturer
Inns of Court School of Law
City University

Cavendish
Publishing
Limited

London • Sydney • Portland, Oregon

Fifth edition first published in Great Britain 2003 by
Cavendish Publishing Limited, The Glass House,
Wharton Street, London WC1X 9PX, United Kingdom
Telephone: + 44 (0)20 7278 8000   Facsimile: + 44 (0)20 7278 8080
Email: info@cavendishpublishing.com
Website: www.cavendishpublishing.com

Published in the United States by Cavendish Publishing
c/o International Specialized Book Services,
5804 NE Hassalo Street, Portland,
Oregon 97213-3644, USA

Published in Australia by Cavendish Publishing (Australia) Pty Ltd
3/303 Barrenjoey Road, Newport, NSW 2106, Australia

© Allen, CJW	2003
First edition	1994
Second edition	1996
Third edition	1998
Fourth edition	2000
Fifth edition	2003

British Library Cataloguing in Publication Data
Allen, Christopher, 1944–
Evidence – 5th ed – (Q&A series)
1 Evidence (law) – England – Examinations, questions, etc
2 Evidence (law) – Wales – Examinations, questions, etc
I Title
345.4'2'06

Library of Congress Cataloguing in Publication Data
Data available

ISBN 1-85941-736-1

1 3 5 7 9 10 8 6 4 2

Printed and bound in Great Britain

PREFACE

A reviewer of the first edition of John Pitt Taylor's *Treatise on the Law of Evidence* (1848) described the writer's subject as one:

> ... that peculiarly requires to be read in the spirit rather of the philosopher than of the mere lawyer. It has the unchanging laws of nature and reason for its foundation; it is less liable to the infringements of legislation; there is less of reference to cases, and more of principle, than in almost any other subject to which the studies of the lawyer extend; and in its practical application he is almost always obliged to adduce the principle in support of his argument, instead of finding refuge for fallacy within the all-compassing defence of cases.

This was no idiosyncrasy. In 1834, Phillip Williams KC, the Vinerian Professor at Oxford, had strongly recommended to law students the study of divines and ethical writers as furnishing to an advocate some of the best specimens not only of style but of legal argument. He made special reference to the writings of Isaac Barrow, the 17th century English mathematician, and divine, because of 'the models they offer for the investigation of truth, in the application of the rules of evidence'.

That was one perspective. By 1861, Fitzjames Stephen was commenting that:

> The law of England in the present day may be not altogether unfairly described as a mass of details which no memory can embrace, and which hardly any understanding can reduce under the heads to which they properly belong ...

But evidence law, particularly criminal evidence, was slow to follow this pattern. True, for a considerable part of the 19th century, a body of exclusionary rules made incompetent as witnesses many who were in the best position to give an account of the facts in dispute. But it was not until the advent of the Court of Criminal Appeal in 1907 that evidence law can truly be said to have become rule based. The technicalities of similar fact evidence before *Boardman* were, for example, wholly unknown in the 19th century, when argument in such cases turned on broad questions of relevancy.

Whether or not this development was of advantage to defendants is arguable. What is certain is that it made learning evidence law a rebarbative chore.

Now, the balance is beginning to be redressed. Despite the ever-growing incursion of statute law, the study of evidence is quite often not the banausic task that it once was. It is coming increasingly to be recognised that a lawyer who deals with evidence is not going to be able to solve all, or even the majority, of his problems by looking at a textbook. His primary job is to tackle problems of proof and, as Thayer said, 'the law has no mandamus to the logical faculty'. This is reflected in the problem questions found in evidence examinations of all kinds, where the ability to reason with facts is a prerequisite for the application of law. We realise, with a start, that the writers of the first half of the 19th century have something to say to us.

The problem questions and answers which appear in the chapters that follow reflect this development. But as well as being able to deal with facts, some ability to deal with theory is required of the law student. As long ago as 1851, a leading article in *The Times* pointed out that legal education should not be restricted to 'mere technical knowledge', but should treat law 'as a liberal science reducible to true principles, pointing out its shortcomings and anticipating its improvements'. Those who like to imagine that there are two distinct entities called 'practical' and 'academic' legal education might care to reflect that they are out of date by over 150 years.

Such a distinction would be particularly absurd in the teaching of evidence law. Just as the object of problem questions is to test a candidate's ability to reason with facts and legal principles, so the object of the essay questions in the examination is to give candidates an opportunity for reasoning with ideas. A creative lawyer – the only sort worth having – must be able to do both. But some wider reading is necessary to tackle an essay question effectively. In the bibliography I have listed the main works to which I have referred; I hope that this will be a useful starting point for further reading.

Since the last edition of this book, case law has been developing rapidly, and many answers have had to take this into account. In particular, the influence of the Human Rights Act 1998 has been experienced in several topics, including reversal of the burden of proof in criminal trials, the exclusion of improperly obtained evidence, and the operation of s 41 of the Criminal Justice and Public Order Act 1994. There have also been important developments affecting identification evidence, the Criminal Evidence Act 1898, s 78(1) of the Police and Criminal Evidence Act 1984, and s 34 of the Criminal Justice and Public Order Act 1994. As in the last edition, I have assumed the Youth Justice and Criminal Evidence Act 1999 to be fully implemented.

I hope that this book may be of value as a way of achieving an overall view of a subject that all too often can appear to be only a gallimaufry. The emphasis on criminal evidence is intentional; it is here that the subject is most lively and this is reflected in examination questions. I hope that the book may also be a means of revision, and a guide in the practice of answering examination questions. I considered dedicating it 'to those who have better things to do', but gravitas prevailed. I like to think, though, that it will be helpful not only to those whose devotion to their mistress the law is total, but to those who spread their favours more widely: to student poets and musicians, to actors and oarsmen and to many more. Nor do I forget those mature students, often with widely different concerns in their daily work, whose opportunity for study is inevitably limited. To all my readers I wish enjoyment and success.

CJWA
Gray's Inn
October 2002

CONTENTS

TABLE OF CASES

TABLE OF STATUTES

CHAPTER 1

BASIC CONCEPTS

Introduction

The biggest obstacle to doing well in an evidence examination is failure to realise that this is very largely a practical subject, and that when you are faced with a problem question you need to think as carefully about the facts as about the law – perhaps even more carefully, because quite often what you think about the facts will affect the legal position. It would therefore be a good idea to make it a rule that you think about a problem question first as a story.

Somebody is trying to prove something. How is he doing this? First, he should have in mind a clear idea of what is to be proved. Suppose we take a famous murder trial which took place in 1910 – that of Dr Crippen. The prosecution was trying to prove that Crippen had murdered his wife. The story, according to them, was that Crippen had fallen in love with his young secretary, Ethel Le Neve, and had decided to kill his wife so as to leave him free to marry Ethel. One night, therefore, he put poison in a glass of stout – his wife's regular nightcap. The poison might have been sufficient to kill her, or it might merely have rendered her unconscious. At any rate, by the time Crippen had finished with the body she must have been dead. According to the prosecution, he cut the flesh from the bones and buried it in pieces in the cellar of the house where they lived. He burned the bones, and the head was never found. To explain his wife's absence, he told friends at first that she was staying with relations. Later, when the police began to make inquiries, he told them that she had left him and that he had been too embarrassed to tell people this. Crippen had not yet been arrested, and shortly after his interview with the police, he hurriedly left the country with Ethel Le Neve. Meanwhile, the police dug up the cellar floor and discovered the human remains that had been buried there. Crippen was followed and brought back to England to stand trial.

You know, of course, what constitutes murder in English law. But from the standpoint of someone studying evidence, you must now decide precisely what it was that the prosecution had to prove in this particular case.

The first thing they had to prove was that Mrs Crippen was dead. Crippen maintained throughout that his wife had left him and that he knew nothing of the remains in the cellar. It was therefore necessary for the prosecution to establish that the remains were those of Mrs Crippen. They had also to show that her husband had killed her intentionally.

It is at this stage that the prosecution had to start thinking carefully in terms of relevance. Ideally, each item of evidence they presented should have had a probative job to do in the overall task of proving that Crippen had murdered his wife. For example, by proving that Mrs Crippen had had the mark of an operation on her body, and by showing that one of the pieces of buried flesh had the same mark, the prosecution was able to establish that the remains in the cellar were those of Mrs Crippen and that therefore she was in fact dead.

The evidence of Crippen's flight was also relevant, but it's worth pausing to consider why this was so. What probative job did this item of evidence do for the prosecution? The prosecution suggested that it showed guilty knowledge. But why should it do that? One answer is that people who suddenly leave the country when the police are making inquiries about them are likely to do so because they fear that their criminal activities are about to be discovered.

Notice two important points at this stage. The first is that if you press sufficiently the question why an item of evidence is relevant, your explanation will often take the form of a generalisation about the way things are in the world *which itself may or may not be true.* I tried to make my explanatory generalisation about people who run away appear true by using the words/'are likely to do so'. It leaves room for alternative explanations – they may be innocent but fear that the police will frame them; they may have a rich aunt dying in Brazil – but I put my explanation forward as one that is likely. If I am right in this, it follows that the evidence of the flight was relevant, admissible and had significant probative weight.

Now, let's look at a question of relevance in another famous murder case. Edith Thompson and her husband were not very happily married. They took in a young lodger, Freddie Bywaters. One night, when Mr and Mrs Thompson were walking home, Freddie sprang out from a place where he had been waiting and stabbed Mr Thompson to death. But the prosecution story was that Freddie was not the only culprit. He and Edith, it was alleged, were having an affair, and she had plotted the murder with him and had encouraged him to carry it out.

Among the many items of evidence relied on at trial by the prosecution was the disparity in age between Freddie and Edith. She was 28 years old at the time of the murder; he was only 20. What was the relevance of this? What probative job did this information do? At the time, nobody seems to have had any clear thoughts on the matter. But we need to ask this question: what generalisation about the way things are in the world has to be true for this item of evidence to be relevant? Here is a suggestion: 'In a sexual relationship, an older woman is likely to dominate a younger man.' That, if true, would help the prosecution because it would add to the probability that

Edith persuaded Freddie to murder Mr Thompson. But *is* it true? If it is not true, and no satisfactory substitute can be found, then surely the evidence is irrelevant, and so inadmissible. (See Twining, W, *Theories of Evidence: Bentham and Wigmore*, 1985, pp 143–44; and Twining, W, *Rethinking Evidence: Exploratory Essays*, 1994, pp 290–93.)

This is the sort of problem that classically arises in relation to what is known as 'similar fact evidence'. More will be said later on that subject (see Chapter 8), but it is worth emphasising now that in all such cases, you should be asking the following two vital questions. What is the probative job that this bit of evidence is being put forward to do? What generalisation about the way things are in the world has to be true for this evidence to be able to do that job?

I said earlier that there were two important points to be made about the sort of answer which I suggested to the question of why evidence of Crippen's flight was relevant at his trial. One was the point which I have just been making about the *form* the answer takes – that of a generalisation. The second important point is this. The weaker a generalisation is, the more likely it is to be true. But the weaker the generalisation, the less probative weight will attach to the item of evidence in question. This may be very important where admissibility depends on assessing the probative weight of a piece of evidence and the improperly prejudicial effect that it might have on a jury if they heard it (see, generally, the law relating to similar fact evidence). For example, some cats are Siamese. I have three cats. But, this is not much evidence that I have a Siamese cat. One or more of them *may* be a Siamese, but the likelihood is not great because there are many other breeds, as well as non-pedigree cats.

Later, you will see the importance in other areas of evidence law of the question: what is the probative job that this item of evidence is put forward to do? (Hearsay is a particularly good example. See Chapters 4 and 5.) But being able to answer this question, and being able to say why an item of evidence is relevant by pointing to an appropriate generalisation, can be done only if you have first thought carefully about the *story* the examiner is telling you in the particular problem question.

If you get a question directly on relevance in the examination, it will almost certainly be an essay question involving theory, and I have tried in the answer to Question 1 to give some idea of how such an essay might be tackled. But you don't *have* to be able to write an answer to a theoretical question about relevance to do well in an examination. What you *do* have to be able to do is understand how the idea *works*.

As well as relevance, there are a few other basic concepts which you ought to know about; I have referred to these in the Checklist and you should find them adequately dealt with in your textbook. You will find that this is a subject that has attracted quite a complicated terminology, about the use of which there is not complete agreement on the part of either judges or writers. A lot of this terminology can in practice be avoided, but you should take care to understand how the writer of the textbook you are using employs his terminology, and you should be particularly careful when reading cases to make sure that you understand what a particular judge is getting at by the language he uses.

Checklist

Students should be familiar with the following areas:

- relevance;
- admissibility;
- what facts are in issue in criminal cases;
- how to discover what facts are in issue in a civil case;
- formal admissions in civil and criminal cases;
- judicial notice.

Question 1

Is a concept of legal relevance useful in the law of evidence?

Answer plan

Begin by setting out the two different ways in which a legal concept can be 'useful': one is connected with what the law is, the other with what it ought to be. The question raises a classic problem on which the two great American writers on evidence, Thayer and Wigmore, had different views; these are outlined. Note that there are some cases where judges do appear to have laid down rules about what is or is not relevant. Note also the practice of the courts of rejecting evidence of only minimal weight on the ground that it is 'irrelevant'. But, the point is then made that none of this justifies acknowledging a concept of 'legal relevance' in existing law because:

- such a concept would be impossible to define; and
- it would be difficult to develop a body of case law on the subject.

In addition, such a concept would be undesirable because:

- if a body of case law could after all be developed, it would be cumbersome and restrictive;
- it would make it even more difficult than it is at present for the law to respond to changing conditions.

In summary, therefore, the essay is constructed as follows:

- two ways in which a legal concept can be 'useful';
- outline of the argument to be put forward;
- Thayer's rejection of 'legal relevance';
- Wigmore's contrary view;
- judicial decisions about relevance, for example, *DPP v Camplin* (1978); *DPP v Majewski* (1977);
- the connection made by courts between relevance and weight;
- apparent 'rules' about relevance: *Grant* (1996); *Halpin* (1996); *Guney* (1998);
- difficulties presented by 'legal relevance'.

Answer

A legal concept may be useful either because it helps us to understand the law as it is, or because if it were to be introduced, it would improve the state of the law. I shall argue that a concept of legal relevance is not to be found in the existing state of the law and that it would not be useful to introduce it.

Thayer defined the law of evidence as 'a set of rules and principles affecting judicial investigations into questions of fact', but he pointed out that these rules and principles do not regulate the process of reasoning, save to the extent of helping to select the factual material upon which the processes of reasoning are to operate. Chiefly, in addition to prescribing the manner of presenting evidence and fixing the qualifications and privileges of witnesses, these rules and principles determine what classes of things shall not be received in evidence. There is one principle of exclusion, however, which Thayer described as not so much a rule of evidence as a presupposition involved in the very conception of a rational system of evidence: this was the principle which forbids receiving anything irrelevant.[1] But the law, according to Thayer, furnishes no test of relevance. For this, it tacitly refers to logic and general experience, the principles of which are presumed to be known.

Wigmore, on the other hand, questioned the idea that the law furnished no test of relevance. He argued that although relevance is originally a matter of logic and common sense, there are still many instances in which the evidence of particular facts as bearing on particular issues has been so often the subject of discussion in courts of law, and so often ruled upon, that the united logic of a great many judges and lawyers may be said to furnish evidence of the sense common to a great many individuals, and so to acquire the authority of law. It is thus proper, he argued, to talk of legal relevance.

It is certainly the case that in some instances, judges have laid down rules about what is relevant or irrelevant. For example, they have decided that age and sex are always relevant when considering the defence of provocation (*DPP v Camplin* (1978)). And intoxication is, as a matter of law, irrelevant in considering whether the *mens rea* for a crime of basic intent was present (*DPP v Majewski* (1977)).

But, apart from specific rules such as these, it is necessary to take into account the practice of the courts of rejecting evidence that has minimal weight on the ground that it is 'irrelevant'. Is this because the evidence falls short of the minimum requirement of something which can be called 'legal relevance'? There are good reasons why data of very slight weight should be excluded. Doing justice according to law is not the same as doing a piece of historical research. Concessions have to be made to what Justice Holmes referred to as 'the shortness of life', as well as to the financial resources of the litigants or the legal aid fund. Moreover, if the field of judicial inquiry were too wide, it might make decisions more unreliable because a mass of evidence would more readily lead to confusion.[2]

It is also possible for the courts to develop something that can appear at first glance to be a rule about relevance in a particular type of situation, but which is really something else. Over the last few years, there has been a cluster of cases concerned with the precise significance to be attached to the discovery of large sums of cash in the possession of persons charged with possession of drugs with intent to supply. In one of these cases, *Grant* (1996), it was said in the Court of Appeal that if there was any possible reason other than drug dealing for the defendant's possession of cash, the finding of the cash was to be treated as irrelevant, and juries should be so directed. And, in *Halpin* (1996), the Court of Appeal said that evidence of a defendant's possession of large amounts of money, or of his extravagant lifestyle, could not be relevant where the issue in the case was possession, rather than intent to supply. However, this was later rejected in *Guney* (1998), where the Court of Appeal said that although evidence of cash or lifestyle might only rarely be relevant where there was a charge of simple possession of drugs, such evidence could not be excluded as irrelevant as a matter of law. The relevance of any item of evidence is to be decided 'not on abstract legal theory but on the circumstances of each individual case' (see also *Griffiths* (1998)). It appears that the courts, at any rate, are reluctant to acknowledge a concept of 'legal relevance', higher and stricter than logical relevance. In fact, two main difficulties lie in the way of such development.

The first is that a concept of this kind would defy definition. The second is that since each case would be decided on its own facts, there would be considerable difficulty in developing a body of case law about what was legally relevant. The examples cited earlier of *DPP v Camplin* and *DPP v Majewski* are better seen as defining the substantive law in relation to particular offences than in saying something about a concept called 'legal relevance'.[3]

Not only does there seem to be little support for the proposition that a concept of legal relevance – despite the language of some judges – can be found in the law; there appear to be good reasons why such a concept should not be recognised.

In the first place, there is an inherent conflict between a theory that all logically relevant evidence should be admitted unless excluded by a clear ground of policy, and a theory of legal relevance, which would require a minimum quantity of probative value for each item of evidence in any particular case. There is a danger that a concept of legal relevance, if consistently applied, would exclude logically relevant evidence unless legal precedent authorised its admission. If, despite difficulties, a body of case law were to develop, it would give rise to a large number of cumbersome rules and exceptions.

The second reason why a concept of legal relevance ought not to be recognised is that to fix relevance in a straitjacket of case law would make it even more difficult than it already is to adapt the law to changing circumstances.

Necessarily, judges' decisions about relevance reflect the prevailing value judgments of the society in which they live. Relevance can become a useful instrument for discarding arguments and evidence that challenge important, though perhaps unexpressed, values. Thus, in the 19th century, the courts upheld a notion of freedom of contract which allowed them to argue that an aggrieved worker could have protected his position by insisting on an appropriate contractual stipulation. Evidence of inequality of bargaining power would have been ruled 'irrelevant'. That what is relevant depends on the basic assumptions of a particular society becomes even clearer when one considers the evidential significance of marks on the bodies of those formerly suspected of witchcraft, or of the appearance in their vicinity of such creatures as a cat, a toad or a wasp.[4]

No one, of course, could argue a case from a standpoint wholly outside the beliefs of his own society. And it may well be that arguments about relevance will be constrained by the way in which the substantive law is defined. What one can reasonably hope is that the ability to argue from a critical standpoint in particular cases should not be easily frustrated. A further obstacle in the way of such arguments would be likely to emerge if a concept of legal relevance were to become fully developed in the law of evidence.[5]

Notes

1   Cf *Turner* (1975) *per* Lawton LJ: 'Relevance, however, does not result in evidence being admissible: it is a condition precedent to admissibility.'

2   Cf the observations of Lord Bridge in *Blastland* (1986).

3   But see s 41 of the Youth Justice and Criminal Evidence Act 1999. It looks very much as if the government is accepting that some facts may be *logically* relevant, but, to preserve a 'balance' between the interests of the complainant and the defendant, they are not allowed to be *legally* relevant.

4   Thomas, K, *Religion and the Decline of Magic*, 1971, p 530.

5   See Thayer, JB, *A Preliminary Treatise on Evidence at the Common Law*, 1898, Chapter 6; James, GF, 'Relevancy, probability and the law' (1941) 29 California L Rev 689, pp 689–705; Trautman, HL, 'Logical or legal relevancy – a conflict in theory' (1952) 5 Vanderbilt L Rev 385, pp 385–413; Weyrauch, WO, 'Law as mask – legal ritual and relevance' (1978) 66 California L Rev 699, pp 699–726.

Question 2

How satisfactory is the law on judicial notice?

Answer plan

The law on this subject is in a mess – albeit an interesting one. The following points should be made:

• the distinction (if any) between taking judicial notice and using local or special knowledge;

• the different rationales that have been suggested for judicial notice;

• the effect of those rationales on the way the law is viewed;

- the failure of English law to commit itself unequivocally to a single rationale;
- the ambiguity of the relationship between judicial notice and evidence.

Answer

The problem with the law of judicial notice is that it is underdeveloped. As a result of this, there is confusion about the principles on which it rests and about its scope.

There is confusion about its scope because it is unclear whether a distinction should be made between taking judicial notice and using special or local knowledge. In *Wetherall v Harrison* (1976), the Divisional Court held that magistrates were entitled to use their own special or local knowledge when trying cases, but Lord Widgery CJ saw this as a necessary concession to the layman's inability to exclude such factors from his deliberations. He thought that, in this respect, magistrates were unlike trained judges, and were more like members of a jury. In line with this approach, the Divisional Court in *Bowman v DPP* (1990) said that a bench of magistrates using its local knowledge of a particular piece of land was not taking 'judicial notice'. But in *Mullen v Hackney LBC* (1997), the Court of Appeal held that a county court judge had been entitled to take judicial notice of his own special or local knowledge about the defendant council's failure to honour undertakings given to the court in other cases. This decision was almost certainly wrong. There is a line of cases to the effect that county court judges can rely on their own local knowledge 'properly and within reasonable limits': see, for example, *Reynolds v Llanelly Tinplate Co Ltd* (1948). But all these cases were decided under the Workmen's Compensation Acts, under which the county court judge sat as an arbitrator. There is no doubt that an arbitrator can, in certain circumstances, make use of his own knowledge and experience to determine issues in dispute between the parties to the arbitration, without hearing expert evidence. This was held to be within the judge's powers under those Acts: see, for example, *Peart v Bolckow Vaughan & Co Ltd* (1925). But the cases do not establish that county court judges sitting in any other capacity have the same freedom that they had as arbitrators in workmen's compensation cases. Nor do those cases suggest that judges were taking 'judicial notice' of anything.

There are two main theories about the rationale of judicial notice. On one view, it is a device for filtering out evidence about matters that are really unarguable. If you regard judicial notice in this light, you will tend to want its scope to be restricted to notorious, or readily ascertainable facts; its application to be mandatory rather than discretionary; and the effect of its application conclusive.[1]

Another view is that judicial notice is simply a labour saving device in litigation. If seen in this way, its scope can be wider, and its application discretionary. Its effect can even be defeasible in the light of further evidence.[2] A controversial variant of this view is that any process of judicial reasoning about facts assumes the truth of a mass of material that has not been formally proved. For example, a judge assumes that trains run on rails, that France is outside the United Kingdom, and that there is a law of gravity. If this analysis is right, 'the tacit applications of the doctrine of judicial notice are more numerous and more important than the express ones'.[3] But this is a controversial view. Others have acknowledged that both judges and juries must make use of general knowledge to interpret evidence. But, they argue, this is not a question of judicial notice; it is the tribunal relying on its own experience of the ordinary course of human affairs.[4]

A limited view of judicial notice should require mandatory application. This line has been taken in cases relating to political and constitutional matters. For example, in *Duff Development Co Ltd v Government of Kelantan* (1924), the House of Lords said that where the question of the sovereignty of a foreign state is in issue, it is the practice of the courts to treat as conclusive the information that they obtain on the matter from a Secretary of State. But in other cases, the courts have taken the view that they have a discretion whether or not to take judicial notice of a particular fact. In *George v Davies* (1911), for example, it was tacitly accepted by the Divisional Court that a judge had a discretion to decide whether to take judicial notice of an employment custom that had been established by evidence in earlier cases.

A further problem with judicial notice is its relationship to evidence. Where judicial notice is taken without inquiry, for example, that cats are kept for domestic purposes (*Nye v Niblett* (1918)) or that people who go to hotels do not like having their nights disturbed (*Andreae v Selfridge & Co Ltd* (1938)), it is clear that no process of proof is involved, because no material containing information is produced by either party. But is judicial notice after inquiry based on a process of proof? The opinions of judges have been divided. In *McQuaker v Goddard* (1940), at least one member of the Court of Appeal (Clauson LJ) took the view that a judge was entitled to disregard the rules of evidence and look at materials that would otherwise have been inadmissible, on the basis that he was merely 'refreshing his memory' about the ordinary course of nature – a subject of which, by a legal fiction, judges had complete knowledge.

It is clearly unsatisfactory to have a situation where it is unclear whether rules about admissibility are going to be applied or not. The truth of the matter is that, in principle, scope and effect, the law about judicial notice is underdeveloped and ripe for clarification.

Notes

1   Morgan, EM, *Some Problems of Proof under the Anglo-American System of Litigation*, 1956, p 42.

2   Thayer, JB, *A Preliminary Treatise on Evidence at the Common Law*, 1898, p 278.

3   Tapper, C, *Cross & Tapper on Evidence*, 9th edn, 1999, p 77.

4   See, for example, Eggleston, R (Sir), *Evidence, Proof and Probability*, 2nd edn, 1983, pp 143–44.

CHAPTER 2

BURDEN AND STANDARD OF PROOF

Introduction

The burden and the standard of proof are matters that must be kept distinct, and judges have a duty to direct the jury in respect of each of them. Problems are therefore most likely to arise in criminal jury trials because a wrong direction, or no direction at all, could provide a successful ground of appeal.

You must be able to distinguish between a legal and an evidential burden. The latter is not strictly a burden *of proof* at all. It is best seen as a rule of common sense which says that there must be *some* evidence for a particular issue to become a live one, so that it is fit for consideration by a jury or other tribunal of fact. Because of this, whether an evidential burden has been satisfied or not in a jury trial is a matter for the judge alone, and consequently there should never be a need to refer to it in a summing up.

In civil cases, it will generally be clear from the statements of case where the burden of proof lies. Although you will find fascinating cases where it wasn't clear at all discussed in the textbooks, don't get bogged down with them when you first approach this topic.

It is important to understand why in criminal cases it is impossible to say for certain when the well known *Woolmington* principle will *not* apply. As you will see from the answer to Question 3, there can be no simple list of exceptions. This popular essay topic can be presented in many forms. All the examiner has to do is reproduce a pro-defence excerpt from Lord Sankey's speech and either ask the sort of question which appears below, or simply say 'Discuss'. Obviously, you must read any question carefully, but if you see something on these lines in the examination paper, it is likely that you are being asked to write about this problem.

The *standard* of proof is less likely to occur as an essay topic because it raises too many theoretical issues. For example, should we reduce the standard of proof in (some) criminal cases if there were to be a significant increase in a particularly unpleasant type of crime? Does it make sense to talk of 'standards' of proof at all? Aren't things either proved or not, more or less easily, depending upon their inherent probability? All good fun, but not to be attempted in the examination if you haven't studied these problems as part of your course.

What you may get is a 'dud direction' question, covering both burden and standard of proof, where you are asked to examine an excerpt from a summing up and say whether there are grounds for appeal. It is important to remember that there is no magic form of words about either the burden or standard of proof that *must* be used, though judges are wise to follow one of the two accepted forms and it is clear that certain directions will not suffice. It's a good idea to look at the cases which have approved some forms of words so as to get their general sense and compare those with cases where there was held to have been a misdirection.

It is particularly important to remember that the legal burden of proof remains with the prosecution where defences such as provocation, self-defence, duress, non-insane automatism and alibi are in issue. In cases where the defendant *does* have the legal burden of proving something, that burden will be discharged if the civil standard of proof is satisfied. Remember also that where there is a burden on the defence on a particular issue, there cannot also be a burden on the prosecution on that same issue. Sometimes, candidates try to have the best of both worlds and say, for example, that the defence in an offensive weapon case has to prove on the balance of probabilities that there was a reasonable excuse, and the prosecution has to prove beyond reasonable doubt that there was not. This is gibberish.

Checklist

Students should be familiar with the following areas:

- the distinction between the burden and standard of proof;
- the meaning of 'evidential burden';
- factors affecting the burden of proof in civil cases;
- the burden of proof in criminal cases;
- the standard of proof in civil and criminal cases.

Question 3

'No matter what the charge or where the trial, the principle that the prosecution must prove the guilt of the prisoner is part of the common law of England and no attempt to whittle it down can be entertained.'

To what extent has this principle been maintained in the years following *Woolmington v DPP*?

Answer plan

Something has already been said about this topic in the Introduction. The first paragraph should put the quotation in context and fill an important gap by referring to what Lord Sankey said about exceptions. The essay proceeds as follows:

- examples of post-*Woolmington* express statutory exceptions;
- s 101 of the Magistrates' Courts Act 1980 – its place in the *Woolmington* story; its content; its extent;
- the haphazard application of s 101;
- the failed attempt to secure greater certainty in *Edwards*;
- the effect of *Hunt*;
- the impact of the Human Rights Act 1998.

Answer

In his speech in *Woolmington v DPP*, Lord Sankey said that this principle was subject to the defence of insanity and subject also to any statutory exceptions. It seems clear that this was a reference to both express and implied exceptions. There were at the time several long standing decisions which interpreted certain statutes as impliedly putting a burden on the defence.[1]

A statutory provision which has considerable potential for narrowing the scope of Lord Sankey's principle is s 101 of the Magistrates' Courts Act 1980, though it is right to point out that a similar provision was in force when *Woolmington* was decided and so might be thought to have been covered by Lord Sankey's reference to statutory exceptions.[2] On its wording, s 101 applies only to summary trials, but in *Hunt* (1987), the House of Lords held that it reflects the common law rule about the incidence of the burden of proof in trials on indictment.

The problem with this section is that the courts have operated it in such a haphazard way that it is impossible to say to what extent it limits Lord Sankey's principle. Two Highways Act cases illustrate the point. In *Gatland v Metropolitan Police Commissioner* (1968), the Divisional Court had to interpret a provision of the Highways Act 1959 under which it was an offence, 'If a person, without lawful authority or excuse, deposits any thing whatever on a highway' (s 140). The court held that the effect of the predecessor of s 101 was that it was for the accused to prove the lawful authority or excuse. But another section of the Highways Act provided that it was an offence 'if a person, without lawful authority or excuse, in any way wilfully obstructs' a highway (s 121(1)). In *Nagy v Weston* (1965), the Divisional Court held, without referring to the predecessor of s 101, that it was for the prosecution to prove that there was no lawful authority or reasonable excuse.

Section 101 is also ignored in the interpretation of legislation relating to drinking and driving. This makes it an offence to fail 'without reasonable excuse' to provide a specimen of breath or laboratory specimen (ss 6(4) and 7(6) of the Road Traffic Act 1988). Although the courts have taken a strict view of what is a reasonable excuse, they have held, without reference to s 101, that the accused bears an evidential burden only, so that where a defence of reasonable excuse is raised, it is for the prosecution to negative it (*Cotgrove v Cooney* (1987)).

Section 101 is therefore a very uncertain guide to whether a burden will be held to fall on an accused. In *Edwards* (1975), it was argued for the appellant that at common law, the burden of proving an exception, exemption, proviso, excuse or qualification is borne by the accused only if the facts constituting it are peculiarly within his own knowledge. This might, if accepted, have gone some way towards producing greater certainty, but the Court of Appeal rejected this submission.

The House of Lords in *Hunt* may be said to have widened still further the scope for operating outside Lord Sankey's principle. Although Lord Griffiths said that Parliament can never lightly be taken to have intended to impose on an accused an onerous duty to prove his innocence, and that a court should be very slow to draw such an inference from the language of a statute, the House of Lords nevertheless laid down wide principles of construction. In the final analysis, it was said, each case must turn on the construction of the particular piece of legislation with which it was concerned in order to determine whether the defence was an exception within s 101. Moreover, in construing an enactment to determine where the burden of proof lies, the court is not restricted to the form or wording of the statutory provision, but is entitled to have regard to matters of policy, although these were said to include the ease or difficulty that the respective parties would encounter in discharging the burden.

There are also express statutory provisions which place a burden of proof on the defendant. However, both implied and express burdens must now be considered in the light of the Human Rights Act 1998 and Art 6(2) of the European Convention on Human Rights. The latter provides that everyone charged with a criminal offence shall be presumed innocent until proved guilty according to law. The European Court of Human Rights has held that this does not amount to an absolute prohibition on reverse burdens. The interests of the individual have to be balanced against those of society, and in *DPP ex p Kebilene* (2000), Lord Hope suggested that it may be useful to consider three questions: (1) what does the prosecution have to prove in order to transfer the burden to the defendant?; (2) what is the nature of the burden on the defendant?; (3) what is the nature of the threat faced by society that the provision is designed to combat?

A good example of the effect of the Human Rights Act 1998 can be seen in the decision of the House of Lords in *Lambert* (2001), where it was held that s 28(2) of the Misuse of Drugs Act 1971, when interpreted in the light of s 3(1) of the Human Rights Act 1998, imposed only an evidential burden on a defendant and not, as had been previously thought, a legal burden. It is possible that this shows the beginning of a retreat from the imposition of legal burdens on defendants in criminal trials, but the significance of *Lambert* is not yet clear. Thus, in *L v DPP* (2002), the Divisional Court upheld the traditional interpretation of s 139 of the Criminal Justice Act 1988, saying that there was a strong public interest in bladed articles not being carried in public without good reason, and that it was not obviously offensive to the rights of the individual to require him to prove a good reason for carrying one.

The conclusion must be that it does not appear with any clarity to what extent Lord Sankey's principle has been maintained since the decision in *Woolmington*. It may be that the most objectionable feature of the law in this area is not that legal burdens are sometimes put on defendants, but that it is impossible to predict with any certainty whether a court will interpret a particular piece of legislation as imposing such a burden.

Notes

1 See the speech of Lord Griffiths in *Hunt* (1987).

2 Section 39(2) of the Summary Jurisdiction Act 1879. See, generally, Smith, JC, 'The presumption of innocence' (1987) 38 NILQ 223, pp 223–43.

Question 4

Answer all FOUR parts of this question:

(a) Alice was convicted of theft. In her summing up, the judge said to the jury: 'The prosecution brings this case and it is for the prosecution to prove it. Unless, having heard all the evidence, you are sure that the defendant is guilty, she must be acquitted.' Advise Alice whether she has grounds for appeal.

(b) Bertha was convicted of having an offensive weapon with her in a public place, contrary to s 1 of the Prevention of Crime Act 1953. In her summing up, the judge said to the jury: 'Members of the jury, it is not contested that this defendant had with her an offensive weapon in a public place. But she says she had it with her for her own protection. She has to satisfy you that that was a reasonable excuse for having the weapon with her, and unless you are satisfied of that, you must convict.' Advise Bertha whether she has grounds for appeal.

(c) Charlene is charged with murder. There is medical evidence suggesting that she is under a mental disability which renders her unfit to plead and stand trial. What is the law relating to the burden and standard of proof in this situation?

(d) Dora was convicted of wounding with intent to do grievous bodily harm. In her summing up, the judge said to the jury: 'The defence in this case is self-defence. That means that the defendant has an evidential burden, but no more, to satisfy you that what she says about acting in self-defence is more probable than not.' Advise Dora whether she has grounds for appeal.

Answer plan

It is very unlikely that you would get a whole question like this in the examination devoted to one area of law. But you can use this question to test your knowledge of the topic, and something like this could appear in the examination as part of a wider question.

Part (a) obviously deals with the burden and standard of proof. The question is whether the judge has directed the jury adequately. The answer is that she has, but note how you can show your knowledge effectively to the examiner when saying so. Without being at all irrelevant, the following points can be made:

• the need to provide a correct direction on both the burden and the standard of proof;

- the proper direction on the burden of proof;
- the application of that test to what was said in this case;
- the proper direction on the standard of proof;
- it is not a particular formula but the effect of the summing up as a whole that matters;
- *Kritz* (1950) and *Walters v R* (1969).

Don't forget to advise Alice – this is done in the final sentence.

Part (b) is a bit more complicated. You need to know about s 1 of the Prevention of Crime Act 1953, but this is a fairly well cited example of a statutory provision that expressly puts a burden of proof on the defendant. It is important to remember that a direction on the *burden* of proof and a direction on the *standard* of proof are two different things. The following points should be made:

- whether there has been a correct direction on the burden of proof;
- standard of proof where a burden is placed on a defendant in a criminal trial;
- ambiguity of the language used in Bertha's case.

Part (c) provides an example of the operation of different standards of proof, depending on which side raises the issue.

Part (d) requires you to make the following points:

- basic rule about burden of proof;
- self-defence available as a defence;
- no *legal* burden on the accused;
- the evidential burden.

Answer

(a) Every summing up should contain a correct direction on both the burden and the standard of proof (*Bentley (Deceased)* (2001)). Here, there is a direction on each. The judge has rightly told the jury, in effect, that the burden is on the prosecution. No particular form of words is necessary, and this is the clear sense of the words actually used. There has also been a correct direction on the standard of proof. Again, it is not the particular formula that matters, but the effect of the summing up (*Allan* (1969)). One of the well established forms of direction, however, is to tell the jury that in order to find the accused guilty they must be 'sure', or 'satisfied so that they feel sure' (*Kritz* (1950); *Walters v R* (1969)). Here, the former expression has been used. It is entirely adequate and Alice has no grounds for appeal on this part of the summing up.

(b) Section 1 of the Prevention of Crime Act 1953 provides a defence of reasonable excuse to a charge of having an offensive weapon in a public place, but the section places the burden of proving this defence on the accused. It would be possible to argue, following *Lambert* (2001), that the effect of s 1 is to impose only an evidential burden on defendants. But this interpretation is unlikely to be applied. In *L v DPP* (2002), the Divisional Court upheld the traditional interpretation of s 139 of the Criminal Justice Act 1988, saying that there was a strong public interest in bladed articles not being carried in public without good reason, and that it was not obviously offensive to the rights of the individual to require him to prove a good reason for carrying one. The same approach is very likely to be adopted towards having an offensive weapon in a public place. The judge has almost certainly got her direction on burden right. However, in all cases where the law puts a burden of proving something on a defendant, it can be discharged merely by proof on the balance of probabilities – the civil, rather than the criminal standard (*Carr-Briant* (1943)). What has happened here is that the judge has told the jury that Bertha has to 'satisfy' them that she had a reasonable excuse. But this is ambiguous, for it could refer either to the civil or to the higher criminal standard (*Hepworth* (1955)). Thus, the jury might have applied the wrong standard in deciding whether Bertha had made out her defence. Accordingly, she has a good ground of appeal.

(c) The answer depends on who raises the issue.[1] If the prosecution says that Charlene is under this disability and the defence disputes this, the burden of proof will be on the prosecution to satisfy the jury beyond reasonable doubt that its contention is correct (*Robertson* (1968)). If, on the other hand, it is the defence which puts forward this contention and the prosecution disagrees, the defence will have the burden of proof, but only to the civil standard – on a balance of probabilities (*Podola* (1960)).

(d) Where the defendant is charged with wounding with intent to cause grievous bodily harm, the burden of proof, as is usual in criminal cases, rests throughout on the prosecution. In certain circumstances, self-defence may be a defence to this charge, but the accused bears no legal burden on the issue. Thus, in *Lobell* (1957), where the appellant had been convicted on such a charge after the trial judge had directed the jury that it was for the defence to establish its plea of self-defence, the conviction was quashed on the ground that there had been a misdirection. What the defendant does have is an evidential burden, but this means no more than that he must be able to point to some evidence in the trial which makes self-defence a live issue for the jury's consideration. As Lord Morris put it in *Bratty v Attorney General for Northern Ireland* (1963), where the accused bears the evidential burden alone, he must adduce such evidence as would, if believed and left uncontradicted, induce a reasonable doubt in the mind of the jury as to whether his version might not be true.[2]

Whether a party has discharged an evidential, as opposed to a legal, burden is a matter for the judge and not the jury. It was therefore wrong of the judge to refer to the evidential burden in her summing up. If possible, it was even more wrong to refer in that connection to the standard of proof which is applicable where a defendant has a *legal* burden. The jury have been misled, and Dora has a good ground of appeal.

Notes

1   Either the prosecution or the defence may do so: see s 4(1) of the Criminal Procedure (Insanity) Act 1964.

2   Although Lord Morris used the word 'adduce', this does not mean that the defendant must call such evidence himself. It could be obtained from prosecution witnesses under cross-examination, or it might even emerge during their examination-in-chief.

Question 5

Annie hired a removal firm, XY & Co, to move the contents of her house in Plymouth to a house which she had bought in Worcester. The removal van and all its contents were destroyed by fire in a layby just outside Exeter. Some time after the loss, Annie was told by an employee of XY & Co that the van had been deliberately set on fire so that XY & Co could claim from their insurers for its loss.

Annie is suing XY & Co for the value of her destroyed property, which she estimates to be £250,000. She claims first in respect of their deliberate destruction by the defendants; alternatively, she alleges that they were destroyed by reason of the defendants' negligence. By their defence, XY & Co deny deliberately setting fire to the van and plead that their contract with Annie had an exclusion clause, which said that they would not be liable for loss by fire provided that their servants were not negligent. They also plead that it was a term of the contract that they would not be liable for any loss in excess of £5,000. Annie says that she never agreed to this term and that XY & Co are liable for the full loss.

Discuss the burden and standard of proof in relation to the issues that arise.

Answer plan

The first step is to sort out what the issues are likely to be. A rough and ready way of doing this is to think of what matters each side would have to prove in order to win, assuming there is no response from their opponents.

Annie must prove the existence of the agreement with the defendants for the carriage of her goods, the consignment of her goods to the defendants in accordance with the agreement, the fact that non-delivery was due to deliberate destruction of the goods by the defendants, and the amount of the loss. In view of the exclusion clause, the burden of proof in relation to negligence is uncertain.

The defendants must prove the existence of the exclusion clause, and, if need be, that the loss falls within it. They may also have to prove that they exercised all proper care of the goods while they were in their possession. In addition, they will have to show that the provision limiting their liability to £5,000 was part of the contract.

Broadly speaking, it will be seen that this ties in with the maxim that he who asserts must prove, but there are problems with the interpretation of the exclusion clause which require discussion of bailment.

The allegation of arson raises the question of the standard to be applied where a crime is alleged in a civil action.

Answer

Although the burden of proof in any particular case depends on the circumstances under which the claim arises, in a civil action, the burden normally lies on the party who affirms something to be the case, and not upon the party who makes a denial. As Viscount Maugham said in *Constantine (Joseph) Steamship Line Ltd v Imperial Smelting Corp Ltd* (1942), it is 'an ancient rule founded on considerations of good sense and it should not be departed from without strong reasons'.

Annie will therefore bear the legal burden of establishing the essential elements of her claim. With one exception, these are readily defined.

She will first have to prove the existence of a contract made between herself and the defendants for the carriage by the defendants of her goods from Plymouth to Worcester. She will then have to prove that, pursuant to this contract, she consigned her goods to the defendants. Her principal claim is that the defendants deliberately destroyed her goods by fire whilst they had possession of them. Clearly, the burden of proving this rests on Annie. She will also have to prove the value of the goods which have been lost.

Since this is a civil action, all these matters will have to be proved according to 'the preponderance of probability' (*Miller v Minister of Pensions* (1947)). Even where Annie is alleging matters that would amount to the criminal offence of arson, she does not have to prove them beyond reasonable doubt. In *Hornal v Neuberger Products Ltd* (1957), the plaintiff was sold a lathe by the defendants. One of their directors was alleged to have stated falsely that the machine had been reconditioned by a named firm. Had this representation been made by the director with knowledge of its falsehood, he would have been guilty of fraudulent misrepresentation. In a civil action for damages for breach of warranty, alternatively for fraud, the trial judge found that the claim in respect of fraud had been proved on the balance of probabilities, but added that he would not have been satisfied had the criminal standard been applicable. The Court of Appeal held that he had correctly applied the civil standard.

In *Hornal*, Denning LJ said that the more serious the allegation, the higher the degree of probability required, and in some later cases, the judge appears to have applied a slightly loaded civil standard.[1] However, Morris LJ said in *Hornal* that the gravity of the allegation was simply part of the whole range of circumstances that had to be weighed when deciding on the balance of probabilities. He did not favour variations of standard in civil cases, and current opinion prefers his view. In *Re H and Others* (1996), the majority of the House of Lords supported the view that the more serious the allegation, the less likely it was to be true, and the weightier the evidence needed for a court to find it proved. But it was emphasised that where a serious allegation was in issue, the standard of proof was not higher than the ordinary civil standard. If a third standard were to be substituted in some civil cases, it would be necessary to identify what that standard was, and when it applied. Confusion and uncertainty would result. Any earlier observations to the contrary were not accurate statements of the law.

As an alternative to deliberate destruction, Annie pleads negligence on the part of the defendants. Does she have the legal burden of proving this? Two arguments might be used to show that she does. It could be said that this is just another instance of the application of the basic maxim that it is for the person who affirms something to be the case to bear the burden in respect of that issue. The defendants might also argue by analogy from the way in which an exclusion clause was interpreted in *The Glendarroch* (1894). In that case, the plaintiffs claimed damages from shipowners for the latter's failure to carry goods safely. The shipowners relied on an exemption clause which excluded their liability for loss or damage occasioned by perils of the sea. It was held that the defendants had the burden of proving this provision and that the loss fell within it, but that the plaintiffs, who wished to rely on a proviso to the exemption clause which excluded its operation in the event of the shipowners' negligence, had the burden of establishing that the facts were such as to bring the proviso into effect.

There is, however, an argument that, instead of Annie's having to prove negligence, the defendants have a burden to show that they used all proper care in the carriage of the goods. This is the basic common law rule in cases of bailment for reward, of which this contract is an instance. It could be argued that any ambiguity as to the burden of proof should be resolved in Annie's favour because this basic principle has not been clearly excluded, and its rationale is clearly present here: after the goods were consigned to the defendants, they, and not Annie, were in a better position to explain what happened to them. This was a consideration which proved persuasive in *Levison v Patent Steam Carpet Cleaning Ltd* (1978). In this case, the defendant carpet cleaners lost the plaintiff's Chinese carpet in unexplained circumstances. A clause in the contract would have exempted them from liability for negligence, but not for any fundamental breach of contract. The burden of proof on the latter issue was held by the Court of Appeal to lie on the defendants. They had to show that they had not been guilty of fundamental breach because they could more easily discharge this burden than could a plaintiff who had a burden to prove that there had been such a breach.

It will of course be for XY & Co to establish the existence of the exclusion clause and, if need be, that the goods were destroyed by fire. Similarly, if they wish to rely on the limitation of damages clause, they will have to prove it formed part of the contract.

Note

1   See, for example, *The Michael* (1979).

CHAPTER 3

PRESUMPTIONS, COMPETENCE AND COMPELLABILITY

Introduction

Presumptions fit awkwardly into an evidence course. When lawyers first started to write books on evidence, they used to include large amounts of substantive law on such subjects as trespass, nuisance, bailment, actions on the case and so forth. The object of these writers was to include not only what we should recognise as rules of evidence, relating to such matters as the competence of witnesses and hearsay, but rules about what had to be proved in order to establish particular claims or defences. There was no unifying principle other than the convenience of the arrangement for practitioners. (See, for example, Gilbert, G (Sir), *The Law of Evidence*, 2nd edn, 1760. This was the leading work on the subject in the second half of the 18th century; the last edition was published in 1801. See, generally, Twining, W, 'The rationalist tradition of evidence scholarship', in *Rethinking Evidence: Exploratory Essays*, 1994, pp 32–91.)

Modern evidence textbooks deal with some, but by no means all, presumptions. (See the Checklist for details.) However, this is really no more than a hangover from the older way of writing. No successful attempts have been made to find an all-embracing theme that would make 'presumptions' a true part of evidence law. What you will be looking at will be several quite distinct bits of substantive law that have little or no connection with each other.

Because this is an area where attempts to find unifying features have been made so unsuccessfully, you may find classification confusing. When a writer refers to a presumption, you need to be sure about how he is using the word. The sort of presumption that you will be trying to learn about (of death, legitimacy, etc) is what is often called a 'rebuttable presumption of law'. In my view, it confuses things to talk about anything else as a 'presumption'. If someone refers to a 'presumption of fact' he should mean an *inference* about facts which is part of an ordinary reasoning process, having nothing specially to do with law at all. And, if he refers to an 'irrebuttable presumption of law', that is just the same as referring to some rule of substantive law. Thus, to refer to 'the presumption of innocence' is the same thing as referring to the rule which places the burden of proof on the prosecution.

Questions of competence and compellability are mainly governed by statute. You should note that the Youth Justice and Criminal Evidence Act 1999 contains new provisions relating to the competence of witnesses and their capacity to be sworn in criminal trials (ss 53–56). It also amends s 80 of the Police and Criminal Evidence Act 1984. Spouses and children are the obvious subjects for examination questions; for details, see the Checklist.

Checklist

Students should generally be familiar with the following areas, but check your syllabus, because it may provide a narrower or wider range:

- classifications of presumptions;
- presumption of marriage;
- presumption of legitimacy;
- presumption of death;
- presumption of regularity;
- *res ipsa loquitur*;
- conflicting presumptions;
- general rule of universal competence and compellability;
- how a co-accused can become competent for the prosecution;
- comment on an accused's failure to testify;
- competence and compellability of an accused's spouse: for the prosecution, the accused or a co-accused;
- competence of children in civil and criminal cases.

Question 6

'The theoretical basis for recognising presumptions is that the presumed fact would, in the usual course of events, flow naturally from the existence of the primary fact, so that there is a rational connection between the two so strong that it is unnecessary to require evidence of the presumed fact in the absence of unusual circumstances.'

Discuss.

Answer plan

This is an essay question which requires you to consider a subject that has already been referred to in the Introduction. Is it possible to say something that is true about the way in which all rebuttable presumptions of law behave? If it is, is this the common factor which is to be found? It is important to emphasise that this question, like many other essay questions, cannot be answered on knowledge of statutes and cases alone. You need to have read something of the theory of the subject, and in order to answer this question, you should at least have read what is said in Tapper, C, *Cross & Tapper on Evidence*, 9th edn, 1999, pp 122–24, and in Zuckerman, AAS, *The Principles of Criminal Evidence*, 1989, pp 110–21.

You need to cover the following topics:

- the superficial attractiveness of the proposition;
- presumptions that appear to increase artificially the probative worth of the basic facts, for example, presumption of death;
- presumptions designed simply to resolve difficulties of proof, for example, s 184(1) of the Law of Property Act (LPA) 1925;
- the argument that all presumptions may operate simply as techniques for allocating the burden of proof;
- the diversity of ways in which the 'same' presumption can operate.

The conclusion is that at best, the quotation tells only part of the story, and it may be positively misleading.

Answer

The theoretical basis suggested in the quotation is superficially attractive. For example, according to the presumption of legitimacy, it is presumed that a child born during lawful wedlock is legitimate in the absence of evidence to the contrary (*Hetherington v Hetherington* (1887)). Given the fact of a birth in those circumstances, it would seem most unreasonable not to presume the legitimacy of the child.

But not all presumptions provide such a ready illustration of this sort of rational process. According to the presumption of death, a person will be presumed to have died if it is proved that: (a) there is no acceptable evidence that he has been alive at some time during a continuous period of at least seven years; (b) there are persons likely to have heard of him, had he been alive, who have not heard of him during that period; and (c) all due inquiries have been made with a view to finding the person in question, but without success (*Chard v Chard* (1956)).

The presumption in this case appears to operate so as to increase artificially the probative value of the basic facts in the absence of any contrary evidence. So far as probative worth goes, there is nothing special about seven years' absence as opposed, say, to one of six years. Yet, the former period gives rise to a rebuttable presumption of law, while the latter gives rise to no more than an inference of fact that may be made or not.[1]

In other cases, it seems clear that a presumption has been designed simply in order to resolve a difficulty of proof. An example is s 184(1) of the Law of Property Act 1925. This provides that where two or more persons have died in circumstances rendering it uncertain which of them survived the other or others, such death shall (subject to any order of the court), for all purposes affecting the title to property, be presumed to have occurred in order of seniority and, accordingly, the younger shall be deemed to have survived the elder. Here the probative worth of the basic fact is non-existent; the whole effect of the presumption is to allocate the burden of proof.[2]

It has been suggested in fact that a presumption is in all cases simply a technique whereby the substantive law distributes the risk of losing on a given issue, and that it is misleading to try to develop a rationale based on the probative force of the basic facts of the presumption. This misleading approach, it is argued, leads to the conclusion that presumptions such as that of death are simply presumptions of fact to which the law gives artificial weight. If, however, the rationale of presumptions is to be found in the allocation of the burden of proof, the charge of artificiality is misconceived. The rights of someone who has disappeared cannot remain suspended indefinitely; what the law does is to provide, by a rule affecting the burden of proof, a limitation period. The basic fact may, of course, have some probative weight, but it has this by virtue of common sense and experience rather than by virtue of the presumption.[3]

This view of presumptions as devices for allocating the burden of proof receives considerable support from the fact that a particular presumption does not always affect the burden of proof in exactly the same way; the way in which a presumption operates depends on the context in which it may be relevant. This would not be the case if, from a primary fact, there flowed naturally in the usual course of events a particular presumed fact. One would expect a rational process such as that to operate regardless of context.

That this is not the case is shown by the operation of presumptions in a criminal context. According to the presumption of regularity, upon proof of the fact that some official or public act has been performed, or that a person acted in an official capacity, it is presumed that the act which was done complied with any necessary formalities, or that the person so acting had been properly appointed. In *Dillon* (1982), a police officer had been charged in Jamaica with the offence of negligently permitting two prisoners, lawfully in his custody, to escape. The prosecution failed to call any evidence to show that the officer had authority to hold the prisoners in custody, a matter which they had the burden of proving. On a defence submission of no case to answer, the magistrate held that the prosecution was entitled to rely on the presumption of regularity to establish that such authority existed. This decision was upheld by the Court of Appeal of Jamaica but rejected by the Privy Council, which held that the prosecution was not entitled to rely on a presumption to establish a central element of the offence.

There seems little doubt that the presumption of legitimacy would also affect the burden of proof in different ways, depending on the nature of the proceedings. In a civil case, once birth in lawful wedlock is established, the court must find the child legitimate unless the party opposing legitimacy proves on the balance of probabilities that the child is illegitimate.[4] But suppose a defendant is charged with committing incest with his daughter and his defence is that, though conceived and born in wedlock, she is actually the child of another man. It is most unlikely to be held that the defendant has a legal burden of proof on that issue. It would surely be enough to raise in the minds of the jury a reasonable doubt about whether the woman in question might have been the daughter of another man.[5]

It might be objected that in these criminal examples, there is a conflict of presumptions which produces a different outcome, the presumption with which the others conflict being the presumption of innocence. But this would be to mislead by language. The so called presumption of innocence is not a rebuttable presumption of law like the others, but is simply a way of stating the rule that in criminal cases, the burden of proof is on the prosecution.

At best, therefore, it appears that the theoretical basis for recognising presumptions which is suggested in the quotation does not tell the whole story. At worst, it may be positively misleading.

Notes

1   Tapper, C, *Cross & Tapper on Evidence*, 9th edn, 1999, p 123.

2   Tapper, C, *Cross & Tapper on Evidence*, 9th edn, 1999, p 123.

3   Zuckerman, AAS, *The Principles of Criminal Evidence*, 1989, pp 119–21.

4   Section 26 of the Family Law Reform Act 1969.

5   Tapper, C, *Cross & Tapper on Evidence*, 9th edn, 1999, p 124.

Question 7

Charlie, while driving his motor car, was involved in a collision with Doris, a cyclist aged 14, who suffered a broken leg as a result.

(a) Charlie is charged with dangerous driving. The CPS wish to call the following, both of whom have made statements to the police, as witnesses for the prosecution:

(i) Ethel, Charlie's wife. She was travelling in the car with Charlie. Shortly after the accident, she made a statement saying that her husband was distracted by a violent argument with her just before he hit Doris's bicycle. Recently, she has been in touch with the officer in the case and has told him that she does not want to give evidence because she loves her husband despite everything.

(ii) Freddie, aged nine, who saw the accident while he was waiting for a bus to take him to church, where he sings in the choir.

Advise the CPS on the competence and compellability of Ethel and Freddie.

(b) Charlie has been prosecuted and acquitted. Civil proceedings have now been begun against him on behalf of Doris for negligence. The claimant's solicitors wish to call Ethel and Freddie as witnesses. Advise the solicitors on the competence and compellability of these potential witnesses.

Answer plan

This is one of the topics where evidence law depends on whether the proceedings are criminal or civil. Deal with the criminal trial first, and then the civil trial.

The criminal trial

(i) *Ethel.* For competence, see s 53(1) of the Youth Justice and Criminal Evidence Act (YJCEA) 1999. For compellability, see s 80 of the Police and Criminal Evidence Act 1984, as amended by the YJCEA 1999. Is this a 'specified offence'? Note Doris's age at the time of the accident. How should 'involves' in s 80(3)(a) be interpreted?

(ii) *Freddie.* For competence, see s 53(1) of the YJCEA 1999. Note s 55(2)(a).

The civil trial

(i) *Ethel.* For competence, see *Ex p Fernandez* (1861). For compellability, see s 1 of the Evidence Amendment Act 1853.

(ii) *Freddie*. Note the possibility of giving sworn evidence. Your starting point will be the *Hayes* test, with s 96(2) of the Children Act 1989 as a fall-back position.

Answer

The criminal trial

Ethel is competent by virtue of s 53(1) of the Youth Justice and Criminal Evidence Act 1999, which provides that, at every stage in criminal proceedings, all persons are (whatever their age) competent to give evidence.

Her compellability will be governed by s 80 of the Police and Criminal Evidence Act 1984, as amended. She will be compellable only if the offence with which her husband is charged is a 'specified' offence. At the time of the accident, Doris was under the age of 16. It might be arguable that the offence fell within s 80(3)(a), and so was a specified offence, because it involved injury to a person who was at the material time under the age of 16. The interpretation of 'involves' in this provision is uncertain. It might mean 'involves as a matter of legal definition', as robbery, for example, involves the use of force or a putting in fear of force.[1] If this approach is adopted, dangerous driving is clearly not a specified offence. On the other hand, 'involves' could mean 'involves as a matter of fact in the circumstances of the particular case'. If that were the interpretation adopted, the offence with which Charlie is charged would be a specified offence, and Ethel would be compellable.[2]

Freddie is in principle competent by virtue of s 53(1) of the Youth Justice and Criminal Evidence Act 1999. There is nothing to suggest that he falls into the category of persons who are not competent that is set out in s 53(3). However, because he is under 14, his evidence will be given unsworn: see s 55(2)(a).

The civil trial

The basic rule, set out in *Ex p Fernandez* (1861), is that all persons are competent to give evidence and may be compelled to testify. By s 1 of the Evidence Amendment Act 1853, it is specifically provided that the husbands and wives of the parties to civil proceedings are competent *and compellable* to give evidence on behalf of *any* of the parties to the proceedings. Ethel will therefore be a compellable witness for the claimant.

Because this is a civil action, Freddie may give either sworn or unsworn evidence. The question whether he understands the nature of an oath so as to be able to give sworn evidence will presumably be decided by applying the tests formerly used when children gave evidence in criminal proceedings. The judge will question Freddie in open court before he gives evidence. In *Khan* (1981), the Court of Appeal said that, although much depended on the type of child before the court, generally, inquiry should be made in the case of a child under 14. The conditions to be satisfied were stated in *Hayes* (1977) to be that the child had a sufficient appreciation of the solemnity of the occasion, and understood that an oath involved an added responsibility to tell the truth over and above the social duty to do so. Understanding of a divine sanction is not required.

If these conditions are not satisfied, Freddie may give unsworn evidence. Section 96(2) of the Children Act 1989 provides that a child's evidence may be heard, even if he does not understand the nature of an oath, if he understands that it is his duty to speak the truth, and he has a sufficient understanding to justify his evidence being heard. Freddie is likely to be competent, and so also compellable (*Ex p Fernandez* (1861)).

Notes

1   See s 8 of the Theft Act 1968.

2   For further discussion, see Tapper, C, *Cross & Tapper on Evidence*, 9th edn, 1999, pp 220–22.

Question 8

Eight years ago, Mr and Mrs Austin set off from England to spend an indefinite period of time travelling in South America. They left behind them three adult children: Basil, Cynthia and Darren. At first Mr and Mrs Austin wrote regularly to all the children, but after a time they did so erratically and infrequently. After two years, nothing further was heard from them by any of the children. The letters that had been received showed that Mr and Mrs Austin were travelling through parts of South America where from time to time there was civil unrest and also danger from natural disasters such as flooding and earthquakes.

Some years before leaving England, both Mr and Mrs Austin had made wills. Mr Austin left everything to his wife, but he also provided that, if she should predecease him, his estate should be divided equally between 'the legitimate children of my family'. Mrs Austin left everything to her husband; in the event of his predeceasing her, the estate was to be divided between various charities.

Basil and Cynthia say that their parents must by now have died and wish to know what rights of inheritance they have. They say also that Darren, though born to Mrs Austin during her marriage, was not the child of Mr Austin but of a man with whom Mrs Austin was having an affair while their father was in prison.

Discuss the evidential issues that arise.

Answer plan

Three problems of law need to be considered here:

- the presumption of death;
- the presumption created by s 184 of the Law of Property Act 1925;
- the presumption of legitimacy.

In dealing with these points, you should bear in mind the inferences that might be drawn from the evidence without the aid of presumptions, and also any gaps there may be which necessitate requests for further information.

Answer

A person will be presumed to have died if it is proved that:

(a) there is no acceptable evidence that he has been alive at some time during a continuous period of at least seven years;

(b) there are persons likely to have heard of him, had he been alive, who have not heard of him during that period; and

(c) all due inquiries have been made with a view to finding the person in question, but without success (*Chard v Chard* (1956)).

In the case of Mr and Mrs Austin, nothing has been heard for the last six years only, so the presumption cannot be applied. In any case, it does not appear whether there are any other persons who might have heard from Mr and Mrs Austin, or what inquiries, if any, have been made. Thus, even if Basil and Cynthia were to wait for a period of seven years to have elapsed, a court might not be satisfied that all conditions for the operation of the presumption had been complied with.

Quite apart from the presumption, it would be open to a court to infer from appropriate circumstantial evidence that Mr and Mrs Austin had died, but Basil and Cynthia would have the burden of proving their parents' death on the balance of probabilities. Thus, if the evidence were sufficient, there would be no need to wait for the expiry of seven years.[1] Whether the evidence is sufficient is likely to depend largely on what inferences can be drawn as to the presence of Mr and Mrs Austin in areas of natural disaster or insurrection and their likelihood of survival in such circumstances.

Section 184 of the Law of Property Act 1925 provides that, in all cases where two or more persons have died in circumstances rendering it uncertain which of them survived the other or others, such death shall (subject to any order of the court), for all purposes affecting the title to property, be presumed to have occurred in order of seniority, and accordingly the younger shall be deemed to have survived the elder. For the children to inherit, it would be necessary for Mr Austin to have survived his wife. By s 184, he will be presumed to have done so if he was the younger of the two; it will therefore be necessary to discover their respective ages. There appears to be no reason why s 184 should not apply where the court makes a finding of death by virtue of the presumption of death.

On the assumption that Mr Austin was younger than his wife and that he therefore survived her, the question of Darren's legitimacy arises. There is a presumption of legitimacy in respect of any child who is proved to have been born or conceived in lawful wedlock. However, s 26 of the Family Law Reform Act 1969 provides that this presumption may be rebutted by evidence which shows that it is more probable than not that the person in question is illegitimate or legitimate as the case may be. Darren will have the advantage of the presumption because he was born while his parents were lawfully married. It will therefore be for Basil and Cynthia to prove on the balance of probabilities that he is illegitimate in order to exclude him from sharing in the distribution of Mr Austin's estate.

One item of evidence in their favour may be the provision itself in Mr Austin's will; it suggests that he believed that there was at least one child of the family who was not legitimate. Clearly, the evidence of his imprisonment will be of the utmost importance. If, for example, Darren was conceived at a time when Mr Austin could have had no access to his wife, this would seem to rebut the presumption conclusively.

Note

1   See, for example, *Re Watkins* (1953) for a case where the presumption of death could not be applied, but where the fact of death was nevertheless inferred.

CHAPTER 4

HEARSAY: THE SCOPE OF THE RULE

Introduction

It will be helpful to start with a statement of the rule against hearsay. As good as any is that given in *Cross & Tapper on Evidence* and adopted by Lord Havers in *Sharp* (1988): 'An assertion other than one made by a person while giving oral evidence in the proceedings is inadmissible as evidence of any fact asserted.' In order to get to grips with this idea, several points need to be considered. The order in which they are tackled is important:

(1) The rule against hearsay will exclude an item of evidence only if the purpose of adducing that evidence is to establish the truth of the matters asserted. It follows that in relation to any item of evidence which you suspect may be caught by the rule, you need first to ask: 'What is the job of proof that this item of evidence is put forward to do?' Another way of raising the same issue is to ask what is its relevance. At this stage, don't think about law at all. Think about the problem of proof. Only when you have dealt with this can you say whether somebody wants to call the evidence to prove the truth of something that has been asserted. You ought to be in no doubt about why a party wants to call a particular piece of evidence. If you *are* in doubt, it will usually be a sign that you haven't thought carefully enough about the facts.

Don't think you can save the situation by saying that the item of evidence might be excluded for offending the rule against hearsay, but it might be admitted to prove that the assertion was made. This evades the issue and will discredit you in the eyes of the examiner. If you think that somebody might want to show simply that an assertion was made, you *must* explain to the examiner why you think that it might be relevant to show that. For example, in a case like *Subramaniam v Public Prosecutor* (1956), you would explain that the evidence ought to be admitted because the threats are likely to have affected the state of mind of the defendant, thus making the evidence relevant to his defence of duress.

(2) Once you have grasped the importance of relevance in the rule against hearsay, you need to consider what is meant in this context by an assertion. In its most obvious sense, an assertion gives an account of events or describes a state of affairs, however briefly. For example:

- 'He flung his empty revolver down the slope';

- 'It's a long way to go';
- 'No more firing was heard at Brussels – the pursuit rolled miles away. Darkness came down on the field and city; and Amelia was praying for George, who was lying on his face, dead, with a bullet through his heart';
- 'It is a truth universally acknowledged that a single man in possession of a good fortune must be in want of a wife.'

But words can be used for purposes other than the making of assertions. For example, they can be used to ask questions, to give orders or to greet somebody. There may also be ways in which to utter a form of words is to *do* some sort of *act*. This may be governed by a religious or social convention, as when words are uttered as part of the ceremony of baptism or that of launching a new ship. Alternatively, the law may say that the utterance of a form of words in certain circumstances amounts to an act; for example, where words are uttered by way of contractual offer or acceptance. A difficulty arises because from all apparently non-assertive utterances it is possible to make inferences about the surrounding circumstances. Where such inferences can be made, it is tempting to say that the utterance, though not an express assertion, is an implied one as to the circumstances which may be inferred. Thus, if someone overhears my asking the guide the way to Larissa, he might infer that I do not know the way, and a lawyer might argue that the question operates as an implied assertion of my ignorance of the way to Larissa.

These possibilities have to be considered because of the decision of the House of Lords in *Kearley* (1992) to the effect that implied, as well as express assertions are caught by the rule against hearsay. It is unfortunately not clear what will count as an implied assertion for this purpose, and you will need to pay particular attention to any cases or articles to which you may be referred which discuss this problem.

(3) When stages (1) and (2) have been covered, you might think that it is time to move on to the established exceptions to the rule. But before that, you need to appreciate that despite what was said in *Myers v DPP* (1965), there have been occasions when the rule against hearsay has just been conveniently ignored. The best introduction to this topic is Ashworth, A and Pattenden, R, 'Reliability, hearsay evidence and the English criminal trial' (1986) 102 LQR 292, pp 292–331. See also *Ward* (2001).

Checklist

Students should be familiar with the following areas:

- the justifications for the rule against hearsay;

- the place of relevance in the rule against hearsay;
- the distinction between express assertions and other things that may be done with words;
- the future application of *Kearley*, for example, whether there could be hearsay by conduct;
- cases which do not fall within established exceptions, but where the rule against hearsay has apparently been ignored.

Question 9

Albert Crippen and Charlie Haigh are charged with dishonestly receiving stolen goods, namely 20 bottles of gin belonging to Umbrages plc, knowing or believing the same to be stolen goods. The case for the prosecution is that they bought the gin from a neighbour, Bridget, who was employed by Umbrages, from whom she had stolen the gin. Albert's defence is that he had no idea that the goods were stolen. When questioned by the police, he said that Bridget had told him that the bottles of gin were 'perks' which her employers allowed her and which she did not want to keep because she was teetotal. If Albert testifies in his own defence, will he be allowed to repeat what Bridget told him?

Charlie told the police that he had never taken part in the deal and that he did not even know Bridget. While DS Shovel was lawfully searching Bridget's house, the telephone rang. He picked up the receiver and heard a female voice say: 'Bridget, are you and Charlie Haigh coming to David's party on Saturday?' DS Shovel said nothing and the caller rang off after a few seconds. May evidence of the telephone call be given by DS Shovel to establish a connection between Charlie and Bridget and to show that Charlie lied to the police?

Answer plan

The first part of this question requires you to decide Albert's purpose in wanting to give evidence of what Bridget had told him. It would, of course, be a defence to the charge if what Bridget said was true because the gin would not then have been stolen. But Albert doesn't need to go that far. He need only raise a doubt about whether he knew or believed the goods to have been stolen. So he wants to give evidence of his innocent state of mind at the time of the sale and show that his account of the matter is likely to be true because of what Bridget said to him. You need therefore to describe how the rule against hearsay operates and to show that this is a situation, like the one in *Subramaniam* (1956), where the basic condition for applying the rule is absent.

The second half of the question requires you to think about the admissibility of Charlie's statement to the police that he did not know Bridget, and the relevance of what was heard on the telephone. In connection with the latter, you need first to sort out what might be inferred from the caller's question and then to apply the decision in *Kearley* (1992).

Answer

The general rule is that an assertion other than one made by a person while giving oral evidence in the proceedings is inadmissible as evidence of any fact asserted (*Sharp* (1988)). This rule applies just as much to defence evidence as it does to prosecution evidence. For example, in *Sparks v R* (1964), the Privy Council held that a complaint by a child who was too young to testify could not be repeated in court by the person to whom it had been made, even though the contents of the statement showed that 'a coloured boy' had committed the crime and the defendant was a white man.

However, evidence of a statement made outside court will be admissible if the purpose of calling the evidence is not to prove the truth of the matters asserted, but some other matter which is relevant in the proceedings. In this case, the purpose of adducing the evidence would not be to prove the truth of what Bridget said, but simply the fact that she made the statement to Albert. This would be relevant because the prosecution must show that Albert knew or believed the gin to have been stolen. If Bridget told him that she had acquired the gin with her employers' consent, the prosecution case in this respect is less likely to be true. For this purpose, it does not matter whether Bridget was telling the truth or not. What matters is the effect her words may have had on Albert's mind.

This distinction was brought out by the Privy Council in *Subramaniam v Public Prosecutor* (1956). The defendant had been charged with unlawful possession of ammunition; his defence was duress. In support of this defence, he wished to give evidence of what had been said to him by terrorists, but was prevented from doing so by the trial judge on the basis that such evidence would offend the rule against hearsay. The Privy Council said that the evidence should have been admitted, emphasising that the fact that a statement had been made was frequently relevant, quite apart from its truth, in considering the mental state and subsequent conduct of someone in whose presence the statement had been made.

Albert may therefore give evidence of what Bridget told him.

The first question in relation to the telephone call taken by DS Shovel concerns what it is able to prove. The words constituted not an assertion but a question. The words uttered by the caller cannot therefore be said to have been either true or false. What could be inferred from what the caller said? Amongst the possibilities are:

(1) the caller knew Bridget;

(2) the caller believed that Bridget and Charlie Haigh knew each other;

(2a)Bridget and Charlie Haigh did know each other;

(3) the caller believed that Bridget was in the habit of going out with Charlie Haigh;

(3a)Bridget was in the habit of going out with Charlie Haigh.

If (2a) or (3a) were true, it could be shown that Charlie had lied to the police when he said that he did not know Bridget. His lie would be relevant because it would be something from which a jury might infer Charlie's guilt.

The fact that Charlie had denied knowing Bridget would be admissible because the rule against hearsay applies only where evidence of an out of court statement is adduced to prove the truth of what was said. It does not apply where the purpose of adducing the evidence is to show that the speaker said something that was false. For example, in *Mawaz Khan v R* (1967), the two defendants were charged with murder. The Crown relied strongly on the fact that each defendant had made a statement in which he had tried to set up a joint alibi with his co-defendant. Those alibis could be shown to be false. The Privy Council held that the statements were relevant because they tended to show that the makers were acting in concert and that this showed a common guilt. Evidence of these statements was not affected by the rule against hearsay because the prosecution had proposed to establish not their truth, but the fact that they had been made.

However, in the light of the decision of the House of Lords in *Kearley* (1992), evidence of the telephone call would be inadmissible to enable the jury to infer either (2a) or (3a). In *Kearley*, a majority of the House of Lords held that the beliefs of a number of telephone callers to the defendant's premises that drugs were available from the defendant were irrelevant to the question of whether the defendant could or would supply them. This is a much weaker case than that because the prosecution has to rely on the belief of one caller only that Charlie knew Bridget. Even if relevant, the decision in *Kearley* would make the evidence an implied assertion, and so inadmissible hearsay.

DS Shovel will therefore not be permitted to give evidence of the telephone call.

Question 10

Has the hearsay rule become divorced from its rationale?

Answer plan

You need to begin by stating the traditional rationale – in fact, a collection of reasons – for the rule against hearsay. Lord Normand in *Teper v R* (1952) is as good a source as any. Then go on to show ways in which the rule was applied despite the fact that the rationale didn't operate. It would be appropriate to make some reference to challenges to the rationale, and to the effect of *Kearley* (1992) in divorcing rule from rationale. Finally, some reference could be made to attempts to find a new rationale.

In summary, therefore, the essay is constructed as follows:

- reasons for the rule against hearsay;
- application of the rule when some reasons were absent: *Sparks v R* (1964); *Myers v DPP* (1965);
- questionable validity of some reasons against hearsay;
- effect of extending the rule to implied assertions;
- an alternative rationale: a right of confrontation and a right to challenge witnesses;
- conclusion: slender links between rule and rationale.

Answer

In *Teper v R* (1952), Lord Normand explained the rationale of the rule against hearsay in this way. Hearsay is not the best evidence, and it is not delivered on oath. The truthfulness and accuracy of the person whose words are recounted by another witness cannot be tested by cross-examination, and the light that the original speaker's demeanour would have thrown on his testimony is lost.

But it is clear that the rule against hearsay has been applied when some of these criticisms have been inapplicable. In *Sparks v R* (1964), for example, the trial judge refused to allow the mother of a girl aged three to give evidence that her daughter had told her that she had been assaulted by 'a coloured boy'. This decision was upheld by the Privy Council. But there was no significant hearsay danger. The child's statement was unambiguous, she was unlikely to have been mistaken, and the danger that she might have lied was surely non-existent.

Another example is *Myers v DPP* (1965). In order to show that cars sold by the defendant had been stolen, the prosecution wished to call an employee who was in charge of records kept by the car manufacturers. These records were microfilms of cards that had been filled in by production line workers. They showed details of numbers stamped on the cylinder blocks of the cars on the production line. The House of Lords held that this evidence was hearsay, and so inadmissible. But the manufacturers' records must have been far more reliable than the memories of the workers, even if they could have been identified and called.

The hearsay rule was made to accord more with its rationale by the provisions permitting documentary hearsay in the Criminal Justice Act 1988. But the position in relation to oral hearsay remains unchanged, and the result in *Sparks v R* (1964) would be the same today.

It is arguable that the hearsay rule has become divorced from some elements of its rationale because these elements have become obsolete, or at least questionable. The argument that hearsay is not the best evidence has always been unsatisfactory. Where hearsay is the only evidence of some matter, it will be the best evidence of that matter. The Law Commission concluded that there is no clear evidence that an oath or affirmation in itself promotes truthful testimony.[1] Wigmore thought that the oath added little to cross-examination, which he thought was the real test.[2] In any case, the argument that hearsay is not on oath addresses only the danger that the person reported might have made a false statement deliberately. It can be no safeguard against an original observation that was mistaken. Opinions have differed about the value of a witness's demeanour in testing reliability.[3] The difficulty in recapturing the emphasis and tone of voice of the original utterance may be a more significant objection to admissibility. The main element in Lord Normand's explanation that survives today is the absence of an opportunity to cross-examine the original speaker.

The extension of the hearsay rule to implied assertions in *Kearley* (1992) has divorced the rule even from the rationale based on absence of cross-examination. Lord Normand's objection was that the truthfulness and accuracy of someone whose words are reported by another witness cannot be tested. But where the words relied on are non-assertive, they cannot have a truth value, and this objection cannot apply. The real objection here is that the original speaker may be mistaken (though hardly dishonest) in the underlying belief that prompted the non-assertive utterance. If A is overheard asking B, 'Have you any bananas for sale today?', that utterance cannot be true or false. What is true or false is A's underlying belief that B is in the business of selling bananas.

Lord Normand's explanation of the rule against hearsay relies solely on the limited probative weight to be given to hearsay evidence. A different kind of argument is based not on rectitude of decision, but on concern for procedural rights.[4] There are two rights that may be relied on in support of the hearsay rule. One is the right of confrontation, by which evidence cannot be given against a defendant behind his back. The other is the right of challenge to witnesses. Although these rights make for rectitude of decision, they also maximise the defendant's participation in his own trial, and so promote the legitimacy of the verdict in his eyes and in the eyes of the public generally.

Hearsay evidence appears to infringe both the right of confrontation and the right of challenge. But it is difficult to argue that these rights are part of the rationale of the rule. There is no absolute right of physical confrontation in English law. Evidence may be given by video link, for example. And European decisions show that hearsay evidence can be used against defendants in certain circumstances, despite Art 6(3)(d) of the European Convention on Human Rights, which provides that everyone charged with a criminal offence has the right to examine or have examined witnesses against him.

A complete divorce has probably not yet taken place between the hearsay rule and its traditional rationale, but the links that remain are slender.

Notes

1   Law Com No 245, Cm 3670, para 3.13.

2   *Wigmore on Evidence*, 3rd edn, 1940, vol 5, para 1362.

3   Law Com No 245, Cm 3670, paras 3.9–3.12.

4   See Dennis, IH, *The Law of Evidence*, 1999, pp 515–18.

Question 11

Oliver Mellors is charged with the murder in London of Connie Chatterley. The case for the prosecution is that they met at Connie's house, and that during a quarrel Oliver struck Connie repeatedly with a cricket bat, thereby causing her death. There is medical evidence that Connie died between 1 pm and 2 pm. The police found a gold cigarette case engraved with the initials 'OM' beside the body. They subsequently interviewed Mellors, who claimed to have been in France on the day that Connie was killed. Later, a neighbour told the police that she had seen Mellors in London on the day in question, but no statement was taken and the witness cannot now be traced. Connie's gardener has told the police that at about 10.30 am on that day he overheard a conversation between Connie and a man. He did not see either of them, but he recognised Connie's voice and he thought he recognised that of Mellors. He says that Connie said: 'Don't forget to buy some fish, Oliver.' The man replied, 'I'll get some on the way home'.

Discuss the evidential issues that arise.

Answer plan

You must first decide what items of evidence have to be discussed. They are:

- the discovery of the cigarette case. What is its relevance? Is there a hearsay problem? If there is, can it be avoided?;
- the relevance of a false alibi. Is hearsay involved in relating what Mellors said about being in France?;
- can evidence be adduced of what the neighbour said to establish that the alibi was false?;
- the gardener's evidence. Note that there are two ways in which what he says may be relevant. There are hearsay problems with only one of them.

Answer

The first issue concerns the discovery of the engraved cigarette case. This may assist the prosecution by showing that the defendant was present at the scene of the crime at about the time when the murder took place. For this purpose, it would have to be established that the cigarette case belonged to the defendant, and the engraved initials suggest that this was so. But is there a hearsay problem? It is arguable that the context in which the initials appear shows that their function is to assert ownership; this appears to make the prosecution rely on an assertion for the truth of its contents, contrary to the rule against hearsay. A similar situation arose in *Patel v Comptroller of Customs* (1966), where labels on goods which stated the country of origin were held by the Privy Council to be inadmissible as proof of where the goods came from.[1]

The country of origin of the goods was one of the matters in issue in the case of *Patel*, and this serves to distinguish it from *Lydon* (1986). In the latter case, the prosecution wished to adduce evidence that a piece of paper bearing the words 'Sean rules' had been found near the scene of the crime. This was alleged to be relevant because it tended to connect the defendant, whose first name was Sean, with the commission of the offence. The Court of Appeal held that this evidence was admissible because although the words on the paper constituted an assertion, it was not in itself an assertion of anything that was relevant to the facts in issue. The fact that something relevant to a fact in issue might be inferred from this item of evidence did not affect admissibility.[2]

Here, however, the inscription arguably does amount to an assertion of a matter which the prosecution wishes to establish as part of its case – the ownership of the cigarette case. In principle, therefore, admissibility seems to be in doubt because of the rule against hearsay. However, it may be possible for the prosecution to rely on evidence from acquaintances of Mellors who can recognise the cigarette case as one that Mellors used to carry. *Miller v Howe* (1969) suggests that something that is written will not be caught by the rule against hearsay when it is an identifying part of an object, the identity of which is in issue, and not merely an assertion of a characteristic of the object. This was a case where the question arose whether a particular breath testing device had been the one approved by the Home Secretary, an 'Alcotest 80'. The Court of Appeal indicated that a label to that effect on the device would have been sufficient evidence of its identity, and that even the presence of such a label on the box containing the device would have been enough.

The giving of a false alibi may be an indication of guilt. The prosecution will have no difficulty in adducing evidence that Mellors told the police that he was in France on the day of the murder. No breach of the rule against hearsay is involved because the prosecution wishes to rely, as in *Mawaz Khan* (1967), not on the truth of what was said, but on its falsity.

Had the neighbour made a written statement to the police, that might have been admitted as evidence under the Criminal Justice Act 1988 (see Chapter 5). But there are no provisions which would allow oral hearsay evidence to be given, and for further proof of the falsity of the alibi, it will be necessary to rely on the evidence of the gardener.

The probative force of the gardener's testimony is that Mellors was not in France, but with Connie in London on the day in question. Two factors suggest this. First, the fact that Connie addressed 'Oliver' suggests that it was Mellors to whom she was talking. There are hearsay problems with this. The fact that the words 'Don't forget to buy some fish, Oliver' were not intended as an assertion but as an exhortation, or perhaps a command, appears now to be irrelevant to the question of whether or not the utterance is affected by the rule against hearsay. A jury would be asked to infer from these words an implied assertion by Connie that Mellors was present. But this is not permissible. An express assertion to that effect made by Connie to the gardener would be inadmissible as hearsay, and, since *Kearley* (1992), it is clear that the same principle applies to an implied assertion. In that case, a majority of the House of Lords held to be inadmissible evidence that callers at the defendant's premises had made requests involving implied assertions that the defendant supplied drugs.

Secondly, however, the fact that the gardener heard a voice which he thought he recognised as that of Mellors also suggests that the latter was in London and not in France. What is relied on here to prove that Mellors was present is not the truth of what the man who made a reply to Connie said, but the fact that whatever words were uttered were in tones which the gardener identified as those of Mellors. No hearsay problem arises, and the gardener should be able to testify that he heard, at the time and place referred to, the voice of Connie and a voice which he thought he recognised as that of Mellors.

Notes

1   See also *Comptroller of Customs v Western Lectric Co Ltd* (1966).

2   Would this decision be the same after *Kearley* (1992)?

Question 12

How satisfactory are the proposals of the Law Commission on the reform of hearsay?

Answer plan

The important thing here is not to get bogged down in too much detail – remember the time constraints of an examination. You ought to have some knowledge of the main recommendations of the Law Commission in its report, *Evidence in Criminal Proceedings: Hearsay and Related Topics*, 1997, Law

Com No 245. However, you are not expected to remember all the possible options that the Commission considered, with arguments for and against. What you need to have is an understanding of the criticism that can be levelled against the Commission's overall approach, which has been to recommend the retention of an essentially rule based system. Have a look at the articles by Zuckerman, and perhaps also Spencer in [1996] Crim LR for ideas. It would then be a good idea to find something in the Commission's recommendations that you can approve of. The reversal of *Kearley* is an obvious example. Note, incidentally, the reference to the Schedule in the Criminal Procedure and Investigations Act 1996. This is probably in practice going to have little, if any, significance, and the Law Commission has recommended its repeal. But it shows the examiner that you are up to date with your statute law, and it does provide another useful example to support the argument put forward. The result is a critical but well balanced essay that shows, in the limited time allowed by an examination, knowledge of the existing law and of the Commission's main proposals.

In summary, therefore, the essay is constructed as follows:

- the major issue of principle: rules or discretion;
- summary of the Law Commission's recommendations;
- its reasons for rejecting an inclusionary discretion;
- Zuckerman's argument against a hearsay rule;
- predictability in evidence law;
- equal treatment of defendants;
- potential complexity of rules of exclusion;
- the Law Commission's recommendation that *Kearley* (1992) be reversed;
- the major problems arising from *Kearley*;
- concluding comments on the Law Commission's recommendations.

Answer

The major issue of principle that the Law Commission had to consider when reviewing the rule against hearsay was whether to adopt an approach that was rule based or discretionary. The Commission decided to preserve a rule based approach. It recommended that there should be an exclusionary hearsay rule, with specified exceptions and a limited inclusionary discretion. The four classes of exception were as follows:

- categories of automatic admissibility where the declarant's oral evidence is, for one of certain specified reasons, unavailable;

- an exception under which statements made by witnesses who are in fear may be admitted with leave of the court;
- a business documents exception;
- certain preserved exceptions, such as confessions, statements that are part of the *res gestae*, and statements made by parties to a common enterprise.

The Commission recommended a limited inclusionary discretion to admit hearsay that fell within no other exception. Its purpose would be to prevent the potential injustice that could arise through the exclusion of hearsay evidence. It should extend to oral as well as documentary hearsay, and to multiple as well as first hand hearsay. It should be available to both prosecution and defence if the court is satisfied that, despite the difficulties there may be in challenging the statement, its probative value is such that the interests of justice require it to be admissible.

The recommended reform is therefore a cautious one. The Commission did not recommend the abolition of the exclusionary rule and its replacement by an inclusionary discretion. At the heart of this decision was a fear of judicial discretion, based on experience of the varied judicial approaches to the discretions given in respect of documentary hearsay by the Criminal Justice Act 1988. The Commission argued that uncertainty about the admissibility of evidence meant that the prosecution could not confidently assess the prospects of a conviction when deciding whether to prosecute. Nor could defence lawyers confidently advise their clients on their pleas, or the conduct of their cases.

Zuckerman has cogently objected that the prospect of conviction or acquittal hinges not on admissibility, but on credibility, and, most of the time, this must be right.[1] The purpose of rules of evidence ought to be, among other things, to protect the innocent from conviction, to safeguard the defendant from prejudice, and to maintain proper standards of behaviour in criminal investigations. It is not the business of rules to assist in the determination of truth or falsehood. The hearsay rule has little or nothing to contribute to the positive functions of rules of evidence, and the history of the subject has shown the failure of previous attempts to regulate proof and achieve predictability by establishing categories of admissibility. The law relating to witness capacity is a vivid example of that.

Even if rules of law could create certainty and predictability, that would have no special significance in evidence law. Despite the arguments of the Commission, it is unlikely that in practice the conduct of prosecutions or defences is much inhibited by inability to predict a judicial decision on a point of evidence. Predictability is useful when people are going to plan their future actions, as in the world of commerce. However, by the time a lawyer gets hold of a case, all relevant events are in the past.

A stronger argument, perhaps, in favour of the Law Commission's stance, is the need to be seen to treat defendants equally. Whether a relevant item of evidence is admitted ought not to depend on which judge happens to be trying the case. There certainly appears to have been a significant division in judicial approaches to the documentary provisions of the 1988 Act. But because matters of proof turn so much on the facts of the particular case before the court, it may not be simple to set up comparables, and this argument may therefore lose some of its force.

Certainly, under the Law Commission's recommendations, the law would be simplified. But for how long would the law remain simple? However tight a definition may appear to be, gaps will inevitably appear. Problems of interpretation will arise with equal inevitability, and an essentially rule based system may become rigid. Instead of wasting time and money over arguments about admissibility, there is much to be said for Zuckerman's suggestion that the admissibility of evidence should be governed by reliability, not rules, and should be settled at a pre-trial review.

A more welcome recommendation is the reversal of *Kearley* (1992). The Commission has proposed that, subject to the exceptions, in criminal proceedings, a statement not made in oral evidence in the proceedings should not be admissible as evidence of any matter stated. But a matter should be regarded as stated in a statement if and only if the purpose, or one of the purposes, of the person making the statement appears to the court to have been to cause another person to believe the matter, or to cause another person to act, or a machine to operate, on the basis that the matter is as stated.[2]

This should deal effectively with two major problems arising from *Kearley*. The first is that it substantially extended the hearsay rule. Once it is accepted, following Parke B in *Wright v Doe d Tatham* (1837), that an utterance may be inadmissible because of the assertions that it may imply or, more accurately, because of the inferences that may be drawn from it, it becomes difficult not to follow Parke B's opinion that evidence of conduct may be caught by the rule against hearsay because of the 'assertions' that such conduct might 'imply'. Yet, from any human action, it is possible to infer a belief by the person performing the action in the existence of a state of affairs that justifies the conduct in question. Clearly, not all evidence of conduct can be excluded on the basis that it involves an implied assertion. Stephen Guest's example of A, who approaches B with knife in hand and arm upraised, is an obvious example.[3] But how is a line to be drawn?

The second problem is that the wide interpretation of the rule against hearsay is at odds with other developments in case and statute law limiting the operation of the rule. For example, the rule has been successfully avoided in cases such as *Cook* (1987) and *Constantinou* (1989), where artist's sketches and photofit images were held to be admissible. The effect of ss 23, 24 and 26 of the Criminal Justice Act 1988 can be to let in, under certain conditions, direct assertions in the form of statements made by potential witnesses to the police. Schedule 2 to the Criminal Procedure and Investigations Act 1996 provides for the admissibility, under certain conditions, of written statements admitted in evidence in proceedings before examining magistrates. Yet *Kearley* reinforces the decision in *Harry* (1988), which showed how the hearsay rule can operate against the interests of defendants, as well as in their favour. Proof of incriminating acts by an accused would be allowed because of the exception to the hearsay rule in favour of confessions.[4] But proof of the acts of third parties, on which the accused might wish to rely, might now be excluded. So might acts of the accused from which exculpatory inferences could be drawn.[5]

There are other points of detail where the Law Commission has tried to improve on existing law. The conclusion must be that in the definition of hearsay, and in some simplifications of existing law, the recommendations are welcome. But the overall approach, retaining an essentially rule based system, has been overly cautious.

Notes

1   Zuckerman, AAS, 'The futility of hearsay' [1996] Crim LR 4.

2   Law Com No 245, paras 7.17–7.41.

3   Guest, S, 'The scope of the hearsay rule' (1985) 101 LQR 385.

4   See ss 76(1) and 82(1) of the Police and Criminal Evidence Act 1984.

5   Tapper, CFH, 'Hearsay and implied assertions' (1992) 109 LQR 524.

Question 13

Percy is being prosecuted for the murder of Edith. He is an Australian visitor to England who was staying in a flat on the third floor of a block known as Shearman Court in West London. Edith lived alone in another flat on the ground floor. The prosecution says that Percy and Edith were having an affair, but that on the evening of 14 July, there was a quarrel between them at Edith's flat, during which Percy strangled her.

Percy was first implicated in the crime when a police tracker dog led detectives to his flat on the third floor. In a properly conducted police interview, he told the police that he had not killed Edith, had never had an affair with her and had never been inside her flat.

Curtis, who lived in another flat on the ground floor of Shearman Court, told police that on the evening of the murder, he had heard a loud argument going on in Edith's flat between Edith and a man with an Australian accent.

When the police lawfully searched Percy's flat, they found an opened letter in a desk drawer. It was addressed to Percy and read as follows: 'Don't be fooled by that tart Edith. She's been screwing Frederick for the last month. Give her up – she's not worth it. With love from Rose.' The prosecution does not wish to call Rose, but it wants to put the letter in evidence as part of their case against Percy.

Lilian, a friend of Edith, was interviewed by Percy's solicitor. She told him that after the murder, she took away from Edith's flat a parrot called Max, which Edith had kept as a pet, in order to look after it. She said that during the day Max was silent, but that when evening came, the bird repeatedly called out, 'Frederick, no, no, no!'.

Discuss the evidential issues that arise.

Answer plan

The first thing to emphasise is that all the evidence you have been asked to consider is circumstantial and highly inconclusive, *but it is not, merely for this reason, inadmissible.* If you think about it, there is no evidence that proves something conclusively, for there will always exist possible alternative explanations for the item of evidence in question. Far too many students think that a defendant cannot be convicted on purely circumstantial evidence, or at least that such evidence is bound by its very nature to be less substantial than direct evidence, such as the evidence given by a witness of what he saw or heard. This too is completely wrong. In *Taylor, Weaver and Donovan* (1928), Lord Hewart CJ said: 'It is no derogation of evidence to say that it is circumstantial.' His words should be remembered.

With this in mind, you need to consider five points:

- *Tracker dog evidence.* There is an English authority on this. Note what has to be proved to establish the reliability of such evidence. Of course, there is no hearsay problem here.

- *What Percy said to the police.* What is the purpose of adducing this in evidence? The answer to that question will solve any hearsay difficulties.

- *Curtis's evidence.* Again, what will the prosecution be adducing this to prove? Your answer should be: (a) There was a quarrel that night. (b) It took place at Edith's flat. (c) It was between Edith and a man. (d) The man was Australian. None of this, of course, points inevitably to Percy, but see the opening paragraph above, and remember that this is only a part of the prosecution case.

- *The letter.* This is an example of what is sometimes called the distinction between hearsay and real evidence. If you treat these expressions as labels which can be instinctively slapped on various items of evidence, you are heading for disaster. The starting point, as always, is not the *label* but the *job of proof* that the evidence can do. Putting it another way, the problem of admissibility can be solved only if you consider carefully what inferences can be drawn from the evidence in question. As part of its case, the prosecution wants to prove a number of propositions. Which of those propositions, if any, does the letter support? The answer to this will tell you if it is relevant. What arguments are needed to move from the letter to the propositions that the prosecution wants to prove? The answer to this will tell you about admissibility.

- *Lilian's evidence.* Is it relevant? Is there a hearsay problem? If it is relevant and there is no hearsay problem, what is to stop it from being admitted?

Answer

The tracker dog presumably led the police to Percy's flat because the animal picked up Percy's scent in Edith's flat. There might have been a perfectly innocent explanation for this but, in view of Percy's denial that he had ever been inside the flat, the evidence is capable of supporting the prosecution case. *Pieterson* (1995) established that evidence of the activities of tracker dogs will be admissible, provided a proper foundation can be laid to establish reliability. The dog's handler should give evidence about its training, and should also establish that over a period of time, it behaved reliably as a tracker during controlled tests.

Evidence can be given of what Percy said to the police. The prosecution will wish to show that Percy lied about his association with Edith and will invite the jury to infer guilt from this. The purpose in adducing evidence of what Percy said will be to show its falsity, not its truth. In these circumstances, the rule against hearsay does not apply (*Mawaz Khan v R* (1967)).

Curtis can give evidence of the sounds that he heard coming from Edith's flat on the evening of 14 July. A jury would be entitled to infer from this that an argument was going on at the time. Curtis could also say that he heard the accents of an Australian male to show that such a person was present on that occasion. Neither of these items of evidence infringes the rule against hearsay because the purpose of adducing the evidence is not to establish the truth of what was said, but the fact that there was an argument and that one of the participants was an Australian man.

The evidential value of the letter found in Percy's desk is not that it establishes the truth about Edith's love life, but that it enables us to infer that Percy had been having some sort of relationship with a woman called Edith and that he probably had a vengeful state of mind towards her. The fact of the relationship is not to be inferred from the fact that the writer of the letter thought that there was one; to argue on these lines would be to fall foul of the prohibition against implied hearsay established in *Kearley* (1992). But the argument can be put thus: why should Percy have such an interest in the letter that he kept it in his desk if he did *not* have any such relationship? In other words, it is Percy's reaction to what was written that is relied on, not the truth of what was said in the letter. Evidence was admitted for a similar purpose in *McIntosh* (1992) where the defendant was charged with importing drugs. In a house where he had been living before his arrest, the police found a piece of paper which contained calculations, not in the defendant's hand writing, of the purchase and sale prices of 12 oz of an unnamed commodity. The Court of Appeal held that this evidence had been properly admitted as circumstantial real evidence tending to connect the accused with the crime charged. Though not spelled out by the court, the reason appears to have been that the person in possession of the document kept it because he was interested in the information which it contained.

Given that there was a relationship between Percy and Edith, then, *regardless of the truth of what was said about Edith in the letter*, the fact that the allegation was read and the letter kept suggests that Percy took it seriously, and from that it can be inferred that he may have had vengeful feelings towards Edith.

One possible inference from the parrot's behaviour is that the bird was repeating what it heard Edith shout on the evening when she was murdered. From this it could be inferred that, because Frederick is named rather than Percy, it was not Percy who murdered her. The first point to be made is that what the parrot 'said' was not an assertion, on the assumption – perhaps arrogant – that a human brain is required for articulation to amount to something so sophisticated. Because some parrots tend to repeat human language which they hear, Max might be seen as a recording device. Had a tape recorder been operating at the time, the tape could well have been admissible as direct evidence of what was going on. In *Maqsud Ali* (1966), the Court of Appeal held that a tape recording is admissible in evidence provided, *inter alia*, the accuracy of the recording can be proved and the voices properly identified. It was held by Shaw J in *Robson and Harris* (1972) that if there is a challenge to the accuracy of a tape, the court must be satisfied that a *prima facie* case of originality has been made out before allowing it to go to the jury.

The real difficulty here is not one of hearsay, for the parrot made no assertion and, by analogy with *Taylor v Chief Constable of Cheshire* (1987), Lilian should be allowed to give evidence of what she heard if Max is properly seen as a recording device but cannot be made to operate in the presence of the jury. The prosecution could legitimately object, however, that as a recording device Max is most unreliable. How could the court be satisfied, even on a *prima facie* basis, that Max did not pick up this expression on some quite different occasion and from someone other than Edith? The truth of the matter is that even if Max does not have a mind, he has a brain, and thus is quite different from the sort of mechanical recording devices whose products have been admitted hitherto by the courts as real evidence. Lilian's evidence is therefore most unlikely to be admissible for the defence.

CHAPTER 5

HEARSAY EXCEPTIONS

Introduction

You need to keep two categories clearly in mind: common law exceptions, and statutory exceptions for documentary hearsay. Both categories affect criminal cases only. The Civil Evidence Act 1995 effectively abolished the rule against hearsay in civil proceedings. The Act has certain procedural provisions but, unless your examination covers procedure as well as evidence, these are of minimal concern.

The main common law exceptions are:

- *Res gestae* statements. These are often taken to include four different situations:
  (a) Where the statement accompanies and explains the acts of the person making it, for example, *McCay* (1990).
  (b) Spontaneous exclamations by the victim of an offence or an observer. The leading case is *Andrews* (1987) and you should know what Lord Ackner said in that case about the general test of admissibility.
  (c) Declarations of a person's own contemporaneous state of mind or emotion. This is a favourite with examiners. Pay particular attention to the cases about statements of intention; they may be capable of being reconciled, but you will need to think about this. Don't forget that the cases deal with declarations of intention to do specific things. Examiners are fond of something more vague, so you may have to think about relevance too.
  (d) Declarations about the speaker's physical sensations. The statement must be approximately contemporaneous with the physical state, and remember that the statement may not be used to prove the cause of that state.
- Statements of deceased persons. These include the following:
  (a) Declarations against pecuniary or proprietary interest. Remember that a declaration in this category may be admitted not merely to prove the fact that is against the declarant's interest, but also to prove collateral facts which are part of the declaration, provided they are necessary to explain the nature of the transaction about which the declaration has been made. See *Higham v Ridgway* (1808); *Rogers* (1995).

   (b) Dying declarations in homicide cases. Remember to make it clear that the declarant must have a settled, hopeless expectation of imminent death.

   (c) Statements in the course of duty. These are most likely to be written, and so do come within a statutory exception. But exceptionally, such a statement may be oral, in which case you will need to know the common law.

- Statements made in furtherance of a common purpose. The law on this topic has become lively in the last few years. A statement made in the course or furtherance of a common purpose by one party may be admissible against another, and this rule is not confined to conspiracy cases. It applies wherever the prosecution alleges a joint enterprise. But you should make sure that the statement you are dealing with is one that has been made *in the course or furtherance of the common purpose*. The exception does not, for example, apply to a confession of one conspirator after his arrest: *Walters* (1979).

- Confessions. This topic is separately considered in Chapter 7.

The hearsay provisions of the Criminal Justice Act 1988 (ss 23–26) have to be understood. You should note that they apply only to *documentary* hearsay. Remember that, when you have considered ss 23 and 24, you must go on to consider which of ss 25 and 26 applies, and you should appreciate the difference between them. An important case is *Derodra* (2000), in which the Court of Appeal refused to follow the decision of the Divisional Court in *Brown v Secretary of State for Social Security* (1994). The Court of Appeal said that when, in the latter case, the Divisional Court had drawn attention to the distinction in s 24 of the Criminal Justice Act 1988 between the supplier of the information and the maker of the statement, the court had been wrong to assume that the 'maker of the statement' meant the maker of the document, however mechanical a role he played. The correct view of the 'maker of the statement', according to the Court of Appeal, is that it is the person who makes, or vouches for, the representation of fact that the statement consists of. Who that is will depend on the circumstances of each case. It is now, therefore, far more likely to be the supplier of the information who has to be unavailable or unable to remember (see ss 23(2), (3) and 24(4)).

Checklist

Students should be familiar with the following areas:

- *res gestae* exceptions;
- statements of deceased persons;

- statements made in the course or furtherance of a common purpose;
- documentary hearsay provisions in ss 23–26 of the Criminal Justice Act 1988;
- the special provision for experts' reports in s 30 of the Criminal Justice Act 1988.

Question 14

Harold is charged with the murder of his wife, Irene. The case for the prosecution is that he stabbed her with a bread knife because he believed that she was having an affair with the local vicar. Irene died later in hospital from the wounds that she received. Consider the evidential issues that arise in the following circumstances:

(a) A month before she was stabbed, Irene called in a distressed state on her neighbour, Joan. Irene brought with her a meat axe and a chainsaw, and she asked Joan to look after them for her. When Joan asked why, Irene replied: 'Harold keeps threatening me with these and I'd feel safer if they were out of the way.' She added: 'I've been feeling sick after meals; I think he's already trying to poison me.'

(b) In the ambulance on the way to hospital, Irene said to Larry, a paramedic: 'It was all because of the vicar. He'd only come about the choir outing.' She then lost consciousness.

(c) At the hospital, Irene regained consciousness and asked to see the hospital chaplain. On his arrival, the chaplain said: 'Do you know what's happening to you, Irene?' Irene replied: 'Yes. I don't think I've much chance, have I? I'm going, and if there were any justice in this world that bastard Harold would be coming with me.' She then fell into a coma and died six weeks later without regaining consciousness.

Answer plan

In part (a), you need to ask why the prosecution would want to adduce evidence of Irene's visit to Joan. Obviously, they would like it to be admitted, if possible, to show Harold's intention to kill his wife. This involves considering three elements in the story that Joan might tell:

- the fact that Irene had the meat axe and chainsaw and was in a distressed state;
- what Irene said about her husband's threats;
- what Irene said about feeling sick after meals.

The question involves hearsay exceptions in favour of contemporaneous bodily or mental feelings, and the extent to which reasons may be given for their existence.

Note that there is some authority which might be used to persuade a court to let in evidence of the threats, but it is at first instance only and needs to be questioned.

In relation to the complaint about sickness, the requirement of contemporaneity has to be considered, but note also the objections to repeating what Irene said about the cause. That leaves only the first item, but this by itself could suggest any number of things and lead the jury into mere speculation.

Part (b) also involves relevance; don't forget to refer to this. *Res gestae* arises also. Part (c) tests your knowledge of the law relating to dying declarations. Remember to apply this to the particular facts of the question; the examiner does not want just a repetition of your notes on the subject.

Remember also to consider *res gestae* as an alternative to the dying declaration exception. This may be particularly important because, in at least one case (*Carnall* (1995)), the lapse of time between the attack on the victim and his admissible *res gestae* statement was about an hour.

Answer

(a) The purpose of adducing evidence of what Irene said to Joan would be to establish the murderous intentions of the accused towards his wife. To the extent that it is necessary to rely on the truth of the words uttered by Irene, the rule against hearsay is a potential bar to admissibility.

Although there are circumstances where evidence of a person's distress may be both relevant and admissible, the fact that Irene was in a distressed state when she called on Joan will be relevant only to show her husband's intentions towards her, and this can be done only if Irene's state can be explained by reference to one or more of her utterances. The same principle applies to the fact that Irene had with her a meat axe and a chainsaw. Her possession of these will be relevant only if evidence can be given of her reason for having them, and this can be done only if the rule against hearsay is avoided.

As an exception to this rule, the statement of a person in which she relates her contemporaneous bodily or mental feelings may be admissible. For example, in *Gandfield* (1846), it was held that a person's declarations could be proved in order to show that his fear of some burglars had prevented him from reporting their conduct to the police. And, in *Vincent* (1840), where the question arose whether a public meeting had caused alarm, a police officer was allowed to give evidence that a number of bystanders had told him that the assembly frightened them. It might therefore seem that Joan could give evidence of what Irene had said about the meat axe and chainsaw, and indeed similar evidence was held admissible at first instance in *Edwards* (1872). In this case, as in *Gandfield* (1846) and *Vincent* (1840), reference to the cause of the fear was held to be admissible.

But, in relation to contemporaneous bodily feelings, it seems clear that, while the feelings can be proved, the cause cannot. Thus, in *Gloster* (1888), statements by a woman who was dying from the effects of an illegal abortion, and who named the person responsible, were held inadmissible on the basis that to be admissible such statements must be confined to contemporaneous symptoms and should not include any sort of narrative purporting to say how the symptoms were brought about. Although this was a decision at first instance, it was later approved by the Court of Criminal Appeal in *Thomson* (1912).

A difference between the law affecting statements about physical states and that affecting statements about mental states is unattractive. It is probable, therefore, that the words 'Harold keeps threatening me with these' would not be admissible either to explain Irene's distress or her request. It would, of course, be equally unacceptable to prove the words 'I'd feel safer if they were out of the way' and invite the jury to draw as an inference what could not be proved as an express statement.[1]

It may be doubted whether Irene's complaint that she had been feeling sick after meals was strictly a statement of *contemporaneous* bodily feelings. In *Black* (1922), where the accused was charged with murdering his wife by poison, it was held on appeal that her descriptions of symptoms which she had experienced after taking medicine given to her by her husband were admissible only because they had been made in his presence in such a way as to call for an explanation from him at the time when they were first uttered. Avory J said that had the descriptions not been made in the accused's presence, their admissibility would have been doubtful because they had concerned her past, rather than her contemporaneous, feelings. By contrast, Salter J suggested that 'contemporaneous' ought not to be confined to feelings experienced at the actual moment of speaking.

Even if Irene's statement about feeling sick after meals were to be admitted, it would acquire relevance only when linked to her surmise that Harold was trying to poison her. What she said about this would not be admissible. First, it clearly suggests a cause of her physical condition and case law, as appears above, is against the admission of such evidence. Secondly, there appears to be no other evidence – in particular, no medical evidence – to show that she was being poisoned. Her speculation alone would be both highly prejudicial to the defendant and highly unreliable material with which to establish murderous intent.

(b) This is evidence which, though somewhat ambiguous, is capable of supporting the contention of the prosecution about motive. The question is whether it is likely to be admitted by way of exception to the rule against hearsay as part of the *res gestae*.

According to the decision of the House of Lords in *Andrews* (1987), the primary question to be asked is whether the possibility of concoction or distortion by Irene can be disregarded. To answer this question, the judge will consider the circumstances in which she made the statement. Was the event so unusual, startling or dramatic as to dominate her thoughts, so that her utterance was an instinctive reaction to that event? Irene's case is likely to satisfy these conditions.

There appear to be no special features giving rise to the possibility of honest error on Irene's part such as were referred to in *Andrews*. On the facts given, it seems likely that her statement to the paramedic will be admissible.

(c) The relevance of Irene's words is that by implication they point to her husband as the assailant. Their admissibility may depend on whether they can be brought within the exception to the hearsay rule in favour of dying declarations. Such a declaration must be made when the maker has a settled, hopeless expectation of imminent death. If any vestige of hope remains, the statement is inadmissible (*Gloster* (1888)).

The question therefore is whether the words 'I'm going ... coming with me' should be regarded as qualified by 'I don't think I've much chance, have I?'. If, as seems likely, the latter expression should be seen as an understood acceptance by Irene of her imminent death, her declaration will be admissible. It is irrelevant that in fact she remained alive for some further time before dying. In *Bernadotti* (1869), for example, the declarant lived for nearly three weeks after making the declaration, which was nevertheless held to be admissible.

Another possibility is that the words might be admissible as part of the *res gestae*. Inquiries should be made about the length of time that elapsed between the stabbing and the arrival of the ambulance, and between the latter event and the time when Irene regained consciousness in hospital. In *Carnall* (1995), the victim had been stabbed and beaten with baseball bats, but his account of the incident about an hour later was held by the trial judge, applying the tests in *Andrews*, to be still part of the *res gestae*. The Court of Appeal said he had been entitled to come to that conclusion.

The court added that it was not necessarily fatal to the exception that the statement had been prompted by a question.

Note

1   If any doubt existed about this, *Kearley* (1992) would seem to have resolved it.

Question 15

Charles Peace is charged with the burglary on 15 May of a house in Penny Avenue. On the afternoon of 15 May, PC Moriarty was walking past Penny Avenue when a man whom he did not recognise ran up to him and shouted, 'My God! I've just seen Charles Peace breaking into a house down Penny Avenue! And he was my Sunday School teacher!'. PC Moriarty did not make a note of this at the time or do anything else about it because the man's speech was slurred and he was unsteady on his feet. When the burglary was reported, efforts were made to trace the man who had spoken to PC Moriarty, but without success.

Shortly after Charles was arrested, his brother Martin committed suicide. Martin's girlfriend Nora says that the night before Martin killed himself, he told her that it was he (Martin) who had committed the burglary for which Charles had been arrested. Nora also says that 10 days before the burglary, Martin had told her that there were rich pickings in Penny Avenue and that he was going to do a burglary there very soon. She has now found a diary kept by Martin. The entry for 15 May reads, 'This is the day!'.

Discuss the evidential issues that arise.

Answer plan

The first part of the question involves *res gestae* with the added complication that the eyewitness may have been under the influence of alcohol. There are no documentary statements, so no question of using the Criminal Justice Act 1988 arises.

The second part of the question requires you to deal with the admission of guilt by Martin to Nora, Martin's earlier expression of intention to her, and the entry in his diary.

The admission of guilt appears to be covered by *Turner* (1975). There may be an arguable point based on declarations against pecuniary interest. In relation to expressions of intention, note the different decisions and note how the answer discusses the facts on this point as well as the law. The diary entry requires you to think about relevance again. As well as the obvious reference to s 23 of the Criminal Justice Act 1988, don't forget s 25.

Answer

Can evidence of what the man said to PC Moriarty be adduced in order to establish the truth of what he said, namely, that he had just seen Charles Peace breaking into a house in Penny Avenue? This will be the case only if the evidence can be brought within the *res gestae* exception to the rule against hearsay.

On the face of it, the conditions for the application of this exception appear to be satisfied. According to *Andrews* (1987), the basic question in such a case is whether the possibility of concoction or distortion by the out of court speaker can be disregarded. The initial exclamation 'My God!' and the final words 'And he was my Sunday School teacher!' may well be thought to indicate that the event perceived had been so unusual, startling or dramatic as to dominate the speaker's thoughts, so that his utterance was an instinctive reaction to the event. The words 'I've just seen ...' suggest that there was very little time between perception and utterance.

However, in *Andrews* (1987), Lord Ackner said that there may be special features, apart from the ordinary fallibility of human recollection, which give rise to the possibility of error and which may justify excluding the evidence. He added that the out of court speaker's having drunk to excess would be one such feature. The trial judge in Peace's case would therefore have to consider PC Moriarty's evidence about the speaker's slurred speech and unsteadiness in order to determine whether what would otherwise be admissible as a *res gestae* statement ought to be excluded.

Can Nora give evidence that Martin told her that he, and not Charles, had committed the burglary? Admissions made outside court which incriminate persons other than the accused are generally inadmissible in evidence because of the rule against hearsay. In *Turner* (1975), the Court of Appeal refused to allow a defendant to rely on hearsay evidence to show that someone not called as a witness had confessed to having committed the offence charged, and the House of Lords approved this decision in *Blastland* (1986). The hearsay exceptions permitted by ss 23 and 24 of the Criminal Justice Act 1988 apply only to documentary hearsay. The only other hearsay exception which might be relevant is the one in favour of declarations by a person who has later died against his pecuniary or proprietary interest.[1]

In the *Sussex Peerage Case* (1844), the House of Lords held to be inadmissible evidence tendered of a statement made by a clergyman who had afterwards died, concerning a marriage ceremony at which he had officiated. The ceremony in question could have exposed the clergyman to criminal liability under the Royal Marriages Act 1772. Lord Brougham emphasised that the only declarations of deceased persons receivable in evidence were those made against the pecuniary or proprietary interest of the speaker, and it is sometimes said that a declaration that exposes someone to merely penal consequences will not be admitted. However, it is arguable that the declaration in this case was against the pecuniary interest of the maker, Martin, because it could have exposed him to either a fine or a compensation order in criminal proceedings, or to a civil action for damages at the suit of the owner of the house. It is possible, therefore, that evidence of Martin's confession will be admissible under this exception.

Can Nora give evidence that 10 days before the burglary, Martin said that he was going to do a burglary in Penny Avenue very soon? The case for admissibility is uncertain here also. In principle, a statement of present intention appears to be admissible under the exception to the rule against hearsay, which permits evidence to be given of statements of contemporaneous mental feelings. The cases, however, show that judicial attitudes to such evidence vary.

In *Buckley* (1873), a police inspector was allowed to give evidence that a constable had told him on a particular day that he intended to go that evening to keep watch on the defendant. The purpose of adducing this evidence was to permit an inference to be drawn that the constable had carried out his intention. However, no reason was given for the decision, and it may be that the statement was admitted because it was a declaration made by the constable in the course of his duty.[2] In *Wainwright* (1875), where two brothers were charged with the murder of a woman, evidence was available from someone who had seen the victim leaving her lodgings on the day of the murder. The witness was ready to say that the victim had announced her intention of going to a particular address, which was that of one of the accused. The prosecution appears to have argued that the victim's statement of intention was admissible as part of the act of leaving her lodgings. It appears, therefore, to have relied on a different hearsay exception: that which covers statements relating to the maker's performance of an action, as in *McCay* (1990). But it could be argued that the words of the trial judge were relevant to this exception also. In excluding the evidence as hearsay, he said that it was only a statement of intention, which might or might not have been carried out.

In *Thomson* (1912), where the defendant was charged with using an instrument on a woman for the purpose of procuring a miscarriage, the defence was that the woman (who had died from another cause before trial) had performed the operation on herself. The trial judge ruled inadmissible evidence of her earlier declared intention to do this. In the Court of Criminal Appeal, it was argued that a defendant is entitled to adduce any evidence that would support his defence, whether or not admissible according to the rules of evidence. Not surprisingly, this argument was rejected. No attempt was made to argue on the narrower ground that the dead woman's words were admissible as an expression of her intention. *Buckley* was not cited. The prosecution did cite *Wainwright*, but it is not clear that in that case, the court had this particular exception in mind.

In *Moghal* (1977), however, a statement of intention was held, *obiter*, to be admissible. The defendant was charged with murder and his defence was that the murder had been committed by another person, S. The Court of Appeal took the view that evidence of a statement made six months before the murder by S, in which she had declared her intention to murder the victim, was admissible.[3]

It seems possible that this opinion would be followed in the case of Charles Peace, as Martin's declaration was also of an intention to commit a crime and was made a good deal closer to the event than that in *Moghal* (1977). The only feature that might serve to distinguish Martin's declaration is that it is not as specific as that in *Moghal*. There, a particular victim was mentioned; Martin declared his intention of committing burglary only within a defined area.

The entry in Martin's diary for 15 May is potentially covered by s 23 of the Criminal Justice Act 1988. It is a statement made by a person now deceased in a document. But s 25(2)(c) directs the court to have regard to the relevance of the evidence that the document appears to supply to any issue which is likely to have to be determined in the proceedings. The meaning of 'This is the day!' is most unclear. Something seems to have made the day significant for Martin, but there is little evidence to show what. Perhaps if it is taken in conjunction with Nora's evidence about Martin's statement of intention, it becomes a little less ambiguous, so that a judge might feel able to leave it for consideration by the jury.

Notes

1   A dying declaration must relate to the cause of the declarant's death.

2   For details of this exception, see *Andrews & Hirst on Criminal Evidence*, 4th edn, 2001, pp 615–16.

3   But see the criticism based on relevance in Lord Bridge's speech in *Blastland* (1986).

Question 16

Adrian, Billy and Charlie are charged with possession of drugs with intent to supply. In the house where all three lived, police found a large quantity of cocaine, and £28,000 in used banknotes. When interviewed, all three defendants said that the money had been the proceeds of successful gambling. They said that they had just moved into the house and had no knowledge of the presence of the cocaine, which had been discovered in the loft. The police also found a diary in Adrian's handwriting, in which there appeared inside the back cover a list containing references to first names, to various quantities of something that was unspecified, and to sums of money. Below the list was written: 'Adrian to get half; Billy and Charlie a quarter each.' There were also various entries for the week before the date when all three were arrested. One of these read: 'Billy and Charlie are getting cold feet. I wish they hadn't persuaded me to let them in on the deals.' For two weeks before the arrests were made, DC Kray kept watch outside the house, which was visited by 26 people. He was able to identify 18 of these as persons with previous convictions for the possession of drugs.

Discuss the evidential matters arising.

Answer plan

There are three items of evidence that need your consideration:

- is evidence of finding the money admissible? If so, does the judge need to say anything about it in summing up?;
- are the contents of Adrian's diary admissible? Against whom? Don't forget that the entries should be dealt with separately. Will the judge need to give any special direction?;
- is the evidence of DC Kray admissible for the prosecution?

Answer

In relation to the cash, two questions arise. Is it relevant to the prosecution case? If it is, what directions should the judge give to the jury about it? In *Wright* (1994), the Court of Appeal held that the discovery of £16,000 in cash in the defendant's flat was admissible to support a charge of possessing cocaine with intent to supply, on the basis that drug dealers are known to deal in large sums of cash. However, in *Batt* (1994), the Court of Appeal held that the finding of cash (albeit in that case a much smaller sum) was inadmissible, because it was suggestive only of past dealings. As such, it was unfairly prejudicial because it showed only a disposition to commit such offences. *Batt* seems difficult to reconcile with *Wright*, but later cases have tended to prefer the reasoning in *Wright*. Therefore, the position is that the finding of the cash is likely to be admissible to support the charge, but there are two elements in the charge, both of which the defendants deny. Not only do they deny intent to supply; they also deny *possession* (their case is that they knew nothing of the presence of the cocaine). In *Guney* (1998), the Court of Appeal said that whether evidence is relevant depends on the circumstances of each case. Where possession with intent to supply is charged, there are many circumstances in which evidence of cash and lifestyle might be relevant and admissible in relation to the issue of possession itself, especially to the issue of knowledge as an ingredient of possession. Thus, the discovery of the cash is relevant to possession as well as intent to supply.[1]

However, a careful direction will have to be given to the jury about the use they can make of this information. In *Grant* (1996), the Court of Appeal said that before relying on such evidence, the jury must be satisfied that the money was not in the defendant's possession for any innocent reason that may have been advanced (in this case, as a result of successful gambling) and that, even if they find that it does relate to drug dealing, they must be satisfied that it relates to an ongoing course of dealing, and is not merely the proceeds of past deals.

The entries in Adrian's diary should be separately considered. It was held in *Gray and Others* (1995) that a statement made in furtherance of a common purpose by one defendant is admissible as evidence against the others, though made in their absence. The reason for this is that a combination of persons for the purpose of committing a crime is regarded as implying an authority to each to act or speak in furtherance of the common purpose on behalf of the others. For example, in *Devonport and Pirano* (1996), where the defendants were charged with conspiracy to defraud a bank, a document drawn up by the girlfriend of one of the defendants, at the latter's dictation, showed an intended division of the proceeds of the offence between all the defendants, who were named. It was held that this was evidence against all the defendants, there being evidence in addition to the document to show that they were all parties to the conspiracy. Since the document was a record of *intended* distribution of the proceeds when the conspiracy had been fulfilled, it had been prepared in furtherance of the conspiracy, and was thus admissible. It would have been different if the document had been merely a record, made when everything was finished, of what had happened.

The entries at the back of Adrian's diary show an *intended* distribution between the three defendants, and there is other evidence (the discovery of the drugs and the cash in the house where all three lived) to link Billy and Charlie to a common enterprise, even though not charged as a conspiracy. On this basis, the entry is admissible against all the defendants. But the judge will have to warn the jury that they must be satisfied that the entry was not only evidence of past dealing, but capable of going to intention to supply in the future. In other words, the diary entry must be treated with the same caution as the discovery of the cash: see *Lovelock* (1997).

The second entry about Billy and Charlie getting cold feet is clearly not made in furtherance of the common enterprise. It is admissible as a confession by Adrian, or at least as evidence of his contemporaneous state of mind, but it is not evidence against the other defendants.

The evidence of DC Kray may be relevant because it shows the sort of people frequenting the house, and tends to show that the house was being used for drug dealing. Similar evidence was admitted in *Warner* (1993), where the prosecution's case was that the pattern of visits was consistent with the method of drug dealing testified to by prosecution witnesses. The defence case was that the visitors had been making only social calls, but in *Hasson* (1997), evidence that the defendants, who were charged with being concerned in the supply of cannabis resin, had associated with persons with drug related convictions was held inadmissible. In contrast to *Warner*, it was not part of the prosecution case that the defendants were supplying drugs to those whose convictions were adduced in evidence. The question on these facts therefore appears to be whether there is a nexus between the defendants' association with these visitors and any specific allegation of dealing made by the prosecution. In the absence of such a nexus, the evidence is likely to be inadmissible.

Note

1   See also *Griffiths* (1998).

Question 17

Michael, who runs a car hire firm, is charged with manslaughter. The case for the prosecution is that he rented a car to Nick for one week on 1 April. On 2 April, the car was found at the bottom of a cliff with Nick's body inside. The prosecution alleges that when Michael rented the car to Nick, the steering mechanism was, to Michael's knowledge, so faulty that a driver would be likely to lose control of the car. Michael intends to plead not guilty. He denies that the steering mechanism was faulty. He says that if it was faulty, he had no knowledge of this. He says that fog on the night of the accident made visibility very poor, and that this caused Nick to drive off the road and over the cliff. Another explanation, he says, is that Nick drove over the cliff deliberately because he believed that his wife had left him. Michael wishes to testify that one week before the accident, he rented the same car to Olive, a qualified car mechanic. Michael says that he saw Olive examine the car carefully before getting in and taking it on a test drive by herself. Only when she returned did she allow her children to get in as passengers. Michael also wishes to call Patrick, Nick's best friend, who says that he received a call from Nick's mobile telephone on the night of 1 April. According to Patrick, Nick said: 'I'm driving along a cliff road. The fog is frightening, but I can't find anywhere to stop the car.' The prosecution has disclosed that a note was found on Nick's kitchen table. It was from his wife and was dated 31 March. It said: 'I can't stand living with you any more. I have gone to live with Quentin in Ireland. Don't try to contact me.'

Discuss the evidential issues arising.

Answer plan

There are three items of evidence, to be considered separately:

- the incident involving Olive;
- Patrick's account of the mobile phone call from Nick;
- the note from Nick's wife.

Answer

The significance of the incident involving Olive is that it shows that the car was in good condition only a week before Nick hired it. Olive was a qualified car mechanic, she examined the car carefully before taking it for a test drive, and only on her return did she take her children as passengers. The inference is that she found the car to be in a safe condition. Of course, the fact that the car was safe then does not mean inevitably that there was nothing wrong with it when Nick hired it, but it makes it unlikely. Unfortunately, Michael's evidence about the incident with Olive may not be admissible. Arguably, it constitutes what has been called 'hearsay by conduct'. It has been clear since *Kearley* (1992) that non-assertive utterances are inadmissible to prove inferences as to the existence or non-existence of facts, on the basis that such evidence is caught by the rule against hearsay. In that case, the prosecution wanted to adduce evidence of requests for drugs by telephone callers and visitors to the defendant's house in order to prove that the defendant was engaged in supplying drugs. The House of Lords, relying on *Wright v Doe d Tatham* (1837), held that this evidence was hearsay and inadmissible. Neither *Wright v Tatham* nor *Kearley* was concerned with non-verbal conduct. But in the earlier case, Parke B considered *obiter* whether evidence of actions might be admissible as a way of avoiding the rule against hearsay. He concluded that such evidence also would be inadmissible. In doing so, he gave an example very close to the present facts. He envisaged a trial where the seaworthiness of a ship was in issue. Suppose the deceased captain had first examined every part of the vessel and only then had embarked in it with his family. Such evidence would, said Parke B, be affected by the rule against hearsay just as much as a statement by the captain to a bystander that he had examined the ship and found it seaworthy.

Common sense suggests that this is carrying the hearsay rule too far. Behind every action there is presumably a belief in a state of affairs that would justify the action in question. If rigorously applied, Parke B's opinion would mean that you could not prove that it was raining by giving evidence of seeing persons in the street with open umbrellas. It is an open question whether a court would extend the rule against hearsay so far, but the possibility exists. Much reliance was placed on *Wright v Tatham* in *Kearley*. On the other hand, the evils which the hearsay rule is designed to avoid are not all present in 'hearsay by conduct'. Although the conduct observed may be ambiguous, and may be based on inaccurate perception, the person performing the action is most unlikely to be doing so with the intention of deceiving anybody.

Whether Patrick can give evidence of what Nick said during the telephone call depends on whether it falls under one of the categories of the *res gestae* exception. One possibility is that it would be admissible as evidence of Nick's contemporaneous state of mind or emotion, but the case law on this topic is unsatisfactory, and it might be, by analogy with the exception relating to contemporaneous physical sensations, that although evidence could be given of Nick's fright, the cause of it could not be stated. A better chance of admissibility lies in arguing that what Nick said constituted an 'excited utterance'. The leading authority is *Andrews* (1987). This requires that the circumstances provoking the utterance should have been so unusual, startling or dramatic as to dominate the thoughts of the speaker to the extent that the utterance was an instinctive reaction to those circumstances, with no opportunity for reflection or concoction. The difficulty on these facts is that what Nick appears to have been experiencing, though unpleasant, was not a sudden event; it was, apparently, a continuing state of affairs. As such, it could be argued that it lacked the dramatic quality of something like the sudden and violent attack in *Carnall* (1995). Thus, it is difficult to predict with certainty whether or not Patrick's evidence would be admitted.

The one item of evidence that would almost certainly be admitted is the note that was found on the kitchen table. One of the defence theories is that Nick committed suicide when he discovered that his wife had left him. The evidence of the note will be admissible quite simply for the effect it might have had on Nick's mind. In *Subramaniam v Public Prosecutor* (1956), the Privy Council emphasised that a statement will not be caught by the rule against hearsay where it is adduced merely to establish the fact that it was made. This fact, quite apart from the truth of the statement, is frequently relevant in considering the mental state and conduct of someone to whom the statement was made. That is exactly the relevance of the note on these facts. It might have been quite untrue that the wife had gone to Ireland or had decided to leave her husband for another man. The point is that Nick might have believed what he read, and this might have given him a motive for suicide.

Question 18

Why is the scope of the hearsay rule so difficult to assess?

Answer plan

Start with the basic definition in *Sharp* (1988). Then make these points:

- the test is one involving use of language, and that may present difficulties;
- the discretionary element in the statutory exceptions in criminal cases;
- the undeveloped law in relation to some of the common law exceptions;
- the fact that, from time to time, the courts have ignored the rule.

Then turn to the extension of the rule to cover implied assertions, and the difficulties of its application.

Answer

In *Sharp* (1988), Lord Havers adopted Cross's definition of the rule against hearsay: 'An assertion other than one made by a person while giving oral evidence in the proceedings is inadmissible as evidence of any fact asserted.' This rule is subject to common law and statutory exceptions, but at first glance, there might appear to be little difficulty in assessing its scope. At second glance, however, it will be seen that the rule is essentially one about the use of language. It may not always be easy to determine whether an utterance is being used to establish the truth of its contents, or merely the fact that it was made. An early example showing this difficulty was *Subramaniam v Public Prosecutor* (1956).

Problems also arise in determining the scope of the rule because of the large discretionary element contained in ss 25 and 26 of the Criminal Justice Act 1988, which determine the admissibility of certain documentary hearsay statements. The Law Commission noted this and concluded that the discretionary provisions have not worked satisfactorily because of a wide variety of judicial willingness to admit such evidence (see Law Com No 245, paras 1.29 and 6.36).

Perhaps surprisingly, further difficulties in determining scope have arisen because of the relatively undeveloped state of the law relating to common law exceptions. The cases relating to the admissibility of statements of intention suffer particularly from this defect. In *Buckley* (1873), a decision at first instance, such evidence was admitted, but no reasons were given for the decision. In *Wainwright* (1875), another decision at first instance, such evidence was excluded, but the argument put forward in favour of admissibility may have been a different one, namely that the words uttered explained the speaker's performance of an act. In *Thomson* (1912), the Court of Criminal Appeal held such evidence inadmissible. But *Buckley* (1873) was not cited, and the appellant's argument was based on the much broader proposition that an accused person is entitled to adduce any evidence that is relevant to his defence, whether or not it is admissible according to the strict rules of evidence. A more favourable view of the admissibility of such evidence was taken by the Court of Appeal in *Moghal* (1977). A still more favourable view was taken in *Gilfoyle* (1996), which had the apparent effect of removing the requirement of contemporaneity between the utterance and the state of mind under investigation.

Another problematic decision is *Callender* (1998), in which the Court of Appeal adopted a novel approach to *res gestae*, saying that the *Andrews* requirement of lack of opportunity for concoction or distortion applied in all the *res gestae* categories. This statement of the law is not supported by earlier authorities, and may have been made as the result of a mistaken concession by counsel for the appellant. However, its effect is to confuse further a significant common law exception to the rule against hearsay.

New developments have taken place in relation to other exceptions also. The significance of narratives in declarations in furtherance of a common purpose has been discussed in recent decisions (see *Gray* (1995) and *Jones* (1997)). *Rogers* (1995) limited the circumstances in which collateral words in declarations against pecuniary or proprietary interest can be relied on. The old limitation in the *Sussex Peerage Case* (1844), that declarations against penal interest were not covered by this exception, looks increasingly suspect in view of the wide range of the powers of criminal courts to make orders for compensation and confiscation of property.

Another problem in determining the scope of the rule is that, despite the declaration in *Myers v DPP* (1965) that it was too late for the courts to create any new exceptions to the rule, courts have nevertheless from time to time simply conveniently forgotten its existence. So, for example, they have done so in the rules allowing a witness to 'refresh his memory' from an earlier note. The evidential status given to all the parts of a defendant's out-of-court 'mixed' statement in *Sharp* (1988) is another example. Expert opinion evidence is allowed to be based extensively on hearsay (*Abadom* (1983)), and evidence of an earlier identification probably offended the hearsay rule in *Osbourne and Virtue* (1973). In that case, a witness not only could not remember identifying the defendant; she could not remember identifying anyone. However, someone who observed her earlier identification was allowed to give evidence of what she had done and said on that occasion. Another aspect of identification evidence that appears to ignore the rule is that whereby a sketch or photofit image, based on information supplied by a witness, may be admitted as evidence (*Cook* (1987)).

A case in which the rule against hearsay was evaded rather than ignored was *Ward* (2001), in which a statement as to identity by a driver of a car, who was otherwise unidentified, was held to be evidence of that identity. The Court of Appeal acknowledged that it was *prima facie* hearsay and could not be brought within any relevant hearsay exception. Nevertheless, it held the statement admissible on the basis that if a man gave his full name, a date of birth which was that of the person with the full name, and an address which was also that of the person with that name, the evidence was strong enough to establish an admission.

The difficulties so far discussed in determining the scope of the rule have been added to by the decision in *Kearley* (1992), which gave the authority of the House of Lords to the concept of an 'implied assertion'. This concept is itself muddled, based as it is on something that can be *inferred* by a court rather than on anything *implied* by the maker of a non-assertive utterance. The potential for operation of the hearsay rule was much increased by this decision. It will be increased still more if the *dicta* of Baron Parke concerning hearsay by non-verbal conduct in *Wright v Tatham* (1837) – a decision heavily relied on in *Kearley* (1992) – are followed.

CHAPTER 6

HAZARDOUS EVIDENCE

Introduction

All evidence, without exception, is hazardous. There are several reasons for this.

The first is that all evidence emerges as the result of some sort of selection. One kind may be loosely described as 'natural selection'. Not all the evidence that is relevant to a particular inquiry will have survived. Witnesses may have died; documents may have been destroyed; the physical features of a building may have been altered. Another sort of selection is human selection. In any investigation, someone has to gather the evidence that has survived. But to gather evidence effectively, you have to be intelligent enough to recognise what may be significant, and honest enough to do the job without pre-conceived ideas of what the outcome of the investigation should be. Natural selection and human frailty between them ensure that no jury ever sees more than a part of the whole picture, and that part may be a very small and misleading one.[1]

Another reason for the hazardous nature of evidence is that too much has to be taken on trust. It is not always appreciated that the only direct experience upon which a tribunal of fact can depend in a legal inquiry is its perception of witnesses testifying in the witness box, and perhaps also the perceptions which it experiences from its own examination of an item of real evidence. In relation to a testifying witness, two difficulties arise. The first comes from uncertainty as to whether the witness can trust the evidence of his own senses. He may believe that he saw the defendant stab the victim, but what guarantee has he that things were not otherwise? The second difficulty comes from the fact that the jury has to rely on the witness for an insight into what happened on the occasion under investigation. But all the jury can perceive is the witness in the box giving evidence. What is their justification for inferring from the witness's testimony that the defendant did in fact stab the victim?

A third reason for the hazardous nature of evidence is that, save for some items of real evidence, it is presented through the medium of language. But language is notoriously ambiguous. 'Words ... may easily be misunderstood by a dull man. They may easily be misconstrued by a knave. What was spoken metaphorically may be apprehended literally. What was spoken ludicrously may be apprehended seriously. A particle, a tense, a mood, an emphasis may make the whole difference between guilt and innocence.'[2] But more than this, the very adversary system adopted in our courts tends to perpetuate ambiguity. One of the earliest lessons learned by a student of advocacy is how to avoid giving a witness whom he is cross-examining a chance to explain his testimony. Closed, leading questions which require a 'yes' or 'no' answer are recommended. These may be good trial tactics, but they are ill designed for the discovery of the truth.[3]

Politicians and lawyers have generally turned a blind eye to these fundamental defects. Attempts to make verdicts a little more reliable have been made only erratically and on a piecemeal basis. This chapter deals with attempts that have been made to control the way in which juries think about evidence which at various times has been thought to be particularly unreliable. These gave rise to law which compelled judges to warn juries in a particular way when they had to consider certain types of evidence, or evidence from certain types of witness.

Mandatory warnings to the jury

In the 18th century, when the beginnings of our modern law of evidence can be perceived, both prosecution and defence were often unrepresented by counsel, and the judge played a much larger part in criminal cases than he did in the 19th century and later. In particular, judges had a greater control over juries' deliberations. Summings up could contain much more of the judge's opinion than would now be thought proper. Where it appeared that a deliberation was likely to be short, the jury would often not leave the jury box, and this could provide an opportunity for informal dialogue with the judge about the evidence. Even if a jury returned a verdict with which the judge disagreed, he could persuade them to reconsider.

In time, this informal procedure gave way to a system more like the one we are used to today, though there was one major difference: until 1898, there was no general right for a defendant to testify in his own defence. Prosecution and defence came increasingly to be represented by counsel, possibly because of an increase in the size of the Bar, and the judge's control over the jury's deliberations slackened. But because jurors were free to weigh the evidence without judicial intervention, it became more necessary to warn them in a formal way during summing up about the weight to be attached to certain types of witness and testimony, and of the danger in convicting on the basis of such evidence without some independent support. Warnings were thought to be necessary in three main cases: those involving the evidence of children, of accomplices, and of complainants in cases where a sexual crime was alleged.

For a long time, the manner in which a warning was given, and even whether a warning was given at all, was a matter solely for the trial judge's discretion. But when the Court of Criminal Appeal was set up in 1907, discretionary practices tended to harden into rigid rules of law. Before long, a highly complex law of corroboration had developed. Eventually, it was thought to be so unsatisfactory that Parliament very largely abolished it in s 34(2) of the Criminal Justice Act 1988 and in s 32 of the Criminal Justice and Public Order Act 1994.

Alongside the strict law of corroboration, there had also developed a less formal body of law about warnings that should be given to a jury where a witness might be unreliable even though he did not fall within the limited classes to which corroboration law applied. Thus, it was held that an informal warning should be given where witnesses had a purpose of their own to serve in giving evidence, or suffered from mental disorder (*Beck* (1982); *Spencer* (1986)). This body of law remains unaffected by the statutory provisions abolishing most of the old corroboration law, but it is unlikely now to have an independent existence. In *Makanjuola* (1995), the Court of Appeal emphasised the wide discretion possessed by trial judges to adapt warnings about the testimony of any particular witness to the circumstances of the case. It is possible that the old, less formal law may be suggestive when considering whether a judge should now give any warning to the jury. What is clear is that if he decides in his discretion to give a warning, the exercise of that discretion will only exceptionally be reviewed by the Court of Appeal. *Makanjuola* has also been helpful in killing the notion that the old law about corroboration might still somehow apply once the judge had decided to give a discretionary warning.

There remains one type of evidence where a warning is required which is still governed by a rule based rather than a discretionary system. Identification evidence which falls within the principles set out in *Turnbull* (1977) and subsequent cases must be the subject of a particular type of judicial warning in the summing up.

Code D of the current (1995, amended 1999) Codes of Practice made under the Police and Criminal Evidence Act (PACE) 1984 is likely to be relevant in any problem involving identification. The whole of the Code is important, but you should pay special attention to Annex A (identification parades) and Annex D (showing photographs). You should note that Code D has been modified by SI 2002/615. The officer in charge of a case now has a free choice between a video identification and an identification parade. A group identification may also be offered initially if the officer in charge of the case thinks that it would be more satisfactory than a video identification or a parade, provided the identification officer considers it practicable to arrange. If none of these methods is practicable, the identification officer has a discretion to arrange a covert video or group identification. As before, a confrontation is to be used only as a last resort.

If there has been a breach of the Code, you must be able to advise on the likely consequences. Remember the following:

- what allows the court to look at the provisions of the Code, and what makes them relevant. See s 67(11) of PACE;
- if the quality of the identification evidence is poor and there is no other evidence to support it, the jury should be directed to acquit (*Turnbull* (1977)). Thus, the Code breach may so weaken the identification evidence that a submission of no case to answer will be successful;
- the evidence may be excluded under s 78 of PACE. (See Chapter 7 for further details.)

Notes

1   This is perhaps more obviously true of a historian's work. See Carr, EH, *What Is History?*, 2nd edn, 1987, Chapter 1. But a little reflection should be enough to show that the same is true of the investigation that precedes a criminal or civil trial.

2   Macaulay (Lord), *The History of England from the Accession of James the Second*, 1880, Vol 2, Chapter 5, p 161. Even more hazardous is evidence of statements alleged to have been made on an earlier occasion by a defendant.

3   See, for example, Stone, M, *Cross-Examination in Criminal Trials*, 1988, p 107; Boon, A, *Advocacy*, 2nd edn, 1999, pp 113–14; cf McEwan, J, *Evidence and the Adversarial Process: The Modern Law*, 1992, pp 16–19.

Checklist

Students should be familiar with the following areas:

- the abolition of corroboration law in the Criminal Justice Act (CJA) 1988 and the Criminal Justice and Public Order Act (CJPOA) 1994;
- the effect of this – see *Makanjuola* (1995);
- the guidelines in *Makanjuola* about discretionary warnings;
- *Beck* warnings;
- the rules concerning identification in *Turnbull* (1977);
- Code of Practice D;
- s 62(11) of PACE;
- the possible effects of Code breach;
- warnings where a defendant has lied.

Question 19

Nigel, who has no previous convictions, is charged with raping Millie, whom he knew. The case for the prosecution is that he went with her to a party at Peter's house, that while there, he persuaded her to go into the wine cellar with him, and that there, he raped her on the floor behind a wine rack. Olive saw Millie emerging from the cellar with her hair disordered and dust on her dress. Apart from that, she says, she did not notice anything unusual. Peter says that Millie was initially with other guests in the garden, that he saw her going into the house, and that she was crying when she returned to the garden. He went up to her and said: 'What's the matter? Is it something to do with Nigel?' Millie then said that Nigel had raped her. Later that evening, Millie made a statement to the police in which she repeated her allegation against Nigel. Before making her statement, she was examined by a doctor, who found evidence indicating that she had had sexual intercourse within the previous 12 hours. When Nigel was interviewed by the police, he at first denied going into the wine cellar. Later he admitted that he had been there and that he had had sexual intercourse with Millie behind a wine rack, but said that he had done so with her consent. He has since discovered that last year Millie made separate allegations of rape against Quentin and Richard, which she subsequently withdrew.

Discuss the evidential issues arising.

Answer plan

You need to consider the following items of evidence:

- Olive's observations;
- Millie's distressed state;
- Millie's statement to Peter;
- the medical evidence;
- Nigel's initial lie;
- his previous good character (see Chapter 9);
- Millie's earlier complaints of rape (see Chapter 10).

Answer

Olive's observations will not assist the prosecution case because they are as consistent with consensual intercourse as with rape, and Nigel now admits that intercourse took place, albeit with Millie's consent. The same is true of the medical evidence. To some extent, Olive's evidence supports the defence, for, apparently, she observed no signs of distress when Millie emerged from the wine cellar.

Millie's statement to Peter is possibly admissible as a 'recent complaint'. Although a witness's previous consistent statements are not as a rule admissible, if the complainant in a case involving a sexual offence testifies, a recent complaint will be admissible to show that the witness has given a consistent account, and to rebut the defence of consent (*Lillyman* (1896)). However, the complaint must be voluntary and not elicited by questions of a leading, inducing or intimidating character (*Osborne* (1905)). Here, Peter has not led on the fact of rape, but he has led on the identity of the person responsible for Millie's apparent distress, and this might result in the exclusion of Millie's statement to Peter. If her statement is not excluded, the judge must direct the jury that: (1) it is not evidence of the fact complained of, but only of consistency in Millie's conduct and in the evidence that she has given; and (2) it cannot be independent confirmation of her evidence because it does not come from a source independent of her. Evidence of Millie's distress will be similarly treated (*Islam* (1999)). Another argument against the admissibility of Millie's statement to Peter might be that it did not amount to a recent complaint because it was not made as soon after the event complained of as could reasonably be expected. Millie said nothing to Olive, but Olive might not have been someone in whom she felt that she could confide, and if that is the case, Millie could not reasonably be expected to have said anything to her.

Nigel was caught out in a lie when he denied going into the cellar, and the prosecution can rely on this as evidence of guilt. No hearsay problem arises of course, because his denial is not being relied on for its truth, but for the reverse, as was the case in *Mawaz Khan v R* (1967). However, if the prosecution does wish to rely on this item of evidence, the judge must give a *Lucas* direction to the jury on the lines indicated in *Burge and Pegg* (1996). Since Nigel has admitted the lie, it will not be necessary to warn the jury that they must find it proved beyond reasonable doubt. But the judge must warn the jury that the mere fact that the defendant has lied is not in itself evidence of guilt, because defendants may lie for innocent reasons. Only if the jury is sure that Nigel did not lie for an innocent reason can a lie support the prosecution case. In *Lucas* (1981), Lord Lane CJ said that in appropriate cases, the jury should be reminded that people sometimes lie in an attempt to bolster up a just cause, or out of shame, or out of a wish to conceal disgraceful behaviour from their family. Any or all of these reasons might apply in Nigel's case.

Nigel's previous good character will entitle him to a *Vye* (1993) direction. He has already made a pre-trial statement, and he will almost certainly give evidence at his trial. In such circumstances, the jury should be told that his good character is relevant to his credibility, and also to the likelihood of his having committed the offence.

The relevance of Millie's earlier allegations against Quentin and Richard appears to be that she has a tendency to make unreliable allegations of rape. In *MH* (2002), the Court of Appeal held that questions about a rape complainant's previous false statements are not questions about her sexual behaviour within the meaning of s 41 of the Youth Justice and Criminal Evidence Act 1999, and she may therefore be cross-examined about them. However, a problem would arise if she denied making these allegations. They affect only her credibility, and as such, they would be regarded as collateral to the facts in issue. The result of that would be that evidence could not be called to rebut any denials that she made in relation to them (*AG v Hitchcock* (1847)).

Question 20

Rupert and Edward have been committed for trial, charged with burglary. The case for the prosecution is that they broke into a shop in Brighton owned by Rimsky & Romanov, a firm of jewellers, and there stole a quantity of watches.

Evidence for the prosecution will be given by Tabitha, Rupert's former girlfriend. She has made a statement in which she states that on the evening when the burglary took place, she drove Rupert and Edward to a public house. While drinking there, she overheard Rupert and Edward discussing a plan to break into the premises of Rimsky & Romanov. Later, they all left the public house. Tabitha says that she then drove them in the direction of her house, but that on the way, Rupert asked her to stop, saying that he and Edward needed to relieve themselves. This was near the rear entrance to the shop owned by Rimsky & Romanov. Tabitha states that she waited in the car for about half an hour until Rupert and Edward returned, and that they then drove to Tabitha's house. Tabitha also states that she helped them with some luggage which they had with them, and that the men left the next day. When the police came to ask for Tabitha's help in this matter, they discovered one of the stolen watches in her bathroom.

The prosecution also have a statement from Tabitha's nephew Archie, aged 10, who says that he found the rest of the stolen goods in Edward's garden shed.

When interviewed by the police without a solicitor, Rupert refused to answer any questions. Edward when interviewed denied having any part in the offence. He said that he spent the evening and the night in question at a hotel in Manchester with a woman called Sheila. Sheila has previous convictions for theft, handling stolen goods and for assisting in the management of a brothel.

Discuss the evidential matters arising.

Answer plan

There are six topics which need to be discussed in the answer to this question:

- should there be an informal warning about the reliability of Tabitha's evidence? Note how it is possible to use the old law to argue by analogy, but be careful to avoid any suggestion that it still has any force as binding authority;
- Sheila's previous convictions;
- look at the content of Tabitha's evidence. She is reporting what she heard other people say quite a lot. Is all this admissible? Why?;
- what is the position about Archie's evidence?;
- what is the significance now of Rupert's failure to answer police questions? Try to summarise what the Act says accurately. A student who simply said, for example, that Rupert's silence was evidence of his guilt would not get much credit;
- what are the problems arising from Edward's alibi? Have you read the question carefully enough to deal with this point fully?

Answer

The first question that arises is whether the judge should give an informal warning about the reliability of Tabitha's evidence when summing up to the jury. There are two reasons why such a warning might be desirable. We are told that she is Rupert's former girlfriend. Is there any evidence of antipathy towards him which would make it possible that she is implicating him from a desire for revenge? The rule in *Beck* (1982) was that where a witness might have an 'interest or purpose of his own to serve' in giving evidence, the judge should warn the jury about this. Earlier cases such as *Willis* (1916) and *Evans*

(1965) established that where a wife gave evidence in support of an accomplice, the jury should be warned of the danger in relying on her testimony because she had an interest to serve. It would seem sensible to warn the jury about the different but perhaps equally strong interest of someone giving evidence against a former boyfriend towards whom she felt animosity.

The pre-1994 cases are, of course, no more than suggestive of the way in which a judge might now be persuaded to exercise the wide discretion which, after the passing of s 32 of the Criminal Justice and Public Order Act 1994, he was acknowledged to have in *Makanjuola* (1995). But it is worth noting that under the old law, the jury might have had to be warned that Tabitha was an accomplice and that it would be dangerous for them to convict on her uncorroborated evidence (*Davies v DPP* (1954)). This suggests another reason for an informal warning to be given about Tabitha's evidence. It is possible that, although she was never charged, she was an accomplice. She clearly knew of the plan to break into the shop. She stopped the car near the shop and it is unlikely that she believed that Rupert and Edward took half an hour to relieve themselves in its vicinity. She helped them with their 'luggage', and later one of the stolen watches was found in her bathroom.

No special difficulties are presented by the content of Tabitha's evidence. Her report of what she heard Rupert and Edward saying about their plans to break into the shop will be admissible as an exception to the rule against hearsay as showing the contemporaneous state of mind and intentions of the accused. In *Moghal* (1977), a statement of intention to murder made some six months before the commission of the crime was considered admissible. This particular decision was subsequently criticised by Lord Bridge in *Blastland* (1986) on the ground of relevance. However, the House of Lords emphasised in *Blastland* that such a declaration would be admissible if the state of mind evidenced by it was directly in issue at the trial, or was of direct and immediate relevance to an issue arising in the trial. Clearly, those conditions are satisfied here. Tabitha will be able to report the excuse given by Rupert for stopping the car near the shop because the prosecution will be relying on its falsity, as in *Mawaz Khan* (1967), rather than its truth.

It is just conceivable that the judge would think it appropriate to comment on the weight to be attached to Archie's evidence in view of his relationship to Tabitha if the defence makes a point of this. By s 53(1) of the Youth Justice and Criminal Evidence Act 1999, at every stage in criminal proceedings, all persons are (whatever their age) competent to give evidence. By sub-s (3), a person is not competent to give evidence in criminal proceedings if it appears to the court that he is not a person who is able to understand questions put to him as a witness and give answers to them that can be understood. There is no suggestion that Archie falls into this category, and he will therefore be competent to give evidence. But his evidence will be unsworn. By s 55(2) of the 1999 Act, a witness may not be sworn unless he has attained the age of 14.

Rupert's failure to answer police questions is now governed by s 34 of the Criminal Justice and Public Order Act 1994. The failure of an accused in such circumstances to mention any fact relied on later in his defence, if it was a fact which in the circumstances existing at the time, the accused could reasonably have been expected to mention, will allow the jury in determining whether the accused is guilty of the offence charged to draw such inferences as appear proper. But it is important to know if Rupert was offered a solicitor. Sub-section (2A) of s 34 provides that where the accused was at an authorised place of detention at the time of his failure to mention any fact relied on in his defence, no inferences may be drawn unless he was allowed an opportunity to consult a solicitor before being questioned.

If it is an appropriate case for a s 34 direction, the judge should follow the guidelines set out in *Gill* (2001). He must identify the fact on which Rupert relies and which was not mentioned on questioning. He must direct the jury that it is for them to decide whether in the circumstances, that fact was something that Rupert could reasonably have been expected to mention. He should tell them that if they think it was, they are not obliged to draw any inferences, but that they may do so. Further, he must tell the jury that a suspected person is not bound to answer police questions, that an inference from silence cannot on its own prove guilt, and that the jury must be satisfied that there is a case to answer before they can draw any adverse inferences from silence. Finally, he should tell the jury that they can draw an adverse inference only if they are sure that Rupert was silent because he had no answers, or none that would stand up to investigation.

If Sheila gives evidence to support Edward's alibi, she may be cross-examined about her previous convictions like any other witness, with the exception of the defendant, in order to shake her credibility. Because of the historical connection between criminal convictions and moral standing, the prosecution is not confined to cross-examining her about offences involving dishonesty. In *Clifford v Clifford* (1961), Cairns J said it had never been doubted that a conviction for *any* offence could be put to a witness by way of cross-examination as to credit. There is nothing to indicate that any of Sheila's convictions are spent, so there is no need to ask for leave.

The trial judge should tell the jury that it is for the prosecution to disprove the alibi beyond reasonable doubt (*Johnson* (1995)). In *Burge and Pegg* (1996), it was said that a *Lucas* (1981) direction should be given where, among other cases, the defendant relies on an alibi. It seems, therefore, that the judge should also tell the jury that if they are satisfied so that they are sure that Edward lied about his alibi, then that lie may support the prosecution case, but only if they are sure that he did not lie for an innocent reason.

Question 21

Augustus, Bertram and Claude have been charged with affray, contrary to s 3(1) of the Public Order Act 1986. The case for the prosecution is that all three made a concerted attack on the staff of a nightclub after they had been told to leave the premises.

Donald, a barman, says that he was wounded by one of the men involved. Donald did not recognise him at the time but thought that he would be able to recognise him if he saw him again, despite the fact that the lighting in the club was dim. Eddie, another barman who had seen the attack on Donald, also thought he could recognise the culprit if he saw him again. At the police station, DS Dapper showed both of them several sets of photographs, each containing 10 pictures of men with convictions for violence. After some discussion, Donald and Eddie picked out a photograph of Augustus. Augustus was then arrested and put on an identification parade where Donald and Eddie both picked him out without hesitation.

Fergus, another barman, says that he also was wounded by one of those causing the affray. He was unable to identify anyone from police photographs, but he was able to give information to the police as a result of which a photofit image of his attacker was created, on the basis of which Bertram was later arrested. Fergus failed to pick out Bertram on a subsequent identification parade. Bertram, however, has made several damaging admissions in recorded interviews with the police, and the photofit bears a strong resemblance to him.

Gina, a waitress, was struck by one of those involved in the affray. Her attacker immediately rushed from the club and Gina, who was not seriously hurt, ran after him. The man escaped, but Gina was able to stop a passing police car and explain what had happened. The officers then drove with her round neighbouring streets to see if she could find her attacker. She saw a man standing in a doorway and asked the police to stop. One of the officers went up to the man with her and said 'Is that him?'. She replied 'Yes, I'm positive'. The man, who identified himself as Claude, was then arrested. Claude later asked to be put on an identification parade but was told that this was unnecessary and impracticable because he had already been positively identified.

Gina was later invited to the police station to see if she could identify any others involved in the affray. She was shown a selection of photographs, including one of Augustus. She identified him then, and she subsequently picked out Augustus on an identification parade. Advise the prosecution on the evidential issues that arise in relation to identification.

Answer plan

This question mainly concerns identifications where there may have been breaches of Code D. One of the problems is how to order the rather scattered information which you have been given. The following is a suggestion.

The evidence against Augustus

- Start with the identification parades involving Augustus at which the witnesses were: (a) Donald and Eddie; (b) Gina. Make the point that such evidence is in principle admissible.
- Introduce the relevant Code and, because you are referring to it for the first time, explain its status and relevance.
- Look at what happened prior to the identification parades and explain what breaches have occurred.

The evidence against Bertram

- Deal briefly with the admissibility of admissions (for further details about s 76 of PACE, see Chapter 7).
- Deal with the evidential value of the photofit.

The evidence against Claude

There are two points here:

- Gina's 'on the spot' identification;
- the refusal of an identification parade.

General point

- *Turnbull* warnings in relation to all identification witnesses.

Final check

- If there have been breaches of the Code, what will be the effect on the pieces of evidence to which they relate?

Answer

The facts given do not reveal anything of the circumstances in which the identification parades involving Augustus were conducted. Ordinarily, if the parades had been properly conducted, Donald, Eddie and Gina would give evidence of the assault committed by Augustus in the club and of their subsequent identification of him on the parade. Evidence of pre-trial identification is an exception to the rule against previous consistent statements[1] which is justified on the basis that evidence of previous identification does much to increase the credibility of an identification repeated in court. As Lord Haldane said in *Christie* (1914), evidence of an earlier identification shows that the identification of the defendant in court was not an afterthought. But there is a difficulty with the identification evidence in this case because it may have been affected by breaches of the relevant Code of Practice before the parades took place.

Procedures for the pre-trial identification of suspects are laid down by Code D of the Codes of Practice issued pursuant to s 66 of the Police and Criminal Evidence Act 1984. By s 67(11) of the Act, if any provision of a Code appears to the court to be relevant to any question arising in the proceedings, it shall be taken into account in determining that question. The court is not obliged to exclude the evidence where there has been breach of a Code; the Court of Appeal in *Grannell* (1990) stated that it is necessary to establish whether the breach has caused unfairness.

Paragraph 2.18 of Code D permits photographs to be shown to a witness where the identity of the suspect is not known. Thus, in principle, it was proper to show photographs to Donald, and if he could not have made an identification from them, it would have been proper to show them to Eddie, or vice versa. However, the showing of any photographs must be done in accordance with Annex D of the Code. Paragraph 2 of Annex D states that only one witness shall be shown photographs at any one time. He is to be given as much privacy as practicable and not allowed to communicate with any other witness in the case. By para 3, the witness shall be shown not less than 12 photographs at a time. The police infringed the provisions of both paragraphs when showing photographs to Donald and Eddie. Since a person who picks out a photograph may later pick out someone on a parade with the photograph in mind rather than the original incident, particular care is needed in showing photographs to a witness to ensure that the provisions of Code D are followed. In this case, a strong defence argument could be presented that the evidence of the identification parades involving identifications by Donald and Eddie should be excluded under s 78 of the Act (see Chapter 7) because the reliability of the identifications was significantly weakened by the procedures adopted in relation to the photographs.

Gina should not have been shown photographs at all. Paragraph 2.18 of Code D provides that a witness must not be shown photographs if the identity of the suspect is known to the police and he is available to stand on an identification parade. By the time Gina was invited to look at photographs, the identity of Augustus was known to the police, and he was presumably available to stand on a parade. It seems likely, therefore, that her identification of him will be excluded also.

Subject to anything that the defence might argue, the admissions made by Bertram will be admissible evidence against him under s 76(1) of the Act. The photofit may also be admissible. According to the Court of Appeal in *Cook* (1987) and *Constantinou* (1990), it is analogous to a photograph, and so outside the scope of the rule against hearsay.

In *Kelly* (1992), the Court of Appeal suggested that when a suspect was found within minutes of the crime, and close to the scene, it might well be that the provisions of the Code did not apply and that the best course was for the police to see if the witness thought that the suspect was the offender. This was a case where a woman complained of attempted rape and, as she was talking to police in the street, saw the accused and pointed him out. One of the officers questioned, but did not arrest, him. The complainant was then brought nearer, she confirmed her identification, and the suspect was then arrested. On appeal it was argued unsuccessfully that an identification ought not to have been permitted in those circumstances, but that an identification parade should have been arranged instead.[2]

Gina's identification of Claude is therefore likely to be admissible in principle. But was Claude entitled to an identification parade? Code D, para 2.3, as amended, provides that whenever a suspect disputes an identification, an identification parade or a video identification shall take place if the suspect consents. There are certain express exceptions to this rule, but none applies in this case. In *Forbes* (2001), the House of Lords held that para 2.3 is mandatory, but that a judge who is asked to exercise his discretion under s 78 is not bound to exclude the identification evidence that is available, even though a parade has been improperly refused.

In relation to the admissible evidence of all the identification witnesses, the judge will have to direct the jury in accordance with the principles set out in *Turnbull* (1977). That case requires a judge to do three things when the prosecution case depends wholly or substantially (as it does here) on the correctness of one or more identifications, and the defendant alleges that the identifying witnesses are mistaken. The judge must warn the jury of the special need for caution before convicting the accused in reliance on identification evidence. He must tell the jury the reason why such a warning is needed. Some reference should be made to the possibility that a mistaken witness can be a convincing one, and that a number of such witnesses can all be mistaken. In *Pattinson and Exley* (1996), the Court of Appeal allowed appeals and criticised a direction on identification evidence for failing to make adequate reference to the risk of miscarriages of justice resulting from mistaken identification evidence. The judge must also direct the jury to examine closely the circumstances in which each identification came to be made. Having warned the jury in accordance with these guidelines, the judge should go on to direct the jury to consider if the identification evidence is supported by any other evidence. At this stage he should identify what is, and what is not, capable of providing such support. It was held in *Pattinson and Exley* that it is not essential in every case for the judge to summarise for the jury all the weaknesses in the identification evidence. If he does choose to summarise that evidence, he should point to strengths as well as weaknesses. It was said in *Turnbull* that where the quality of the identification evidence is good, the jury can safely be left to assess it, even without any supporting evidence, subject to an adequate warning. But where the quality is poor, the judge should withdraw the case from the jury at the end of the prosecution case in the absence of any supporting evidence.

Notes

1   Also known as 'the rule against narrative'.

2   See also *Hickin and Others* (1996); *Malashev* (1997); *Anastasiou* (1998).

Question 22

Harold and Jamie have been charged with burglary. The prosecution allege that they broke into Lily's flat intending to steal her collection of silver. When Lily returned home and disturbed them Harold gagged her and tied her to a bed. Harold and Jamie then left the flat with Lily's silver, leaving her tied to the bed.

Lily was asked by police to describe the men she had seen. She was able to describe only the man who had tied her to the bed. On the strength of this, she was then shown a selection of police photographs and she picked out one of Harold. She was asked if she would be willing to attend an identification parade but she refused, saying that she was too frightened. The police later arrested Harold and asked Lily if she would be able to identify the man who had tied her to the bed if she saw him from a position where he would be unable to see her. Lily agreed. At the police station, she was taken to a corridor outside Harold's cell and invited to look through a spyhole in the door. The officer who was with her said only, 'Is that the man who tied you up and gagged you?'. Lily said that it was.

After Lily had left the police station, Mick, the porter at the block of flats where Lily lived, was interviewed by the police. He told them that he had seen two men on the premises at about the time of the burglary. He was shown a selection of police photographs and picked out Harold and Jamie as the men he had seen. Harold and Jamie were later put together on an identification parade with eight other men who were volunteers from a nearby health club. At this parade, Mick picked them out without hesitation.

Discuss the evidential issues that arise.

Answer plan

Not a very difficult question; you need to recognise breaches of Code D. Note, especially, para 2.0. A good way to deal with the problem would be to tackle the points in this order:

- Lily's identification of Harold (a) by photographs, and (b) at the police station;
- Mick's identification of Harold and Jamie (a) by photographs, and (b) by identification parade.

Remember to discuss the results that are likely to follow a finding that there has been a breach of the Code in each case.

Answer

No details are given of the way in which the police photographs were shown to Lily, and it is assumed that the provisions of Annex D of Code D were followed.

However, Lily's subsequent identification of Harold was not in accordance with Code D. This Code provides four methods of identification: a parade, a group identification, a video film, and a confrontation. By Code D, as amended, the officer in charge of a case has a free choice between an identification parade and a video identification. In the light of Lily's fear, a video identification should have been chosen. But identification by confrontation may not take place unless none of the other procedures is practicable (para 2.13).

In any case, the confrontation was improperly conducted. Annex C, para 2 provides that before the confrontation takes place, the identification officer must tell the witness that the person he saw may or may not be the person he is to confront, and that if he cannot make a positive identification he should say so. This warning does not appear to have been given to Lily.

Further, para 2.0 of Code D provides that the police must make a record of the description of the suspect as first given by the witness. This description has to be recorded before the witness participates in any identification procedures referred to in para 2.1 or Annex D of the Code, namely, an identification parade, a group identification, a video film, a confrontation or the showing of photographs. There is nothing on the facts given to show that these requirements have been met.

By Annex C, para 2A, before a confrontation takes place, the suspect or his solicitor shall be provided with details of the first description of the suspect given by the witness who is to attend the confrontation. This appears to have been omitted from the procedure leading to Lily's identification of Harold.

By Annex C, para 3, the confrontation must take place in the presence of the suspect's solicitor, interpreter or friend, unless this would cause unreasonable delay. On the facts given, there appears to be no suggestion that any unreasonable delay would have been caused by arranging for Harold's solicitor or friend to be present.

By Annex C, para 4, the confrontation should normally take place in the police station, either in a normal room or in one equipped with a screen permitting a witness to see the suspect without being seen. To carry out a confrontation when Harold was in a cell might have suggested to Lily that the police were satisfied that they had the right man, and this might have encouraged her to be more positive in her identification than she would otherwise have been. In this connection, the absence of the warning already referred to may be seen as particularly significant.

In the light of these breaches, Lily's identification of Harold at the police station might well be excluded under s 78 of the Police and Criminal Evidence Act 1984.

The breach of paras 2 and 4 of Annex C appears to reduce the weight of Lily's identification evidence to such an extent that exclusion is likely. The question will then arise as to whether Lily's picking out the photograph of Harold might be admissible as being, presumably, the only untainted identification evidence left. It is unlikely that the court would permit this. There is an obvious danger of prejudice if the jury hear this evidence because it would inevitably reveal that Harold had a criminal record. In *Wright* (1934), the Court of Criminal Appeal held that an irregularity had occurred where a witness volunteered in examination-in-chief that he had seen a photograph of the defendant in the 'rogues' gallery' at New Scotland Yard. More recently, in

Lamb (1980), the Court of Appeal condemned the production of an album of police photographs as part of the prosecution case on the basis that it was tantamount to adducing evidence that the accused had a criminal record. Lawton LJ said that generally the prosecution should make no reference to such photographs; they should merely inform the defence of their existence and the use to which they were put, and leave it to the defence to decide whether the jury should be informed of those facts. To involve Harold in this prejudice because the police failed to adopt proper identification procedures at a later stage is unlikely to commend itself to any judge as a fair course of action.

Mick should not have been shown the photograph of Harold because Lily had already picked it out (Code D, Annex D, para 5). There also appears to have been a breach of para 2.0 of Code D; it appears that Mick was not even asked for a description of the suspects. The subsequent identification parade was improperly conducted. Code D, Annex A, para 8 provides that one suspect only shall be included in a parade unless there are two suspects of roughly similar appearance, in which case, they may be paraded together but with at least 12 other persons. Paragraph 8 also provides that the parade shall consist of persons who so far as possible resemble the suspect in age, height, general appearance and position in life. Did the volunteers from the health club satisfy these conditions? If, for example, they were all young, with good muscular development, and the defendants did not fit this description, the parade would not have been properly conducted.

For these reasons the identification evidence of Mick might also be excluded under s 78. No information has been given about the existence of other evidence that might incriminate these defendants. In the absence of any such evidence the defence would be likely to submit, on the basis of the *Turnbull* (1977) guidelines, that the case should be withdrawn from the jury. Such a submission would be likely to succeed, in view of the many breaches of Code D and the consequent reduction in probative value of the identification evidence.

Question 23

'We regard mistaken identification as by far the greatest cause of actual or possible wrong conviction' (Criminal Law Revision Committee, 11th Report, 1972).

Has enough been done to reduce this risk?

Answer plan

Start by identifying the modes of protection: *Turnbull* (1977) warnings and Code D. Then deal with the adequacy of *Turnbull* warnings; some reference to voice identification and to 'evidence of description' would be appropriate here. The problems with the application of Code D should then be considered.

In summary, therefore, the essay is constructed as follows:

- outline of the two ways of protecting against mistaken identification;
- the *Turnbull* (1977) guidelines: *Thornton* (1995); *Slater* (1995); *Pattinson and Exley* (1996); *Qadir* (1998);
- distinction between evidence of identity and evidence of description: *Gayle* (1999);
- voice identification: *Hersey* (1998); *Gummerson and Steadman* (1999);
- Code D: *Kelly* (1992); use of s 78(1) of the Police and Criminal Evidence Act (PACE) 1984; Code D, para 2.3; *Forbes* (2001).

Answer

English law tries to protect defendants from wrongful convictions that are based on mistaken identification evidence in two ways: by a system of judicial warnings to juries; and by a Code of Practice that governs identification procedures.

In *Turnbull* (1977), the Court of Appeal established guidelines that were to apply where the prosecution case depended 'wholly or substantially' on the correctness of one or more identifications of the defendant. The words 'wholly or substantially' have not in practice limited the range of cases in which the guidelines have been considered appropriate. A *Turnbull* direction has to be given in cases where identification is based on recognition as well as in cases where the risk of misidentification might seem greater: for example, where identification is based on a fleeting glimpse. The need for a direction will usually arise when the defendant denies that he was present at a particular place. But the direction may also be necessary where the defendant admits being present at a relevant place but denies involvement in the criminal activity taking place there. So, for example, it was held in *Thornton* (1995), where the defendant was charged with causing grievous bodily harm at a wedding reception, that the *Turnbull* warning ought to have been given because, where others present were similarly dressed, a mistake was clearly possible. As Rose LJ emphasised in *Slater* (1995), the key question is whether there was, in the particular circumstances, the possibility of mistake. Thus, the circumstances in which the warning is required are probably adequate.

Is the nature of the warning adequate? According to *Turnbull*, several stages have to be followed. First, the judge must warn the jury of the special need for caution before convicting on the basis of identification evidence. Secondly, he must tell the jury why such a warning is needed. Some reference should be made to the fact that a mistaken witness can be a convincing one, and that a number of convincing witnesses can all be mistaken. Thirdly, he must direct the jury to examine closely the circumstances in which each identification was made. In *Turnbull*, the court gave examples of topics for comment, such as the light and the length of the period of observation, but in *Pattinson and Exley* (1996), the Court of Appeal said that it was not necessary in every case for the judge to summarise all the weaknesses in the identification evidence. The court added that where the judge does summarise the identification evidence, he should point out strengths as well as weaknesses. Fourthly, the judge should direct the jury to consider whether the identification evidence is supported by any other evidence. Fifthly, he should identify the evidence that is capable, and incapable, of providing such support. Not surprisingly, the Court of Appeal has deprecated rigid formulas for the fulfilment of *Turnbull* requirements. Thus, in *Qadir* (1998), it was said that the form and contents of the summing up should, even when identification is in issue, be tailored to the circumstances of the individual case. Nevertheless, the *Turnbull* procedure appears to provide a strong protection for defendants who challenge identification evidence. Further, it was said in *Turnbull* that cases should be withdrawn from the jury where the identification evidence is poor and there is no supporting evidence.

Turnbull almost certainly does not extend to evidence from a witness who says that he would be unable to recognise the person he saw if he were to see him again, but who remembers some identifying features of that person. But there seems to be no reason why it should be extended in this way to such 'evidence of description'. As Henry LJ pointed out in *Gayle* (1999), the danger of an honest witness's being mistaken as to distinctive clothing, or the general description of the person he saw, are minimal.

But *Turnbull* assumes that most identifications are visual. That is so, but sometimes identification may be by the sound of the human voice. On this topic, the law is undeveloped. In *Hersey* (1998), the Court of Appeal showed support for the equivalent of identification parades for voices, and said that juries should be directed as in cases of visual identification, with appropriate modifications. But, in *Gummerson and Steadman* (1999), the Court of Appeal disapproved of 'voice identification parades', and the content of any warning in the summing up remains unclear.

The protection given by Code D is less satisfactory. Failure to comply with the appropriate procedure will not lead inevitably to the exclusion of identification evidence (*Kelly* (1992)). What has to be shown is that the breach is sufficiently grave to bring the evidence within the scope of s 78(1) of PACE 1984.

Paragraph 2.3 of Code D, as amended, provides that, except in certain stated circumstances, whenever a suspect disputes an identification, an identification parade or video identification shall be held if the suspect consents.

But it seems clear that the Code does not apply to identifications made only a short time after the commission of the offence. Thus, in *Kelly* (1992), the defendant was charged with attempted rape. The offence took place in a street, and the attacker was distracted before he could commit the full offence. The police arrived soon afterwards, and the victim, while talking to the police, saw the defendant, and told the police that she had seen her attacker. An officer questioned, but did not arrest, the defendant. Meanwhile, the victim was brought closer to him in a police car. She then said that she was sure the man she had seen had been her attacker, and the defendant was arrested. The Court of Appeal rejected the argument that this procedure had denied the defendant the benefit of an identification parade. It added that where a suspect is found within minutes of the crime and close to the scene, it might well be that Code D did not apply. Later decisions such as *Hickin and Others* (1996), *Malashev* (1997) and *Anastasiou* (1998) have confirmed this view.

The protection given by para 2.3 was strengthened by the decision of the House of Lords in *Forbes* (2001), in which it was held that para 2.3 is mandatory unless one of the exceptions in the Code applies. However, it was also said that para 2.3 did not cover all situations. It might be futile to have an identification parade if a witness to a crime had made it clear that he would not be able to recognise the culprit if he saw him again, or if the case was one of pure recognition of someone well known to the witness. Formerly, the application of para 2.3 had been in doubt as a result of inconsistent decisions of the Court of Appeal in *Popat* (1998) and *Forbes* (1999), but this reaffirmation of the provision by the House of Lords, combined with the law about *Turnbull* warnings, suggests that much has been done to ensure that the fears of the Criminal Law Revision Committee are laid to rest.

CHAPTER 7

CONFESSIONS AND ILL-GOTTEN EVIDENCE

Introduction

One of the most important of defence counsel's objectives at trial is to ensure that as little of the prosecution evidence as possible reaches the jury – unless, of course, it happens to favour the defendant. This chapter deals with two important statutory weapons in the defence's armoury: ss 76 and 78 of the Police and Criminal Evidence Act (PACE) 1984. These deal with confessions, and with a discretion to exclude for reasons of fairness evidence on which the prosecution proposes to rely. The sections are very often relied on in the alternative; it was decided in *Mason* (1988) that s 78 applies to confessions just as much as to any other evidence.

Students of this topic need an important warning. In reading cases where evidence has been excluded under either section, but particularly under s 78, you are almost never reading precedents which will have to be followed in later cases. The reason for this is that no situation is ever exactly repeated, defendants are not all alike, and the effect of acts or omissions by the police is likely to vary greatly from case to case. Knowledge of previous decisions cannot be a substitute for rigorous thought about the facts of your own particular case, facts which of course include the personal characteristics of the defendant. This is plain enough from looking at the basic law. Sub-section (2)(b) of s 76 – probably the provision in that section which is most relied on – has the effect of requiring the court to attend to the particular circumstances of the individual defendant who relies on the provision. And, in *Jelen and Katz* (1990), the Court of Appeal emphasised that the application of s 78 was 'not an apt field for hard case law and well founded distinctions between cases'.[1]

It is, of course, in relation to a confession that an argument for exclusion will very often have to be made. When a confession appears in a set of prosecution statements or in an examination question, you need to be able to do three things. You must be able to recognise it when you see it, assess its impact on the case as a whole, and work out what arguments are available to you to get it excluded.

Recognising the confession

You may think a confession would be easy to spot: 'OK guv; it's a fair cop. You've got me bang to rights.' Perhaps in real life that sort of thing is said more often than we might expect. But because examiners are interested in grey areas, you are not likely to have to deal with anything so simple in the examination. Your starting point is the partial definition contained in s 82(1) of PACE 1984. With that in mind, you must interpret what has been said. Remember that a favourite topic for questions is the extent to which an accused person can, by something other than an oral statement, *adopt* an allegation against him. Consider some possibilities: he begins to weep; he hangs his head; he blushes violently; he runs away; he says nothing; he attacks the accuser. For a vivid example, see *Batt* (1995).

Impact on the case as a whole

The obvious impact is that of something said by an accused person which inculpates the maker of the statement in relation to the offence in question. But remember to make the point, where appropriate, that an inculpatory statement made by one accused about another outside court, and not in the presence of the co-accused,[2] will not be evidence against the co-accused,[3] and will be admissible only to the extent that it also implicates the person who makes the statement.[4]

There is a very widespread misapprehension that wherever defendants have embarked on a joint endeavour, anything said at any time by any of them, even after arrest, will be admissible evidence against any of the other absent defendants. The case of *Blake and Tye* (1844) is often cited in this connection. This is a totally false understanding of the law, as a reading of *Blake and Tye* would show. Probably because the report is an old one and not readily available, not many students have read it. Fortunately, to understand the law on this point you do not have to read this case because the matter was dealt with more recently by the Court of Appeal in *Gray and Others* (1995). In that case, the court cited and adopted as an accurate exposition of the law a passage from the judgment of Dixon CJ in the Australian case of *Tripodi v R* (1961). In the course of his judgment, in the passage cited and adopted by the English Court of Appeal, Dixon CJ said that the reason for admitting the evidence of the acts or words of one defendant in a joint enterprise against the others was that the agreement to commit the crime was considered as implying an authority to each to act or speak *in furtherance of the common purpose* on behalf of the others. But from the nature of the case, it could seldom happen that anything said by one of the defendants which was no more than a *narrative or account of events that had already taken place* could be admissible against his companions in the common enterprise, though it might be admissible as a confession against the speaker. Usually, Dixon CJ said the question of admissibility would relate to directions, instructions or arrangements, or to utterances accompanying acts.[5]

Another favourite topic for questions is the evidential worth of the exculpatory parts of a mixed statement.[6]

Excluding the confession

In practice, this will involve the operation of s 76(2) of PACE and, as a subsidiary argument in case the first should fail, s 78. Many candidates lose marks because they fail to construct sensible *arguments* at this point in answering a question. The examiner does not want a string of cases; he wants an argument based on the facts of the particular problem. Note particularly that it is foolish to say much in relation to s 76(2)(a) unless there is a proper factual basis for suggesting that there may have been oppression.[7]

In very many cases, you will be relying on breaches of Code C. Remember that even though there may have been a breach, you still need to put an argument on paper about why this is relevant to exclusion. Remember also that this is an area where decisions in other cases are of limited use.[8] This has an advantage for you because it means that you don't have to learn lists of 'authorities'; on the other hand, you will be required to think creatively in the examination about the facts.

Particular attention should be paid to the extent to which the provisions of Code C apply to persons who are at a police station 'assisting the police with their inquiries' but who, technically, are there voluntarily because they have not been arrested (see Question 27).

Notes

1 See also *Roberts* (1997).

2 If made in the presence of the co-accused, you would have to consider whether the latter had adopted what was said.

3 Because of the rule against hearsay.

4 *Gunewardene* (1951). But cf evidence from a co-accused in a joint trial. This, of course, will be given as part of his own defence case, but it may nevertheless implicate another defendant in the commission of the offence. If it does so, it will be evidence which can be used by the jury against that defendant just as much as the evidence from prosecution witnesses. See *Rudd* (1948). Problems arise where one accused makes a statement outside court which implicates both himself and a co-accused. The judge has no discretion to exclude relevant evidence on which a *defendant* proposes to rely (*Lobban v R* (1995)), and a co-defendant will have to make do with a warning to the jury in the summing up that what is said outside court by one defendant is not evidence against another.

5   [1995] 2 Cr App R 100, pp 128–29. But it has been said that an account of events narrated by one of the parties to another while the common enterprise was continuing, in order to bring that other up to date, might be regarded as in furtherance of the enterprise, and so admissible against all the parties referred to in it: see *Jones and Others* (1997).

6   See *Sharp* (1988); *Grayson* (1993).

7   See s 76(8) and look at what was said about the definition of oppression in *Fulling* (1987) and *Parker* (1995).

8   See, for example, observations to this effect in *Jelen and Katz* (1990) and in *Grannell* (1990).

Checklist

Students should be familiar with the following areas:

- the definition of 'confession';
- the adoption by an accused person of allegations made against him;
- the distinction between *Gunewardene* (1951) and *Rudd* (1948);
- the principle in *Sharp* (1988);
- s 76 of PACE 1984;
- s 78 of PACE 1984;
- the provisions of Code C;
- the extent to which Code C provisions apply to persons who have not been arrested;
- ss 34, 35, 36, 37 and 38 of the Criminal Justice and Public Order Act 1994.

Question 24

'The reforms made by the Criminal Justice and Public Order Act 1994 to the right of silence in the police station are more extensive and more difficult to defend than those relating to the accused's failure to testify at trial.'

Discuss.

Answer plan

The question itself contrasts the two different situations where a right to silence has to be considered. In each case, it is necessary to look at the old law to see how much change has been effected by the 1994 Act. It is probably better to take the right to silence at trial first, as the change in this respect seems, in view of the way the common law was developing, far less radical than the provisions affecting the right to silence in pre-trial proceedings. A good summary of arguments for and against the changes that were being debated before the 1994 Act can be found in Greer, S, 'The right to silence: a review of the current debate' (1990) 53 MLR 709, pp 709–30.

In summary, therefore, the essay is constructed as follows:

- comments on failure to testify at common law: *Bathurst* (1968); *Brigden* (1973); *Martinez-Tobon* (1993);
- effect of s 35 of the Criminal Justice and Public Order Act 1994: *Murray v DPP* (1993);
- s 35 and the burden of proof;
- justification of s 35;
- effect of s 34 of the Criminal Justice and Public Order Act 1994;
- arguments in favour of s 34;
- counter-arguments;
- conclusions on ss 34, 36 and 37.

Answer

At common law, the trial judge was permitted to comment on the failure of an accused person to testify at his trial, but he was required by *Bathurst* (1968) to emphasise that the jury must not assume guilt from such a failure. In certain cases, provided this basic point had been made, some criticism was regarded as acceptable. For example, in *Brigden* (1973), the accused's case, put to the appropriate witnesses in cross-examination, was that the police had planted incriminating evidence on him. The accused himself did not testify. The Court of Appeal approved the trial judge's comment to the effect that the jury had not heard from the accused, and that this might help them in deciding whether there was any truth in the allegation against the police. The same sort of criticism could be made where the accused did not testify, but relied on facts which must have been within his knowledge. Thus, in *Martinez-Tobon* (1993), the accused was charged with the illegal importation of cocaine in a packet. The defence was that he had thought the packet contained emeralds, but the accused did not testify. The trial judge commented in his summing up that if the defendant had thought the drugs were emeralds, one might have thought that he would be very anxious to say so. On appeal against conviction, it was argued that the judge's comment had gone beyond what was permissible, but the Court of Appeal disagreed.

Provided the *Bathurst* essentials were complied with, a judge might think it appropriate to make a stronger comment where the defence case involved alleged facts which (a) were at variance with the Crown's evidence or additional to it and exculpatory, and (b) must, if true, be within the defendant's knowledge.

By s 35 of the Criminal Justice and Public Order Act 1994, the court or jury, in determining whether the accused is guilty of the offence charged, may draw such inferences as appear proper from the failure of the accused to give evidence or his refusal, without good cause, to answer any question once he has chosen to testify. However, the section does not make the accused a compellable witness.

How far does this go beyond the common law? It is likely that the section involves a significant change by making it permissible to infer guilt from failure to testify. In *Murray v DPP* (1993), the House of Lords had to interpret a provision in similar terms to s 35 in the law of Northern Ireland. It was held that the inferences that could be drawn were not limited to specific inferences from specific facts, but included an inference that the accused was guilty of the offence charged. As Lord Slynn put it, if the evidence clearly calls for an explanation which the accused ought to be in a position to give, if an explanation exists, then a failure to give any explanation may as a matter of common sense allow the drawing of an inference that there is no explanation, and that the accused is guilty. This looks very much like the law as it was being developed in *Martinez-Tobon*, minus the protection afforded by the *Bathurst* direction. The effect of *Martinez-Tobon* was to create a situation only too familiar to students of evidence law, where a judge follows an approved formula to save himself from the strictures of the Court of Appeal, gives the defendant protection with one hand, promptly takes it away with the other, and thoroughly confuses any thinking members of the jury.

It was sometimes argued that to change the law in this respect would shift the burden of proof. But, there is no reason why changes in evidence law to help the prosecution *discharge* its burden should have the effect of *shifting* it. Even before the 1994 Act, it was not the case that the prosecution's obligation was to establish the accused's guilt beyond reasonable doubt *without any help from the accused*. If it had been so, evidence of such matters as breath tests, fingerprints and handwriting would have had to be excluded, and, s 62(10) of the Police and Criminal Evidence Act 1984 provided that such inferences as appeared proper might be drawn from refusal to provide an intimate sample.

Section 35 can be defended on the basis that it makes sense out of a confusing situation at common law and does not affect the burden of proof.

The change in law affecting the right to silence at the police station is both more radical and far less easy to defend.

At common law, no inference was permitted from the exercise of the right to silence in the face of questioning by the police or others charged with the investigation of offences. By s 34 of the 1994 Act, the failure of an accused in such circumstances to mention any fact relied on later in his defence, if it was a fact which in the circumstances existing at the time the accused could reasonably have been expected to mention, will allow the jury in determining whether the accused is guilty of the offence charged to draw such inferences from the failure as appear proper.

The essence of the argument in favour of this change was twofold. First, there was a gut reaction that anyone who was innocent would trust the police and would want to explain things to them as soon as possible. Secondly, although in the past a very few police had misbehaved, the protection given in the Police and Criminal Evidence Act 1984 of access to legal advice and recorded interviews meant that no suspect who was innocent now had anything to fear.

Unfortunately, recent research suggests that this protection is insufficient. It has been proved that the police use a number of devices to discourage access to legal advisers, such as reading the suspect's rights too quickly or failing to mention that legal advice is free. There have been routine breaches of the Codes of Practice, such as the holding of improper 'informal' interviews before the recorded interview. The style of questioning in at least one interview was so bullying as to be branded oppressive by the Court of Appeal. Legal advisers may be not only unqualified but inexperienced and passive, providing no protection at all for the suspect.[1]

Police do not have to be corrupt for the innocent suspect to fear for his safety. They need only to have made some assumptions about the guilt of their suspect and be prepared to use guile to establish what they believe to be the truth. The innocent citizen probably sees the possibility of making a false confession as remote and so, perhaps, it may be. What is far more likely is that he will give an ambiguous answer which will add to the case against him. And how can he avoid giving ambiguous answers? Not only is language riddled by its very nature with ambiguity, but all the circumstances surrounding a police interrogation conspire to increase the risk. The suspect may be in a highly emotional state. He may feel guilty even though he has committed no offence – for example, feelings of anger or guilt are well established reactions to bereavement. He may be ignorant of a vital fact that explains away suspicious circumstances. He may be frightened, confused or forgetful.

Nor does the innocent suspect have to fear anything so horrific as a miscarriage of justice at trial, though past experience has shown that this is all too possible. A mistake or ambiguity in something said to the police can suggest that there is at least a reason for charging the suspect and a case to answer. That may mean a remand in custody. At the very least it is likely to mean months of anxiety whilst on bail awaiting trial. Much is made of the high standard of proof that is required before a court may convict on a criminal charge. But no such standard applies to other decisions made during the pre-trial stages. Yet these decisions may have terrible implications for an innocent suspect's liberty and for his own and his family's financial security and peace of mind.

At the pre-trial stage, a right to silence is, as things stand now in this country, an essential protection for the innocent. The innovations brought about by ss 34, 36 and 37 of the 1994 Act are indeed *defensible*, but only on the most shortsighted and crudely utilitarian basis, which accepts that it is expedient that innocent people should suffer for the sake of the majority.

Note

1   Greer, S, 'The right to silence: a review of the current debate' (1990) 53 MLR 709, pp 721–22; Sanders, A and Bridges, L, 'Access to legal advice and police malpractice' [1990] Crim LR 494, pp 494–509; Hodgson, J, 'Tipping the scales of justice: the suspect's right to legal advice' [1992] Crim LR 854, pp 854–62. For a particularly gross example of police oppression, see *Paris* (1993).

Question 25

To what extent does s 78(1) of the Police and Criminal Evidence Act 1984 provide a protection for defendants against the use of improperly obtained evidence?

Answer plan

Your starting point is the concept of fairness embodied in s 78. In order to discuss the scope of this provision, it is essential to clarify this concept for the examiner. The points can be made that not all unfairness is relevant for the operation of the sub-section, and that exclusion is, in any case, a matter only of discretion. The next step is to ask how unfairness can arise. Obviously, unreliable evidence can lead to unfairness, and you can show how the sub-section is used to exclude such evidence, with particular reference to unfairness resulting from the way in which evidence has been obtained. Move on then to examples of s 78(1) where factors other than reliability have been taken into account. The object of your argument will be to show that this provision can be used to protect process values as well as reliability. A study of Ian Dennis's article, referred to in the footnote, will be particularly helpful here. You have to face up to the decision in *Chalkley and Jeffries* (1998), and that involves showing, by reference to other appellate decisions, that the limited view of s 78(1) taken in that decision was wrong. Of particular importance is the article by Choo and Nash, 'What's the matter with section 78?' [1999] Crim LR 929. Finally, however, it is necessary to point out that although in principle, s 78(1) can be used to protect process values without regard to reliability, in practice it is unlikely to be used very often to do so, and the protection afforded to defendants is therefore limited.

In summary, therefore, the essay is constructed as follows:

- the concept of fairness in s 78(1): *Mason* (1988); *DPP v Marshall* (1988); *Walsh* (1990); *Christou* (1992);

- unreliable evidence as a source of unfairness: *O'Connor* (1987); *Keenan* (1990); *Smurthwaite and Gill* (1994);

- process values relied on in *Smurthwaite and Gill* (1994);

- the problem presented by *Chalkley and Jeffries* (1998);

- decisions at odds with *Chalkley and Jeffries*: *Matto v Wolverhampton Crown Court* (1987); *dicta* in *Walsh* (1990); *Alladice* (1988); *Khan* (1997); and *Looseley* (2001);

- argument based on s 82(3) of PACE 1984;

- reliability of evidence as a determining factor in practice: *Stewart* (1995);

- conclusion: the limited protection of s 78(1).

Answer

At the root of s 78(1) is the idea that the admission of certain evidence is capable of adversely affecting the fairness of proceedings, but it is clear from cases such as *Mason* (1988) and *DPP v Marshall* (1988) that 'proceedings' refers only to proceedings before a court. It is also clear from the sub-section that fairness is not an all or nothing affair. The exclusionary discretion is to be exercised only if the admission of the evidence in question would have 'such an adverse effect on the fairness of the proceedings that the court ought not to admit it'. Thus, in *Walsh* (1990), it was said that even if evidence had been obtained in breach of the Codes, the breach had to be 'significant and substantial' to lead to exclusion. It follows that the protection afforded by s 78(1) is a limited one. It is limited still further by the fact that the section does not make exclusion mandatory; the judge has merely a discretion to exclude, and the Court of Appeal does not readily upset exercises of judicial discretion. It was said in *Christou* (1992) that exercise of a discretion under this provision can be faulted only for '*Wednesbury* unreasonableness'.

One obvious way in which the fairness of proceedings can be adversely affected is by inviting the jury to convict on the basis of unreliable evidence. We accept that one of the objects of a criminal trial is to secure rectitude of decision, and a criminal trial will therefore cease to be fair to the extent that the likelihood of attaining this end diminishes. Many decisions show the significance of reliability in considering this discretion. In *O'Connor* (1987), for example, the Court of Appeal held that the trial judge ought to have excluded under s 78(1) evidence of a former co-accused's conviction for conspiracy with the defendant. The reason was that the effect of admitting this evidence had been to enable the prosecution to put before the jury a statement made by the co-accused in the absence of the defendant, without having the former co-accused present for cross-examination.

Evidence which might ordinarily be reliable may be rendered unreliable by the way in which it has been obtained, and s 78(1) has been used to exclude it where this has been so. Thus, in *Keenan* (1990), it was said that the provisions of Code C that were designed to ensure that interviews were fully recorded and the suspect given an opportunity to check the record should be strictly followed, and that courts should not be slow to exclude evidence following substantial breaches.

Where evidence has been obtained by entrapment, admissibility has in part depended on reliability. In *Smurthwaite and Gill* (1994), Lord Taylor CJ set out some factors which a judge might take into account. These included whether there was an unassailable record of what had occurred and whether it was strongly corroborated. Other factors were not relevant to reliability, but to the degree of impropriety involved in obtaining the evidence in question. Had the police enticed a defendant to commit an offence which he would not otherwise have committed? Had the police abused their role by asking questions which ought properly to have been asked only at a police station and in accordance with the Codes? This at least suggested that evidence could be excluded under s 78(1) if, although reliable, it had been obtained in a way that showed contempt for what can broadly be referred to as 'process values'. In other words, as Ian Dennis has argued, 'apparently reliable evidence may need to be excluded if it carries significant risks of impairing the moral authority of the verdict'.[1]

An obstacle in the way of this approach was the decision of the Court of Appeal in *Chalkley and Jeffries* (1998), in which the court said that the reference to 'the circumstances in which the evidence was obtained' in s 78(1) was not intended to widen the common law rule stated by Lord Diplock in *Sang* (1980); namely, that save in the case of admissions and confessions and generally as to evidence obtained after the commission of the offence, there was no discretion to exclude evidence unless its quality was or might have been affected by the way in which it was obtained.

Shortly after s 78(1) had become law, there were suggestions that it had not altered the common law as stated in *Sang*, but this narrow construction was rejected in other decisions and quite a number of appellate decisions suggest that the Court of Appeal in *Chalkley and Jeffries* was wrong on this point. It has already been shown that *Smurthwaite and Gill* took into account factors that had nothing to do with reliability. In *Matto v Wolverhampton Crown Court* (1987), the Divisional Court held that evidence of breath specimens should have been excluded under s 78(1) because they had been obtained in bad faith and as the result of oppression. The Court of Appeal has frequently emphasised the importance of bad faith on the part of police in connection with s 78(1). For example, in *Walsh* (1990), it was said that bad faith might make 'substantial or significant' a breach of the Code that would not otherwise have been so. And in *Alladice* (1988), the Court of Appeal said that a distinction was to be drawn when considering the effect of refusing access to a solicitor between cases where the police had acted in good faith and those where they had acted in bad faith. However, bad faith is irrelevant if the court is concerned solely with reliability.

More recently, the House of Lords in *Khan* (1996) accepted that a breach of a defendant's right to privacy under Art 8 of the European Convention on Human Rights was at least a relevant consideration under s 78(1). Yet how could it be so if the sole concern of a court is with the reliability of evidence, however improperly obtained? Further, in *Looseley* (2001), there are several suggestions in speeches of the Law Lords that the s 78(1) discretion is wide enough to exclude evidence on the basis of unfairness, even though the way in which it was obtained had no effect on its reliability. For example, Lord Hoffmann, with whom Lord Hutton agreed on this point, said that an application to exclude evidence under s 78(1) may in substance be a belated application for a stay of proceedings. If so, it should be treated as such and decided according to the principles appropriate to the grant of a stay (which do take into account breach of process values). But to be able to use s 78(1) in this way, its potential scope must be wider than was suggested in *Chalkley and Jeffries*. A final consideration is that in saying that s 78(1) merely restated the common law, the Court of Appeal in *Chalkley* failed to account for s 82(3) of the 1984 Act, which expressly preserves the common law discretion to exclude evidence.

In principle, therefore, s 78(1) appears to be available to protect process values as well as reliability, and so to provide substantial protection for defendants. In practice, however, judges are often reluctant to use it in this way, and reliability will often be the determining factor. For example, in *Stewart* (1995), the defendant was convicted of abstracting electricity and stealing gas. Electricity company officials, accompanied by police, entered the defendant's house in circumstances that were arguably unlawful. There they found a mechanical apparatus used to bypass the meters. The Court of Appeal held that it was unnecessary to decide about the lawfulness of the entry. Even assuming the entry had been unlawful, the admission of the evidence had not had any effect on the fairness of the proceedings because the apparatus had been there for all to see. It was quite a different case from one involving evidence of admissions where there had been a breach of Code C. The basis of the distinction was clearly that in this case, unlike a case where Code C had been breached, there was no doubt about the reliability of the evidence.

Thus, the protection afforded by s 78(1) is a limited one. Not all unfairness comes within its scope; it confers only a discretion and, although it is likely that in principle, the provision is available for the protection of process values regardless of reliability, in practice, if evidence is reliable, it is unlikely to be excluded under s 78(1).

Note

1   See Dennis, IH, 'Reconstructing the law of criminal evidence' (1989) Current Legal Problems 21, pp 35–44.

Question 26

Nigel is arrested on suspicion of murdering Olive. At the police station, he is told of his right to a solicitor but says he does not want one because 'they cost too much and waste a lot of time'. His watch and other personal possessions are taken away from him and he is then locked in a cell for five hours. At the end of that time, he is interviewed by DS Lestrade. After three hours of questioning, Lestrade suddenly produces a photograph. 'Just look at that', he says: 'Now, will you tell me the truth, or do I have to get my box of tricks out?' The photograph, which is in colour, shows Olive's mutilated body. Nigel screams and says: 'For God's sake, my nerves can't stand it. I killed her but I never meant to. She drove me to it.' The next day, he is interviewed again by DS Lestrade, but this time in the presence of a solicitor. He again confesses to the murder.

Discuss the evidential issues that arise.

Answer plan

Here, we have two confessions and the admissibility of each has to be considered.

The first confession

- Application of s 82(1) of PACE 1984.
- The possibility of oppression.
- Causation – always vital when considering s 76.
- Note the use made of the information about the watch.
- Breaches of Code C.

The second confession

- The continuing effect of the first confession – *McGovern* (1991); *Neil* (1994).
- Finally, remember the point based on *Sharp* (1988).

A useful case to remember when dealing with any breach of the Codes is *Elson* (1994), where the Court of Appeal said that the Codes of Practice were there to protect the individual against the might of the State. The individual, the court said, was at a great disadvantage when arrested by the police, and that was so whether or not the police behaved with the utmost propriety.

Answer

Two main questions have to be considered: the admissibility of Nigel's first confession and that of the second confession, made in the presence of a solicitor.

In relation to the first confession, there are two problems: (a) is it likely to be excluded under s 76 of PACE 1984?; (b) if not, is it likely to be excluded under s 78? Although the first confession contains exculpatory matter, it is obviously partly adverse to the maker, and so falls within the definition of 'confession' in s 82(1).

Might the first confession have been obtained by oppression? Once the question is raised, the burden is on the prosecution to prove beyond doubt that the confession was not so obtained. The court is likely to be interested in two matters: the reference to the 'box of tricks' and the showing of the photograph. Oppression is partly defined in s 76(8) of PACE 1984 as including 'torture, inhuman or degrading treatment, and the use or threat of violence (whether or not amounting to torture)'. It is possible that 'box of tricks' could have been understood as a reference to equipment designed for torture, or at least violence, so as to make what was said a threat of violence. However, a causative link has to be established between the threat and the confession and Nigel must be able to confirm that this threat, as well as the shock of seeing the photograph, operated on his mind at the time in question.

Showing the photograph to Nigel does not fall within the partial statutory definition of oppression. However, in *Fulling* (1987), the Court of Appeal approved the *Shorter Oxford Dictionary* definition of oppression as the 'exercise of authority or power in a burdensome, harsh or wrongful manner; unjust or cruel treatment of subjects, inferiors, etc, or the imposition of unreasonable or unjust burdens'. The court added that it would be hard to envisage any circumstances in which oppression would not entail some impropriety on the part of the interrogator. Showing the photograph appears to be on the borderline of oppression. It could be argued that it was psychologically burdensome to show it. There appears to be a good chance of persuading the court that the confession *may* have been obtained by oppression, and an even chance that the prosecution would be unable to prove beyond reasonable doubt that it was not.

Even if the argument on oppression failed, the matters relied on could be used to support an argument for exclusion based on s 76(2)(b). Other matters may be relevant under this head. Nigel may well have been suffering from disorientation after the time spent first in his cell and then in being questioned. His watch had been removed, and he was therefore very likely to have been without any means to measure the passing of time. It is possible that the police acted improperly in removing the watch. Paragraph 4.2 of Code C says that a detained person may retain clothing and personal effects unless the custody officer considers that he may use them to cause harm to himself or others, interfere with evidence, damage property or effect an escape, or they are needed as evidence. Did any of these reasons apply? The police might also try to argue that the watch was an 'item of value', and so excluded from the definition of personal effects under para 4.3.

The detention for five hours before the interview began may have been a breach of para 1.1 of Code C, which requires that all persons in custody must be dealt with expeditiously. What was the reason for the delay? The three hours of interviewing may have been a breach of para 12.7, which requires breaks at recognised meal times and short breaks for refreshment at intervals of approximately two hours, subject to the interviewing officer's discretion. There may also have been a breach of para 11.2 of Code C, which requires the interviewing officer to remind the suspect immediately before the interview begins of his right to *free* legal advice. One of the reasons given by Nigel for not wanting a solicitor suggests that he was not aware of this right.

Section 78 of the Police and Criminal Evidence Act 1984 applies to evidence of a confession (*Mason* (1988)). Thus, all the matters referred to in connection with s 76 could be used, if submissions under that section fail, to support an argument based on s 78. But, under this section, there is only a discretion to exclude, and, as the Court of Appeal acknowledged in *Anderson* (1993), it is not entirely clear where the burden of proof lies.[1]

If the first confession is excluded under s 76, the question arises whether the second confession was so tainted by the circumstances in which the first was made that it should be excluded also. In *McGovern* (1991), the defendant had confessed in two interviews. The first had been without a solicitor and, because of breaches of s 58 of the Police and Criminal Evidence Act 1984 and for other reasons, that confession was excluded. The Court of Appeal emphasised that when an accused person has made admissions at a first interview, the very fact that those admissions have been made is likely to have an effect on the person during the course of the second interview. It was therefore held that the confession in the second interview should have been excluded, as well as that in the first (see also *Ismail* (1990)). In *Neil* (1994), the Court of Appeal said that where there is a series of two or more interviews, and the court excludes one on the ground of unfairness, the question whether a later interview which itself is unobjectionable should also be excluded is a matter of fact and degree. It is likely to depend on whether the objections leading to the exclusion of the first interview were of a fundamental and continuing nature and, if so, if the arrangements for the later interview gave the accused a sufficient opportunity to exercise an informed and independent choice as to whether he should repeat or retract what he said in the objectionable interview, or say nothing. There is clearly room for argument in Nigel's case. Much may depend on what he says about his state of mind in the second interview (see also *Nelson* (1998)).

If the confession is admitted, the evidential value of the exculpatory part will have to be considered. This may be particularly important if Nigel chooses not to give evidence at trial. The Court of Appeal in *Duncan* (1981) held that the jury should be directed that both incriminating and exculpatory parts of a confession must be considered in deciding where the truth lies, and that it was not helpful to try to explain that the exculpatory parts were something less than evidence of the facts they stated. The judge may, however, comment on the relative weight of the two parts. This approach was approved by the House of Lords in *Sharp* (1988) and also in *Aziz* (1995).

Note

1   However, in *Stagg* (1994), very experienced prosecuting counsel accepted that it was for the prosecution to show either that there was no unfairness, or that its degree did not warrant the exclusion of the evidence.

Question 27

Earlier this year, a painting by the well known modernist painter Bruno Hatte was stolen from a public art gallery in Barchester. DS Proudie knew that two local men, Josh and Luke, specialised in the theft of modernist works of art from public galleries. On the day after the theft, he asked them to come with him to the police station to help with police inquiries. They agreed to do so. When they arrived at the police station, they were placed in separate cells.

After about 10 minutes, Josh was taken to an interview room where Proudie was waiting. Josh said at once: 'I want to see a solicitor.' Proudie replied: 'Look, a valuable painting has been stolen. Any chance there may be of its recovery will disappear if we have to wait for a solicitor. Besides, you know the form. You don't need some pimpled trainee to hold your hand.'

He then questioned Josh for 80 minutes, but all Josh would say in answer to questions was 'No comment'. Finally, Proudie said: 'Right. We'll see what your friend Luke has to say. You won't mind waiting in a cell for a few more hours, will you? You won't be lonely; we've just pulled in some skinheads for causing an affray.' Unknown to Proudie, Josh was terrified of skinheads because he had recently been attacked by a group of them. He said to Proudie: 'Look, don't put me with them. Luke and I did it together. But I only got involved because he made me; he's such a bully. We hid the painting in the well in Luke's garden.'

Proudie then visited Luke in his cell. Luke said at once: 'You got nowhere, did you?' Proudie laughed and said: 'In the well in your garden.' Luke shouted: 'Treacherous bastard!' He then refused to say any more.

The painting was later found by police in the well, and Josh and Luke were charged with its theft.

Discuss the evidential issues that arise.

Answer plan

Josh

- Definition of confession.

- Quick reference to ss 76 and 78 – need to refer to Code C.

- Importance of distinguishing between the application of Code C to those who have been *arrested* and those who have not, but are 'assisting the police with their inquiries'.

- Dispose quickly of the possibility of oppression. Don't waste time by going in detail into what is meant by oppression; there are more important things to write about in an answer to this question.
- What exactly was said about a solicitor? Anchor your argument to the facts and ask for further information, as you would in practice.
- Circumstances in which the police can refuse access to legal advice.
- The *Alladice* point.
- The 'special motive' point – *Rennie* (1982).
- The reliability point – note that the emphasis in s 76(2)(b) is on potentiality; it is irrelevant that evidence obtained afterwards confirms the truth of the confession.
- Old favourites: *Gunewardene* (1951) and *Sharp* (1988).

Luke

- Discovery of evidence via an inadmissible confession.
- Is what Luke said a confession within the PACE definition?
- Arguments for exclusion.

Answer

The case against Josh

Josh has made a statement to the police that is partly adverse to him and is therefore a confession within the definition in s 82(1) of the Police and Criminal Evidence Act 1984.

The first matter that has to be considered is whether the confession is likely to be excluded under either s 76 or s 78. In considering this question, it will be necessary to take into account the extent to which there may have been breaches of Code C of the Codes of Practice. It is important to remember that the Code does not apply as fully to someone who is voluntarily assisting police with their inquiries as to someone who has been arrested. But arguments can to some extent be based on the Code, as the following provisions suggest.

Note 1A of the Notes for Guidance to Code C states that although certain sections of the Code apply specifically to persons in custody at police stations, 'those there voluntarily to assist with an investigation should be treated with no less consideration ... and enjoy an absolute right to obtain legal advice or communicate with anyone outside the police station'. However, by para 1.3, the Notes for Guidance are not provisions of the Code.

Caution therefore has to be used in arguing that there have been breaches of the Code in relation to Josh. But it is likely that the provisions of the Code would be taken to provide guidelines as to what makes for fairness and reliability, so that even if the provisions of the Code do not strictly apply, they might well be taken into account in questions arising under ss 76 and 78. In *Christou* (1992), the Court of Appeal took the view that Code C protected persons who had not been arrested, but were being questioned by a police officer about an offence. For the sake of convenience, I shall refer hereafter to 'breaches' of the Code, but that expression should be understood as being qualified by what appears above.

It does not appear that any question of oppression arises in relation to Josh and, accordingly, I shall consider those matters that would be relevant in arguments based on s 76(2)(b) and s 78.

The first of these is the refusal to provide an opportunity for Josh to take legal advice. (I assume from the words uttered that this was a refusal and not just discouragement, but I should like to know whether Josh said anything more about having a solicitor after Proudie's remarks.) It is relevant to ask whether Proudie would have been entitled to delay the opportunity for Josh to obtain legal advice if Josh had already been detained. Proudie would have been so entitled if, amongst other things, Josh had been detained in connection with a serious arrestable offence, and an officer of the rank of superintendent or above had reasonable grounds for believing that the exercise of his right to legal advice would, amongst other things, hinder the recovery of property obtained as a result of such an offence.

Whether the offence was a 'serious arrestable offence' is governed by s 116 and Sched 5 to the Police and Criminal Evidence Act 1984. None of the offences listed in the Schedule is appropriate, and the question will therefore turn on whether the commission of the offence has led to any of the consequences specified in s 116(6), or is likely to lead to any of those consequences. The appropriate consequence appears to be at s 116(6)(e): substantial financial gain to any person. On the basis that the theft of the painting was likely to lead to such a gain, it was a serious arrestable offence and delay in permitting Josh access to legal advice might have been justified.

The question also arises whether, even if delay had not been justified, Josh suffered prejudice as a result. If Josh is experienced in being questioned by the police, the presence of a solicitor might have made no difference. Josh's replies of 'No comment' for 80 minutes suggests that this could well have been the case. In *Alladice* (1988), the appellant admitted that he could cope with being interviewed and said that he was aware of his legal rights. He had requested legal advice because he had wanted a check on the conduct of the police during the interview. The Court of Appeal held that his confession made in the absence of a solicitor was admissible, but the decision in that case was based on findings that the police had made an honest mistake about the appellant's entitlement to legal advice, and that the interview had been properly conducted. It is not clear on the facts given whether the police acted innocently or not.

There is also the problem caused by the suggestion that Josh might share a cell with some skinheads. Paragraph 3.15 of Code C provides that any person attending a police station voluntarily for the purpose of assisting with an investigation may leave at will unless placed under arrest. The police seem to have ignored, or at least to have obscured, this right. In any case, by para 8.1, it is provided that, so far as practicable, not more than one person should be detained in each cell. Was this practicable? Or was the reference to skinheads intended as a threat? If Proudie was acting in bad faith, a court would be more likely to exclude the confession, either under s 76(2)(b) or under s 78, than if he was not. In *Walsh* (1990), it was said that bad faith might make substantial or significant a breach which might not otherwise be so.

The position is more difficult if Proudie was acting in good faith. A confession will not be excluded under s 76(2)(b) merely because the accused had a special motive for making it. As Lord Lane CJ said in *Rennie* (1982), very few confessions are inspired solely by remorse. But what we have here are words uttered by Proudie to Josh which trigger a particular fear, which in turn leads to the confession. Section 76(2)(b) can be used even where there has been no police impropriety (*Fulling* (1987)) and it might therefore be applied here. The fact that the confession is in fact proved reliable by the subsequent discovery of the painting is no bar to the operation of s 76(2)(b).

If the confession is admitted, it will be evidence only against Josh. An extra-judicial confession is generally not admissible evidence against the co-accused of its maker (*Gunewardene* (1951)). The jury will be entitled to treat the exculpatory part as evidence of the facts stated (*Duncan* (1981); *Sharp* (1988)). This may be important if, for example, Josh raises the defence of duress at trial.

The case against Luke

Even if Josh's confession is inadmissible, evidence can be given that the painting was found in the well in Luke's garden (s 76(4) of the Police and Criminal Evidence Act 1984).

Has Luke by his reaction to Proudie's taunt produced a confession? Where the accused is shown to have behaved in a way that indicates awareness of his guilt, it can be argued that his behaviour amounts to an implied confession. If this is correct, the admissibility of the evidence will be subject to ss 76 and 78.

Section 82(1) of the Police and Criminal Evidence Act 1984 provides that a confession may be made 'in words or otherwise' and the concept of an implied hearsay assertion has received a boost from the decision of the House of Lords in *Kearley* (1992). It is likely that in principle, both s 76 and s 78 would be held to apply.

What has happened is that without a caution, Proudie has confronted Luke with a part of Josh's confession in such circumstances as to invite comment on it. He should have cautioned Luke first. The obligation to caution under para 10.1 of Code C was held in *Shah* (1994) to apply where there are grounds for suspicion. These can fall short of evidence supportive of a *prima facie* case, but a mere hunch or sixth sense will not suffice. And, in *Nelson* (1998), the Court of Appeal said that the appropriate time for administration of the caution is when, on an objective test, there are grounds for suspicion, falling short of evidence that supports a *prima facie* case of guilt, that an offence has been committed by the person being questioned. Certainly, after the interview with Josh, Proudie must have had more than a hunch. At that stage, there were grounds to suspect Luke of an offence, and the words 'In the well in your garden' were uttered in circumstances which implied the question 'What do you say about that?'. There appears to be a good basis for a submission that there was an improper failure to caution and that Luke's reaction should be excluded under s 76 or, failing that, s 78. The probative value of the words 'Treacherous bastard!' appears to be much the same, whether they refer to Proudie or to Josh; in either case, knowledge of the significance of the well as a hiding place may be inferred.

Question 28

Benson is charged with obtaining property by deception. The case for the prosecution is that he deceived Miss Prism into agreeing that he should repair some of the windows in her house by falsely telling her that they were in an unsafe condition and that £7,000 was a reasonable price for the work that he did.

After receiving a complaint from Miss Prism's brother, DS Japp went to an address in Anglebury where he saw Benson, who was smelling strongly of alcohol. Japp told him that he wanted to ask some questions about work that Benson had done for Miss Prism. At that moment, Mrs Benson entered the room and shouted at her husband: 'Tell the copper how you cheated the old girl, you bastard! Tell him you'd cheat your own mother for a fiver!' Benson began to weep and said: 'All right. I'll tell you the truth. I cheated her. I told her she couldn't get a cheaper job anywhere else and it wasn't true.'

Benson was then arrested and cautioned and taken to Anglebury police station. As soon as he arrived, he asked to speak by telephone to a local firm of solicitors and was allowed to do so. The firm had no one available to attend the police station except a trainee from their probate department who knew nothing about criminal work. But they did not wish to lose a client, so they sent her without telling Benson of her inexperience. During the course of the interview that later took place between Benson and Japp, she was present and took notes of what was said, but she said nothing herself.

When the interview began, Benson said: 'I must get a drink soon. I've got the shakes and I'm feeling sick. If I make a statement will I get bail?' DS Japp replied: 'You know I can't make any promises, but it costs a lot to keep someone in custody.' Benson then fully admitted the offence.

Discuss the evidential issues that arise.

Answer plan

The two confessions should be dealt with separately. Some comment is needed on the content of the first confession – it is certainly not a full one but is clearly adverse to Benson. The following points should then be made:

- the importance of whether Japp was involved in an interview in Benson's house;
- a quick dismissal of the possibility of oppression;
- the application of s 76(2)(b). Points need to be made about the fact that Benson was prompted to confess by his wife, and about the significance of alcohol consumption;

In relation to the second confession, you should make these points:

- the significance of inadequate legal representation;
- the possibility that if the first confession is excluded, the second one might be also, on the principle in *McGovern* (1991) (see also Question 26);
- the effect of Benson's need for more alcohol – see *Goldenberg* (1988);
- the conversation about bail.

Answer

In relation to the charge against Benson, his words 'I cheated her ... and it wasn't true' appear to be at least partly adverse to him, although they do not amount to an admission of the whole of the prosecution case. They therefore constitute a confession under s 82(1) of the Police and Criminal Evidence Act 1984, and the question of admissibility arises.

Presumably, the prosecution will submit that when Japp went to make inquiries of Benson, he did so only to obtain information or his explanation of the facts, and that he did not at that stage have grounds to suspect him of an offence. This is important because if Japp's inquiry was 'the questioning of a person regarding his involvement or suspected involvement in a criminal offence or offences which, by virtue of para 10.1 of Code C, is required to be carried out under caution', it would have been an interview. As such, it should have taken place at a police station in the circumstances set out in Code C (para 11.1A). In particular, Benson should have been reminded of his entitlement to free legal advice and he should have been cautioned.

In testing the prosecution's submission, the key issue will be the state of Japp's mind. Had things gone beyond the point where he was trying in a general way to discover what had happened, so that it could be said that a crime was at least suspected to have occurred, and Benson was at least suspected of having committed it?[1]

On the facts given, the complaint was not made by Miss Prism, but by her brother, who presumably related his sister's account of what Benson had said and how much she had paid. Had Japp obtained this information directly from Miss Prism, and had he perhaps had this substantiated by a receipt or bank statement to show the sum paid, it is likely that a court would find that he did suspect a crime to have occurred, and Benson to have committed it. Is the position likely to be different where the information came second hand through Miss Prism's brother, apparently without any supporting evidence? This might well change the view a court would take of Japp's state of mind. What may also be of significance is the reason for the complaint's coming from Miss Prism's brother rather than from herself. Was it because Miss Prism was too old or ill to be able to make a complaint herself? If so, might she have been muddled about what happened? This possibility, and the difficulty of assessing the weight to be attached to an account related on behalf of someone else, make it likely that what took place at Benson's house was not an interview.

On that assumption, is the confession admissible? This is not a case where oppression could be relied on, but would a submission under s 76(2)(b) be likely to succeed? The words uttered by Mrs Benson might have amounted to something said which was likely, in the circumstances existing at the time, to render unreliable any confession that Mr Benson might have made in consequence. The words or action do not have to come from the police. In *Harvey* (1988), a woman heard her lover confess to a murder. As this may have led her to make a false confession to protect him, her statement was excluded. In Benson's case, part of the circumstances existing at the time included the fact that he had, probably recently, consumed alcohol. There appears to be no question of his having done so to such an extent that he was unable to appreciate the significance of the question, or of his own answer. But the probability that alcohol had recently been consumed might be thought to add to the likelihood of unreliability. It seems clear that the accused's own mental state may be part of the circumstances under s 76(2)(b). Thus, in *McGovern* (1991), the physical condition and particular vulnerability of the defendant, who was six months pregnant and of low intelligence, were held to have been part of the background against which a submission should have been considered (see also *Everett* (1988)).

If a submission under s 76(2)(b) fails, it is possible that one under s 78 might succeed. *Mason* (1988) establishes that this section as well as s 76 is applicable to evidence of confessions.

If the first confession is excluded, the second confession at the police station may be excluded also on the basis that it is tainted by the defects attaching to the first, as was the case in *McGovern* (1991). But in *Neil* (1994), the Court of Appeal said that whether a later interview, which is in itself unobjectionable, should be excluded is a matter of fact and degree. Exclusion is likely to depend on whether the arrangements for the second interview gave the suspect sufficient opportunity to exercise an informed and independent choice about what, if anything, to say.

Benson's need for another drink is not by itself likely to be of assistance. Under s 76(2)(b), unreliability must come from something said or done by someone other than the defendant. Thus, in *Goldenberg* (1988), where it was argued that admissions were unreliable because the defendant was a heroin addict with withdrawal symptoms who would have done anything to be able to get more heroin, the Court of Appeal held that the unreliability of the confession had nothing to do with anything said or done by someone else, and so was beyond the scope of the provision.[2]

But might Japp's response to the question about bail bring s 76(2)(b) into play? It is arguable that it would. Paragraph 11.3 of Code C provides that if the person being interviewed asks the officer directly what action will be taken in the event of his making a statement, the officer may inform the person what action the police propose to take in that event. That is what Japp did. He implied that bail would probably be granted. But *this* was something said or done by someone other than the suspect. It was not improper, but it does not have to be to trigger s 76(2)(b) (*Fulling* (1987); *Harvey* (1988)). Once s 76(2)(b) has been triggered, all the circumstances can be taken into account (*Everett* (1988); *McGovern* (1991)), and these would include Benson's alcohol withdrawal symptoms. It is therefore possible that for this reason the second confession would be excluded under s 76(2)(b).

Notes

1   See the commentary on *Marsh* in [1991] Crim LR 455, p 456; *Shah* (1994).

2   So, according to *Goldenberg* (1988), s 76(2)(b) requires something which was external to the person making the confession and which was likely to have had some effect on him. Benson's earlier confession was prompted by his wife's remarks. Once these had brought s 76(2)(b) into play, the fact that Benson was affected by alcohol became part of the relevant circumstances. But it appears that without the trigger provided by Mrs Benson's remarks, the defence could not have relied on his condition under s 76(2)(b). But see *Walker* (1998).

Question 29

Simon and Tim are jointly charged with the burglary of a valuable collection of paintings belonging to Ulrica. Simon was the first to be arrested and interviewed by the police. Vivian, a senior police officer, refused his request for a solicitor on the ground that to allow it would hinder recovery of the paintings. He then forced Simon to remain standing while he interviewed him, after cautioning him, between 11 am and 4 pm without a break. Finally, Simon said: 'I'll tell you what you want to know. I was involved in the burglary, but it was only because Tim threatened to kill me if I didn't help him. You'll find the paintings in the house where Wanda, Tim's girlfriend, lives.' Acting on this information, Vivian went to Wanda's house. When he discovered that she had gone away, he broke in unlawfully, ransacked the house, and recovered the paintings.

Tim was later arrested and taken to the police station. When interviewed by the police, he refused to answer any questions. He later instructed solicitors, and told them that he had not been involved in the burglary and that he had no knowledge of the paintings that were found in Wanda's house. He said that he now believed that they had been 'planted' there by Simon, who had a grudge against him because of an affair that Tim had had during the previous year with Simon's wife.

Discuss the evidential issues arising.

Answer plan

Take the defendants separately.

Simon

The first thing to do is to try to get his confession excluded. Try s 76(2)(a), alternatively s 76(2)(b). There's no point in discussing s 78; you are better off with s 76 because of the burden placed on the prosecution by that section, and because it makes exclusion mandatory rather than discretionary. On these facts, any arguments available under s 78 can be used equally well under s 76. Look for breaches of Code C and think about how you can use them to support arguments under s 76. On the assumption that the confession might not be excluded, you need to say something about its evidential status. You might add something about the burden of proof where a defence of duress is raised. Section 76(4) will be important for the discovery of the paintings. A brief discussion of s 78 is appropriate to cover the unlawful entry that led to their discovery.

Tim

You need to discuss the effect of Tim's silence at the police station. Note the importance of discovering if he was offered legal advice. On the assumption that he was, you need to describe how the judge will direct the jury in relation to s 34 of the Criminal Justice and Public Order Act 1994. Another point to consider is whether Tim's theory about planting the paintings is something caught by s 34.

Answer

Although what Simon said to Vivian was partly exculpatory, it was also partly adverse because he admitted taking part in the burglary. It therefore comes within the definition of a confession in s 82(1) of the Police and Criminal Evidence Act 1984 (PACE). The first question to be considered is whether it could be excluded under s 76. Although s 78 is theoretically available also, all the arguments for exclusion are relevant to s 76, and it is better for the defence to rely on s 76 because of the burden of proof that it imposes on the prosecution, and because exclusion under that section is mandatory if the circumstances are appropriate, whereas under s 78(1), exclusion is only discretionary.

By s 76(8), oppression includes, among other things, 'inhuman or degrading treatment'. In *Fulling* (1987), Lord Lane CJ relied on a dictionary definition that included 'exercise of authority or power in a burdensome, harsh or wrongful manner ... the imposition of unreasonable or unjust burdens'. He also emphasised the seriousness of the conduct needed to constitute oppression. This seems to be a borderline case. No violence was involved, although *Paris* (1993) shows that this is not an essential element. It is arguable that it was oppressive to question somebody forced to stand for five hours. There was clearly bad faith; Vivian must have known that by para 12.5 of Code C, persons being questioned shall not be required to stand, and that by para 12.7, breaks from interviewing shall be made at recognised meal times and that short breaks for refreshment shall be provided at intervals of approximately two hours. There is nothing to suggest that the exceptional conditions referred to in that paragraph apply here.

If an argument under s 76(2)(a) fails, the same facts can be relied on under s 76(2)(b). In addition, Simon could rely on the fact that he was wrongly refused access to a solicitor. Under s 58 of PACE, delay is only permitted for limited reasons where someone has been arrested for a serious arrestable offence and where the authorisation of an officer of at least the rank of superintendent has been obtained. The offence is almost certainly a serious arrestable offence. Although burglary is not an offence listed in Sched 5 to PACE, the commission of this offence has almost certainly led to serious financial loss to Ulrica, and this would bring the offence within the category of serious arrestable offences by virtue of s 116(3) and (6)(f) of PACE. We do not, however, know Vivian's rank. If he was not at least a superintendent, was the delay in access to legal advice authorised by someone who was? Even if the delay was authorised by an officer of appropriate rank, it is most unlikely that the s 58(8) condition applied. Section 58(8)(c) does indeed authorise delay where the exercise of the right will hinder the recovery of any property obtained as a result of the offence. But the Court of Appeal stated in *Samuel* (1988) that the right of access to legal advice was one of the most important and fundamental rights of a citizen. The court also said that where the police try to justify denial of access to a solicitor, that can be done only by reference to specific circumstances, including evidence about the person detained or the actual solicitor involved. The officer has to believe, inadvertent or unwitting conduct apart, that if allowed to consult with Simon, the solicitor would commit a criminal offence. There is no evidence whatsoever to support such a belief by Vivian. Provided causation can be shown, there is no reason why an argument based on s 76(2)(b) and relying on the denial of access to a solicitor as well as the matters relied on under s 76(2)(a) should not succeed.

If, by a remote chance, the confession is not excluded, its evidential status will have to be considered. It is evidence only against its maker (see the wording of s 76(1) and *Gunewardene* (1951)), but, following *Lobban v R* (1995), the references to Tim will not be edited out unless Simon agrees. He is unlikely to do so because he will want to show that he raised his defence of duress at an early stage. He does not have the legal burden of proving this defence, but he has an evidential burden in respect of it (*Gill* (1963)).

Even if the confession is inadmissible, the discovery of the paintings will be admissible under s 76(4) of PACE. It would be possible to argue that this evidence should be excluded under s 78 because of the unlawful way in which the paintings were discovered. But although s 78 is probably in principle available to protect process values regardless of reliability, in practice, where the reliability of evidence has not been affected by the impropriety of the way in which it was obtained, it is unlikely to be excluded. For example, in *Cooke* (1995), a case where rape and kidnapping were alleged, the question arose whether s 78(1) should be used to exclude evidence of a sample of hair that might have been improperly taken from the defendant. The Court of Appeal agreed with the trial judge's decision to admit the evidence, regardless of any possible assault. The fact of an assault on the defendant would have cast no doubt on the accuracy or strength of the evidence.

Tim faces the possibility of a direction to the jury under s 34 of the Criminal Justice and Public Order Act 1994 in respect of his silence at the police station. However, if he was not offered legal advice before being questioned no inferences from silence can be made: see s 34(2A). If he was offered legal advice, and he relies at trial on facts that he did not mention to the police, it is possible that a direction would be given. His lack of involvement in the burglary and ignorance of the paintings are facts that might be caught. The defence could argue, following *Mountford* (1999) and *Gill* (2001), that the truth of these facts was the central issue in his trial, and that accordingly, a s 34 direction should not be given. In *Gowland-Wynn* (2002), however, another division of the Court of Appeal rejected this approach and the law is therefore uncertain. Tim's suggestion that Simon planted the paintings is a theory and not a fact and, as such, following *Nickolson* (1999), would not be caught by s 34 unless he could reasonably have been expected to tell the police about the fact of Simon's grudge. If a s 34 direction is given, the judge would have to follow the guidelines laid down in *Gill* (2001), that is to say, he must identify the fact on which Tim relies and which was not mentioned on questioning. He must direct the jury that it is for them to decide whether in the circumstances, that fact was something that Tim could reasonably have been expected to mention. He should tell them that if they think it was, they are not obliged to draw any inferences, but that they may do so. Further, he must tell the jury that a suspected person is not bound to answer police questions, that an inference from silence cannot on its own prove guilt, and that the jury must be satisfied that there is a case to answer before they can draw any adverse inferences from silence. Finally, he should tell the jury that they can draw an adverse inference only if they are sure that Tim was silent because he had no answers, or none that would stand up to investigation.

Question 30

The police suspected that George and Harry were dealing in drugs. Without a warrant, they broke into a house occupied by the two men solely in order to look for evidence while George and Harry were away. They discovered a quantity of cocaine and £30,000 in used bank notes. As a result of their discovery, George and Harry were arrested several days later and taken to the police station for questioning. Both men refused to answer any questions until they had received legal advice. When their solicitor arrived, she advised them to remain silent and accordingly they continued to refuse to answer any police questions. The police later placed them together in a cell in which a listening device had been secretly installed which recorded all their conversation. At one stage, George was overheard saying to Harry: 'One thing's for sure, they can never prove we didn't have the stuff for our own use.' Harry replied: 'I wish I'd made as much out of it as you. I'd be in the south of France by now.' Then came the sound of two men laughing. Nothing further of significance was overheard.

Answer plan

The first point should be a familiar one – improperly obtained evidence and the use of s 78(1) of the Police and Criminal Evidence Act (PACE) 1984. After that, you need to refer to a problem that has occurred recently on several occasions. Is evidence of possession of cash admissible or even relevant on a charge of drug dealing? This is the sort of point which you could deal with perfectly well in an exam if you did not know the cases but thought clearly about basic ideas of relevance and admissibility. It quite often happens that a question will be based, at least in part, on recent decisions. But the examiner looks primarily for an intelligent answer. You are not expected to be an encyclopedia of case law in this subject. Of course, if you have actually read the cases because you read *The Times* or subscribe to the Criminal Law Review or Criminal Appeal Reports, that is a bonus.

There is an easy point about the new law on the exercise of the right to silence. Then we come to evidence obtained by bugging. You ought to be able to deal with this if you've studied the law relating to s 78 efficiently. Finally, some thought is needed about the content of the conversation. Are there any confessions there? If so, how many? And by whom? Note yet again that the examiner is looking to see if you can *analyse* the information you are given.

Answer

The first question that arises is whether the cocaine and cash discovered during the unlawful search will be admissible. The trial judge will have to consider whether, in view of the circumstances in which this evidence was obtained, he should exercise the discretion which he has under s 78 of PACE to exclude evidence of what was found on the ground that its admission would so adversely affect the fairness of the proceedings that it ought not to be admitted.

It is implicit in s 78(1) that it is possible for the way in which evidence is obtained to result in its exclusion. This is particularly likely where the police have acted in bad faith. In *Matto v Wolverhampton Crown Court* (1987), the defendant was convicted of driving with excess alcohol. Police officers had requested a specimen of breath when they were on the defendant's property. This was unlawful, and they knew it to be so. The specimen proved positive. The defendant was then arrested. At the police station, he provided another positive specimen. The appeal was allowed on the ground that because the police had acted in bad faith and oppressively, the Crown Court could have decided to exclude the evidence under s 78 if it had directed itself properly.

However, in cases where improperly obtained real evidence has been considered by the Crown Court in a s 78 application, it is usually admitted because any impropriety in obtaining it is far less likely to have affected its reliability than evidence of an improperly obtained confession. Thus, in *Cooke* (1995), the Court of Appeal pointed out that the vast majority of cases under s 78 had concerned alleged confessions obtained in breach of the Codes. In that case, where a sample of hair had been obtained from the defendant in circumstances that may have been improper, the court held that the trial judge had properly decided to admit the evidence, despite the possibility that there may been a technical assault on the defendant. This did not cast doubt on the accuracy or strength of the evidence.

Two features might make an application to exclude slightly more likely to succeed in this case. It seems very likely that the police were acting in bad faith, and it is clear that their entry was unlawful. But the offence is regarded as such a serious one that the discretion is still not likely to be exercised in the defendants' favour.

Even if an application under s 78 fails, there may be room for further argument about the admissibility of the discovery of the cash.

In *Grant* (1996), the Court of Appeal held that finding money in a defendant's possession is capable of being relevant to whether the defendant intended to supply drugs that have also been found in his possession. It is for the jury to decide whether the presence of the money indicates a continuing trade in the drugs and therefore an intention to supply them. It is necessary, however, to direct the jury that they should regard the finding of money as relevant only if they reject any innocent explanation for its presence put forward by the defendant. But, if they conclude that the presence of money was proof, not merely of past dealing, but of continuing dealing in drugs, they can take the discovery of the money into account.

By s 34 of the Criminal Justice and Public Order Act 1994, if either George or Harry failed to mention when questioned by the police any fact relied on as his defence in subsequent proceedings, and that fact was one which in the circumstances existing at the time he could reasonably have been expected to mention, the jury may draw such inferences from the failure as appear proper. The fact that the defendants' silence was on legal advice may deter the jury from making an adverse inference, but the matter is likely to be left for their consideration. This is an important provision for both defendants because a jury might well think that if there was an innocent explanation either for the cocaine or the cash, it would have been forthcoming at a very early opportunity.

In *Argent* (1997), the Court of Appeal said that when considering whether a fact was one that a defendant could reasonably have been expected to mention, the court must take into account all relevant circumstances at the time of questioning, including the personal characteristics of the defendant. It was also said that legal advice is something the court might have to consider as one of those circumstances. Its significance was more fully considered in *Condron* (1997). In giving guidance, the Court of Appeal said that where a defendant says he failed to answer questions on legal advice, that bare assertion is unlikely to be regarded as a sufficient reason for failure to mention matters relevant to the defence. In practice, a defendant will have to go further and provide, either through his own testimony or that of his solicitor, the reasons for the advice.

If a direction is given under s 34, the judge should follow the guidelines laid down in *Gill* (2001), that is to say, he must identify the fact on which the defendant relies and which was not mentioned on questioning. He must direct the jury that it is for them to decide whether in the circumstances, that fact was something that the defendant could reasonably have been expected to mention. He should tell them that if they think it was, they are not obliged to draw any inferences, but that they may do so. Further, he must tell the jury that a suspected person is not bound to answer police questions, that an inference from silence cannot on its own prove guilt, and that the jury must be satisfied that there is a case to answer before they can draw any adverse inferences from silence. Finally, he should tell the jury that they can draw an adverse inference only if they are sure that the defendant was silent because he had no answers, or none that would stand up to investigation.

In theory, the admissibility of evidence obtained by a trick can be challenged under s 78(1) of PACE, but for a long time, evidence obtained by eavesdropping has been admitted. In *Maqsud Ali* (1966), for example, a tape recorder was used to eavesdrop on a conversation between two suspects, and the evidence obtained was admitted. More recently, in *Bailey and Smith* (1993), the judge admitted evidence of confessions made by the two defendants and tape recorded during conversations between them while they were sharing a bugged cell at a police station after being arrested, charged and remanded in custody. The Court of Appeal upheld the decision to admit the evidence but said that this was a device to be used only in grave cases. Drug dealing for commercial gain is regarded as a grave offence, as was shown recently in *Khan* (1996) where the decision to admit evidence of drug dealing obtained by bugging private property was upheld by the House of Lords.

The exchange between Harry and George is ambiguous. Does it amount to a confession by either defendant? 'They can never prove we didn't have the stuff for our own use' is an observation which is at least partly adverse to both defendants in that it is capable of being interpreted as an admission that the drugs were in the possession of both Harry and George. Harry did not dissociate himself in any way from George's remark, and may therefore be taken to have adopted it. On similar principles, a confession was admitted against both defendants in *Batt* (1995). Ashley and Kerry were convicted of robbery. One of them had appeared to be holding a gun which was partly concealed by material. While on remand in custody, they were sharing a cell. A police officer gave evidence that on one occasion Kerry had said to Ashley: 'They'll fuck themselves if they show that gun in court. It's not the one used.' The Court of Appeal held that this was evidence against Ashley as well as Kerry. Ashley had said nothing, but he had not dissociated himself from his companion's remark.

Harry's remark to George, 'I wish I'd made as much out of it as you', is capable of being interpreted as a confession to dealing, and on the principle just outlined, George's failure to dissociate himself from what was said is capable of being interpreted as an adoption of it.

CHAPTER 8

SIMILAR FACT EVIDENCE

Introduction

Similar fact evidence has a reputation for being an impenetrable subject. Quite often, students who have coped well with other parts of an evidence course reach the examination still feeling that they don't know what it's about or how it works. They are aware of a few slogans – 'striking similarity', 'positive probative value' – but helplessness tends to set in when they are confronted by a problem question.

I think that there are several reasons for this. One is that the very name of the topic – 'similar fact evidence' – is misleading because it is quite possible to encounter cases under this head which do not, strictly speaking, deal with similar facts at all. For example, this subject is generally taken to include cases where the accused is found in possession of incriminating material; there may also be cases where the circumstances surrounding the similar fact evidence are relevant independently of the similar facts. (See the example given by PB Carter of a person charged with theft where the prosecution alleges that he knew the key to a combination lock. Evidence of the fact that he had previously stolen the victim's diary containing a record of that key would be admissible, not to show that the accused was in the habit of stealing, but to show that he knew the key (Carter, PB, 'Forbidden reasoning permissible: similar fact evidence a decade after *Boardman*' (1985) 48 MLR 29, pp 29–30).)

Another reason is that this topic cannot be learned by reading masses of cases and trying to summarise them in a structure of rules, sub-rules and exceptions, which, when properly applied, will provide a correct answer to the question whether any particular piece of disputed evidence is properly described as 'similar fact evidence', and so admissible.

A third reason is that students generally expect a topic in the law of evidence to be about *law*, and this one is not primarily about that at all. It is about facts and problems of proof.

The key to understanding this topic is to realise that it developed because of the need to ensure that juries reached correct decisions. If evidence of significant probative value is kept from a jury, it is likely that the strength of the prosecution case will not be fully appreciated and this may lead to a wrongful acquittal. But there is also the danger of misdecision if a jury hears too much evidence. If a jury hears evidence which has some probative value, but not as much as the jury is likely to think it has, this may lead to a wrongful conviction.

In each case, it is necessary to try to assess the proper probative value of a disputed item of evidence, and to weigh that against any danger there may be that the jury will be misled by it into thinking that the case against the accused is stronger than it really is. The higher the probative value of a piece of evidence, the less will be the danger of misdecision. The reason for this is that although such evidence may still provide some opportunity for the jury to convict for a wrong reason, it is much more likely to persuade them to convict for the right reason, namely, the strength of the case against the accused.

This is shown by the approach taken by the courts to cases that involve a question of the admissibility of what are literally similar facts. When Charlie is charged with burglary of a tobacconist's shop, the jury is not allowed to know of his 27 previous convictions for breaking into other tobacconists' shops. The reason for this is that the jurors might say, 'Well, it's obvious. He's always doing this. He must be guilty'. They might even say, 'This chap needs putting away. The easiest way to achieve that is to find him guilty on this charge'. The fact that Charlie has burgled tobacconists' shops on at least 27 previous occasions is not *irrelevant*; a person with that history is more likely than someone without it to have committed the particular burglary with which the court is concerned. However, that doesn't go very far towards proving that Charlie, as opposed to anyone else, committed the crime in question. It is thought, however, that jurors would be unlikely to appreciate this, so the information is kept from them.

But now suppose rather more. Charlie, when committing his previous burglaries, on each occasion wrote on one of the walls of the premises five lines from Homer's *Odyssey*, in Greek, with accents, and in sequence. A piece of writing which fits this pattern was found in the premises to which this charge relates. At once, the probative value of Charlie's previous history increases greatly because it puts Charlie in a very much narrower range of potential burglars – probably in a class of one. But, you will object, someone might have framed him. That is true. But similar fact evidence, like any other evidence, does not have to be *conclusive* to be admitted. Despite the *possibility* that Charlie was framed, the *probability* is that this evidence points him out correctly as the culprit. Little, if any, of the evidence that is given in court will be conclusive. Not even the testimony of someone who claims to have seen the defendant in the act of committing the crime is conclusive, for the witness may have made a misidentification, or be in some other way mistaken in what he saw, or be committing perjury. Nor is the defendant's own confession conclusive, as some notorious cases have all too clearly shown.

In both cases, we were relying for the relevance of the previous history on an assumption that people tend to follow patterns of behaviour. But the first pattern of behaviour was one followed by quite a large number of persons and so did not point at all clearly to Charlie as having been the burglar on the occasion in question. Yet the second pattern of behaviour was so peculiar to Charlie that it would defy belief to suggest that there might have been someone other than Charlie operating in the same way for his own benefit, and not in order to incriminate Charlie.

I have gone into what must appear to be a rather obvious comparison at some length because I want to show how we set about assessing the probative worth of an item of evidence. Such an assessment depends not on law at all, but on a mixture of logic and general experience. What has already been said in Chapter 1 about relevance is of vital importance here. To argue effectively, you need to clarify those basic assumptions about the way things are in the world that have to be true if a particular piece of information is to be relevant at all. If you need to attack the admissibility of a piece of similar fact evidence, the best approach may often be to attack the generalisation upon which your opponent must rely to establish its relevance. What unexpressed generalisations can you find, for example, in the case of *Butler* (1987)?

You cannot hope to deal effectively with an examination question involving similar fact evidence unless you decide at the outset what part in the story is played by each item of evidence. What precisely is the probative job that a particular item does? Ask not merely *whether* it is relevant, but *why* it is so. And remember that any proper answer to 'Why is it relevant?' should contain a reference to some supporting generalisation. What precisely is that generalisation? Can it be sustained?

How should a candidate use cases in dealing with a similar fact point? Use them as you would if you were arguing a case in court. They don't come first, but they can provide a useful support for your argument.

You will begin with an argument about relevance. In that argument you refer to the overriding principle: if the disputed testimony has greater danger of prejudice than probative weight, it ought not to go in. At that stage, your argument will be confined to the facts, and it may by itself be enough. But, sometimes, a judge may appear reluctant to accept your submissions. At this stage, you may push him in the right direction by drawing his attention to a few decided cases if they are very much in point. But these should *not* be your first line of argument; that is reserved for the facts.

The examiner, like the judge, requires an argument on the facts and not a string of cases. If you have any doubt about this, look at what Sir Ralph Kilner Brown said when delivering his judgment in the Court of Appeal decision in *Butler* (1987). He condemned the citation of numerous authorities and emphasised the need to apply well known principles to the particular circumstances of each case. An intelligent student dealing with a question involving similar fact evidence does not play a game of snap with previous cases, trying to find one where the facts most closely approximate to those of his present problem and then using that as a 'precedent'. He uses previous decisions as illustrations of how basic principles are applied. The cases should be read for their reasoning, not for their results. It follows from this that some of the judgments, and not merely the headnote or a textbook summary, should be read.

You should also note the development of the separate concept of 'background evidence', which is admissible entirely apart from similar fact principles. The case that seems to have started this development was *Pettman* (1985). This remains unreported, but it has been followed in *M and Others* (2000). You should also note *Fulcher* (1995), *Butler* (1999) and *Underwood* (1999).

Finally, a warning. In many problem questions, you are told that defendants have previous convictions. Candidates nearly always assume that this is an invitation to discuss similar fact evidence. Sometimes it is, but very often it is not; what the examiner wants is a discussion about the possibility of cross-examination under s 1(3) of the Criminal Evidence Act 1898 (see Chapter 9). So whenever you are told about previous convictions, think about similar fact evidence *and* the operation of the 1898 Act.

Checklist

Students should be familiar with the following areas:

- relevance;
- application of the principles expressed in *Makin v AG for New South Wales* (1894), *DPP v Boardman* (1975) and *DPP v P* (1991);
- the limited use of 'striking similarity', even in identification cases (*W* (1998));
- the significance of the possibility of concoction by witnesses after *H* (1995);
- new developments in relation to 'background evidence';
- s 27(3) of the Theft Act 1968.

Question 31

'If the inadmissible chain of reasoning is the only purpose for which the evidence is adduced, the evidence itself is not admissible. If there is some other relevant probative purpose, the evidence is admitted.'

How far is this an accurate summary of the basis of the law relating to similar fact evidence?

Answer plan

The quotation is one of a number of attempts that can be found in the cases to express the basis of the law about similar fact evidence. Some familiarity with the context is helpful, and the first paragraph is devoted to this. The 'inadmissible chain of reasoning' was referred to by Lord Hailsham in *DPP v Boardman* (1975). According to his view, what *Makin* (1894) prohibited was any chain of reasoning leading from propensity to guilt. The examiner is therefore asking whether this is an accurate summary of the effect of *Makin*.

The essay then moves on to consider other statements concerning the law of similar fact evidence and brings out the point that emphasis has frequently been placed on the probative force of the evidence whose admissibility is disputed. This sets the stage for the problem posed in the fourth paragraph: might there be cases where evidence of propensity was so strong as to provide sufficient probative force for admissibility – or will evidence of propensity alone, however strong, *never* be sufficient?

The next step is to consider some cases – *Ball* (1911) and *Straffen* (1952) – where it looks as if the only evidence was of propensity, but where it was thought sufficiently probative of guilt to be admitted.

The conclusion might have been simply that Lord Hailsham did not get it exactly right, but that would not have been particularly interesting. He based what he said on *Makin* (1894). If *Makin* is not to be interpreted according to Lord Hailsham, how is it to be interpreted? The essay ends with a summary of CR Williams's suggestion.

In summary, therefore, the essay is constructed as follows:

- the two kinds of evidence referred to in *Makin* (1894);
- the conclusion about an 'inadmissible chain of reasoning';
- the stress on 'positive probative value': *Rance* (1975), *Scarrot* (1978), *Lunt* (1986);
- the effect of *DPP v P* (1991);

- whether evidence of disposition can have sufficient probative value to be admitted: *Ball* (1911), *Straffen* (1952);
- the best interpretation of Lord Herschell's speech in *Makin*.

Answer

In *Makin v AG for New South Wales* (1894), Lord Herschell drew a distinction between two kinds of evidence. On the one hand was evidence which tended to show that the accused had been guilty of criminal acts other than those covered by the indictment 'for the purpose of leading to the conclusion that the accused is a person likely from his criminal conduct or character to have committed the offence for which he is being tried'. On the other hand was evidence which went beyond that and was relevant to an issue before the jury; for example, where it bore upon the question whether the acts alleged to constitute the crime were designed or accidental, or where it rebutted a defence that would otherwise have been open to the accused. According to Lord Hailsham in *DPP v Boardman* (1975), the effect of this distinction is to prohibit a chain of reasoning leading from propensity to guilt. This is the 'inadmissible chain of reasoning', and it follows that similar fact evidence can be admitted only if relevant for some reason other than propensity. Such evidence may in addition possess some relevance via propensity, but the jury should be warned to avoid reasoning based on propensity in reaching their conclusion. In the same case, Lord Salmon said that the test for admissibility must be whether the evidence is capable of tending to persuade a reasonable jury of the accused's guilt on some ground other than his bad character and disposition to commit the sort of crime with which he is charged.

In the later cases of *Rance* (1975) and *Scarrot* (1978), the Court of Appeal emphasised the need for 'positive probative value', and in *Lunt* (1986), Neill LJ made it clear that, notwithstanding the general rule that the prosecution could not adduce evidence that the accused had a propensity to commit crimes of the kind charged, similar fact evidence would be admissible if it was positively probative in relation to the crime charged. More recently, in *DPP v P* (1991), Lord Mackay stated that the essential feature of similar fact evidence was that its probative force in support of the allegation that an accused person committed a crime was sufficiently great to make it just to admit the evidence, notwithstanding its prejudice to the accused in tending to show that he was guilty of another crime.

In the light of these various statements, all emphasising the probative force of proposed similar fact evidence, the question that arises in relation to the 'inadmissible chain of reasoning' quotation is whether there may occasionally be circumstances where evidence of disposition has sufficient probative value to be included.

It seems that there have been cases where similar fact evidence derived its only relevance from an argument via propensity. A clear example is *Ball* (1911), which shows that if the propensity in question is specific enough, it may have sufficient probative force to make evidence of it admissible. In particular, evidence of a propensity towards a particular person will often be admissible. In *Ball* (1911), a brother and sister were prosecuted under the Punishment of Incest Act 1908. The House of Lords upheld the decision of the trial judge to admit evidence of earlier sexual relations between the accused at a time when incest between a brother and sister was not unlawful. It was said that this evidence was admissible to establish the existence of a sexual passion between them. As Lord Loreburn said, this was as much evidence as was their presence together in bed of the fact that when they were there they had had guilty relations with each other. This reasoning suggests that evidence of a mere propensity to commit incest would have been inadmissible. If a man were charged with incest with one sister, a previous conviction for incest with another one would be inadmissible. But in *Ball* (1911), the force of the evidence was that it established a propensity directed exclusively towards the woman implicated in the offence for which the two accused were being prosecuted.

Another example of admissible evidence of propensity is *Straffen* (1952). In this case, the accused had been charged with the murder by manual strangulation of two young girls at Bath. He had been found unfit to plead and had been committed to Broadmoor. A year later, he escaped and was not recaptured for four hours. During that time, another young girl, Linda Bowyer, was murdered by strangulation. Straffen was seen near the place where the body was found, but he denied this killing, although he had admitted those of the girls at Bath. At Straffen's trial for the murder of Linda Bowyer, the judge admitted evidence of the Bath killings. The Court of Criminal Appeal held that this had been right. The evidence of the way in which the earlier killings had been done was relevant because it showed that they had been done in precisely the same way as the killing of Linda Bowyer. The evidence thus identified the killer of Linda Bowyer as the same person who had committed the Bath killings. This was clearly evidence of propensity, albeit of a very particular kind. It showed that Straffen was a strangler of young girls in odd circumstances and with no apparent motive. There had been no sexual interference and no attempt to conceal the bodies. The unusual nature of this propensity gave the evidence its strong probative value.

Given that the courts do admit evidence whose relevance is based on propensity, how should Lord Herschell's speech in *Makin* be interpreted? The best solution appears to be that his formulation refers not to two conflicting rules, but to two competing principles. The first is the principle that evidence which shows the defendant to be of bad character or disposition is not admissible to establish guilt. The second is the principle that relevant evidence ought to be admitted. In each case what has to be determined is which of the two principles should be given the greater weight. If the risk of prejudice is great and the probative value small, the evidence should be rejected. If, on the other hand, the probative value is great and the risk of prejudice slight, the evidence should be admitted. The difficult cases will be those where matters are not so clear cut, but they should be resolved by a combination of common sense, logic and experience rather than by attempts to apply 'legal rules' established by 'precedents'.[1]

Note

1   Williams, CR, 'The problem of similar fact evidence' (1979) 5 Dalhousie LJ 281, pp 281–348. On the difference between principles and rules, see Dworkin, RM, 'Is law a system of rules?', in *The Philosophy of Law*, 1977, pp 38–65.

Question 32

James is charged with indecently assaulting Kate on a coach journey between London and Oxford. The case for the prosecution is that they had not met before, but were sitting next to each other, and that after a while, James began a conversation by asking Kate if she had seen a current exhibition of 20th century American paintings. It is alleged that during the following conversation, James fondled Kate's breasts. James denies the charge. He admits touching Kate's breasts, but says that he did so only by accident when the coach swerved suddenly and he was thrown across his seat.

When James's briefcase was lawfully searched after his arrest, it was found to contain several magazines of heterosexual pornography, and a scrapbook containing photographs of women with large breasts. Last year, James was convicted of indecently assaulting Lily, who had been sitting next to him in a railway carriage on a journey between Worcester and Plymouth. On that occasion, James had begun a conversation with Lily, whom he had not met before, about a current exhibition of paintings by 17th century French painters. A little later, he had fondled Lily's breasts. His defence had been that he had not touched Lily, and that she had invented the whole incident.

Discuss the evidential issues that arise.

Answer plan

The problem concerns the admissibility of potential items of similar fact evidence:

- the magazines and scrapbook (relevance is an important consideration and you should note the nature of James's defence);
- the circumstances of James's previous conviction, to be discussed in the light of *DPP v P* (1991); *Kidd* (1995); *West* (1996); and *Musquera* (1999).

Answer

An argument that the discovery of the magazines is relevant would have to be developed on these lines:

(a) a man in possession of heterosexual pornography is very likely to have heterosexual inclinations;

(b) a man with heterosexual inclinations is more likely than a man without them to commit an indecent assault on a woman.

Even if this argument is accepted, a judge might be persuaded to exclude the evidence on the basis that its probative worth is very slight and is likely to be outweighed by its prejudicial effect. Further, the argument is clearly based on propensity. Evidence of propensity may be admissible to prove guilt where its probative value is very high. Such evidence was admitted, for example, in *Straffen* (1952) to show the propensity of the accused to commit murder in particularly unusual circumstances. It has also been admitted to show the accused's propensity to behave in a certain way towards a particular individual, as in *Ball* (1911), where the object was to show the sexual desire of the accused brother and sister for each other.

In general, however, the prosecution is not allowed to rely on evidence that would merely be evidence of a propensity to commit a crime of a certain type. Cases such as *Lunt* (1986) have established that evidence is admissible as 'similar fact' evidence if, but only if, it goes beyond showing a tendency to commit crimes of the kind charged, and is positively probative in relation to the particular charge. Thus, even assuming the possession of heterosexual pornography to prove a propensity to commit indecent offences against women, the discovery would appear in principle to be inadmissible.

It is possible, however, that the position may be different in view of the nature of James's defence. There is some support for the proposition that evidence of propensity can be admissible to rebut an otherwise plausible defence. In *Lewis* (1982), the defendant had been charged with offences involving indecency with children. Evidence was admitted of his interest in, and qualified sympathy with, paedophilia to rebut his defence of 'innocent association' or 'accident' in relation to one of the counts on the indictment. This decision was in line with earlier cases where similar fact evidence was admitted because of its probative value in putting a different complexion on events that had occurred. Thus, in *Mortimer* (1936), the defendant was charged with the murder of a woman cyclist by deliberately driving a motor car at her. To rebut any suggestion that the death had been accidental, evidence was admitted to show that the defendant had knocked other women cyclists off their bicycles a short time before.

James's defence is a denial that there was physical contact to the extent alleged by Kate, and that to the extent that there was any physical contact, it was accidental. Had he denied any physical contact at all, the evidence of the heterosexual pornography would have been inadmissible (assuming it was relevant), as was the evidence of paedophile interests on the other counts in *Lewis* (1982), in respect of which there was a simple denial. Similarly, in *Wright* (1990), where allegations of sexual offences were made by schoolboys against their headmaster, and his defence was that the stories had been totally fabricated, the Court of Appeal held that evidence should not have been admitted of articles found in his possession that merely tended to show that he had homosexual inclinations. But, because of *Lewis*, exclusion of the heterosexual pornography cannot be relied on.

Even if it is decided that the pornography is irrelevant, or of such slight weight that it ought to be excluded, there remains the scrapbook for consideration. This may be more significant than the pornography. If the jury concluded that it had been compiled by the defendant, they might infer that the defendant had an obsession with women's breasts, and they might believe that a person with such an obsession was more likely than someone without it to assault a woman indecently by fondling her breasts. The case for relevance is thus stronger than it is with the pornography, and it is likely that this evidence would be admitted on the *Lewis* principle to rebut James's defence of accident.

It has been clear since *DPP v P* (1991) that striking similarity is not essential for similar fact evidence to be admissible, and that whether the evidence has sufficient probative worth to outweigh its prejudicial effect must in each case be a question of degree. In particular, it seems that features of the 'stock in trade' of a particular type of offender may now be admissible. This must be a matter of degree. Presumably the decision in *Brown* (1963) would still be upheld, namely, that to admit as similar fact evidence a *modus operandi* common to thousands of other examples of the same offence would effectively abolish the general prohibition against giving evidence of a defendant's bad character. The basic question must be whether the apparent similarities between James's earlier offence and the facts giving rise to the present charge could reasonably be explained as the result of coincidence.

In this connection, it is relevant that only one earlier incident is relied on. But there are some common features:

(a) James began a conversation with a stranger who was sitting next to him on a journey;

(b) he began by referring to a current exhibition of paintings;

(c) there were similarities in the way in which the assaults were alleged to have been carried out.

But there are also dissimilarities:

(a) the paintings were of different styles and periods;

(b) the defences were different;

(c) the locations and modes of transport were different.

Where similar fact evidence of conduct is relied on, the courts must consider any significant dissimilarities when assessing its probative worth. However, as was said in *West* (1996), the mere fact that there are some dissimilarities will not lead inevitably to exclusion. In *Kidd* (1995), the Court of Appeal said that *DPP v P* had considerably broadened this area of law and had given trial judges a much wider discretion than they had been previously thought to have. On the other hand, in *Musquera* (1999), the Court of Appeal said that while *DPP v P* had eliminated the necessity for striking similarity, it was still necessary to point to some common feature or features constituting a significant connection between the similar fact evidence and the evidence in the current trial, and going beyond mere propensity or coincidence. There is therefore at least a chance that a judge would exclude the evidence of James's earlier conviction.

Question 33

Edgar is charged with indecently assaulting Fergus. Fergus, aged 15, was flying his kite at dusk in a public park when he was approached by a man who said that he had a collection of kites and invited Fergus to his house, which he said was nearby, to see them. Fergus agreed to go with him, but while they were walking together, the man made indecent suggestions to him and then indecently assaulted him. Fergus, somewhat hesitantly, picked out Edgar on an identification parade. Garry, aged 17, has made a statement to the police in which he says that he was in another public park in the same town shortly before the date of the assault on Edgar. He said that he was flying his kite when he was approached by a man who said that he had a collection of kites and invited him to his house to see them. Garry agreed to go with him, but while they were walking together the man made indecent suggestions to him. At this, Garry knocked him down and then ran away. Garry identified Edgar on an identification parade as the man who had approached him. Garry and Fergus attend the same school and know each other slightly. Rumours have been circulating at the school about a man who molests boys. When Edgar's house is lawfully searched, no kites are found, but the police find a collection of homosexual videos, some leather masks and several pairs of handcuffs.

Advise the prosecution on the evidential issues that arise.

Answer plan

A classic similar fact problem. Note how the first paragraph of the answer explains the significance of the evidence that the prosecution wants Garry to give; that is, its probative job. His statement requires a discussion of:

- striking similarity (note the analysis of facts; too many candidates at this stage would simply provide a summary of cases);
- danger of collusion (note how this idea might be extended).

Evidence of the search should also be discussed. This part of the problem concentrates on the significance of objects that may be incriminating. For a good summary of the law on this subject, see Tapper, C, *Cross & Tapper on Evidence*, 9th edn, 1999, p 346 and the cases cited there.

Answer

The basic question is whether the rather weak evidence of identification which Fergus is able to give can be supported by the evidence of Garry. It is important that it should be supported because of the special danger that attaches to evidence of identification, and the consequent need for a warning to be given to the jury (*Turnbull* (1977)). But there are two problems in connection with Garry's evidence:

- elements of striking similarity;
- the possibility of collusion.

Since *W* (1998), it is clear that striking similarity is not an essential element in similar fact evidence used to support an identification, but it can be the element that provides sufficient probative weight, and it is therefore necessary to ask if it is available on these facts. 'Striking similarity' really means 'striking peculiarity'; offences can be in all relevant respects identical without providing an instance of striking similarity. Thus, in *Brown* (1963), the court refused to admit as similar fact evidence a method of committing burglary that was common to thousands of other burglaries. Everything depends on the unlikelihood of repetition being mere coincidence. However, the striking similarity may be in relation to the surrounding circumstances of the offence and not merely in relation to the offence itself. Thus, in *Barrington* (1981), the similarities relied on consisted in the appellant's method of approaching young girls to persuade them to take part in acts of indecency.

The relevant similarities in this case are as follows:

(a) both the victims were teenage boys;

(b) both were in public parks in the same town;

(c) both events took place at dusk;

(d) both events took place within a short time of each other;

(e) both boys were flying kites when they were approached;

(f) both boys were told of a collection of kites and invited to view them;

(g) both were subjected to indecent suggestions.

However, only Fergus was actually indecently assaulted. There is no suggestion of physical contact between Garry and the molester until Garry struck him. This has some significance; in *Johnson* (1995), the Court of Appeal said that a judge who has to decide whether each incident bears the signature of the accused should look also at the nature and quality of any disparities that exist. However, it was said in *Johnson*, and later in *West* (1996), that the mere presence of some dissimilarities will not inevitably lead to exclusion.

Item (g) would be significant if the suggestions were sufficiently odd. But at present the only features that begin to look sufficiently idiosyncratic to qualify are (e) and (f). Teenage boys in public parks provide an obvious source of interest for anyone who has it in mind to molest boys, and dusk has obvious advantages from the molester's point of view. The significance of (e) and (f) should not be overestimated. Many boys in a public park will be playing in a group; this will make it difficult for a molester to approach one without being noticed by a number of others at the same time. But flying a kite is a solitary activity, so that a boy who is doing this is more likely to be approached than others who are playing together. It is unlikely that a judge would conclude that there was sufficient evidence of striking similarity here, especially in view of the fact that in the case of Garry, no indecent assault took place.

On the face of it, there seems little risk of collusion because although the boys attend the same school, they know each other only slightly. However, in *DPP v Boardman* (1975), Lord Wilberforce referred also to a risk of falsity arising from 'a process of infection from media or publicity or simply from fashion', and in *Ryder* (1993), the Court of Appeal recognised the possibility of collusion in the sense of a witness's being unconsciously influenced by another. That is not quite this case. What is perhaps present here is a common source of rumour which might have tainted the accounts of both Fergus and Garry so as to make it appear that the incidents in which they were involved, and which they tried to describe truthfully, had more similarities than was in fact the case. This might be of particular importance if anything turned on the detail of the suggestions allegedly made to both boys. Without more information about the nature of the rumours, it is not possible to tell how great a danger of collusion, in the extended sense, there may have been.

However, since the decision of the House of Lords in *H* (1995), it is clear that the judge should rule on the admissibility of similar fact evidence on the assumption that the similar facts alleged are true. If the evidence is admitted, the judge should generally leave questions of weight to the jury, including the consideration of any danger there may be from collusion. Only exceptionally, if no reasonable jury could accept the evidence as free from collusion, should the judge exclude the evidence.

The search

The absence of kites is ambiguous. It may show that the police have got the wrong man; on the other hand, it is quite likely that the account of the kite collection was no more than a ploy. Unless the leather masks and handcuffs can be connected with the indecent suggestions, their discovery will be irrelevant and so inadmissible. The discovery of the videos is more difficult.

If they are in Edgar's possession, they are capable of showing that he has homosexual inclinations. The probative value of the fact that Edgar has homosexual tendencies is that it tends to confirm the identification by Fergus. What a coincidence it would be if the man *misidentified* by Fergus also had homosexual tendencies. A case which may support this argument is *Thompson v R* (1918). The appellant was charged with committing acts of gross indecency with a group of boys. It was not disputed that *someone* had committed these acts and had arranged to meet the boys later near a public lavatory. The appellant was seen with the boys at the time and place that had been agreed and was arrested. All the boys identified him as the offender. His defence of mistaken identity was rebutted by proof of facts tending to show that he was a homosexual with a taste for boys. If the boys had been mistaken, it was an unbelievable coincidence that they should have happened to pick out another man with those inclinations.[1] That would be the prosecution's argument. In response, the defence would argue that homosexuality is now recognised to be a more frequent phenomenon than it was in 1918, and that where there is a complete denial of the offence (as opposed, for example, to a defence of 'innocent association'), evidence of homosexual proclivity is inadmissible, as was the case in *Wright* (1990).

Note

1 But the proximity of the rendezvous in *Thompson* to a public lavatory may weaken this argument. For another case where articles found on the premises of a suspect were able to confirm an identification, see *Reading* (1966).

Question 34

Hector is charged on an indictment containing two counts of handling stolen goods. Count 1 alleges that on 1 February last year, he received 50 bottles of gin, knowing or believing them to have been stolen. Count 2 alleges that on 1 March last year, he received 500 cigars, knowing or believing them to have been stolen. Hector's defence to count 1 is that he purchased the gin honestly from a teetotal friend in the belief that his friend had received it as a gift. His defence to count 2 is that it was not he who had received the cigars, but his identical twin brother. Four years ago, Hector was convicted of handling 500 bottles of stolen whisky. His defence on that occasion was that he had purchased the whisky honestly from a teetotal friend in the belief that his friend had won it as a prize in a raffle. Hector continues to maintain that he received the whisky innocently and says that he was wrongly convicted by the jury.

Advise the prosecution on the evidential issues that arise.

Answer plan

This question is based on the special provisions of s 27(3) of the Theft Act 1968. It also raises basic similar facts points. Note particularly:

- the limited purpose for which evidence can be adduced under s 27(3);
- the discretion to exclude, even though the section is available;
- the notice provision and time limit;
- limits on what can be given in evidence: *Fowler* (1988);
- s 74(3) of PACE;
- the direction that should be given to the jury where there are several counts in the indictment.

Answer

The first matter that has to be considered is whether and to what extent the prosecution can rely upon Hector's conviction for handling whisky to support the present case against him. Section 27(3) of the Theft Act 1968 provides, amongst other things, that where a person is being proceeded against for handling stolen goods, if evidence has been given of his having in his possession the goods which are the subject of the charge, evidence of a previous conviction for handling shall be admissible for the purpose of proving that he knew or believed the goods to have been stolen. In the present case, therefore, evidence of Hector's previous conviction will be admissible in relation to count 1, because on that count receiving is admitted and the only issue is guilty knowledge. Evidence of the previous conviction would not, however, be admissible in relation to count 2 where the live issue is whether it was Hector or his identical twin brother who received the goods. By s 27(3)(b), the conviction must have been within the five years preceding the date of the offence charged. This condition is satisfied. There is also a further condition requiring that seven days' notice in writing be given to the defendant of intention to prove the conviction.

The judge has power to exclude s 27(3) evidence on the ground that its prejudicial effect outweighs its probative value (*Smith* (1976); *Perry* (1984)). Because the conviction will be relevant on one count only, the judge may very well exercise this discretion in Hector's favour. If he does admit the evidence, he will have to explain carefully to the jury the extent to which it is relevant (*Wilkins* (1975)).

The sub-section does not permit details of the earlier conviction to be given; a bare recital of the conviction is all that is allowed. If the prosecution wants to adduce evidence of the details of the previous offence they must rely on the common law relating to similar fact evidence (*Fowler* (1988)). However, the effect of s 73(2) of PACE is that any certificate of conviction following trial on indictment must state the substance and effect of the indictment and conviction, including the type of property involved. In *Hacker* (1994), such a certificate was held by the House of Lords to be admissible in evidence, subject only to the judge's discretion to exclude it if its admission would prejudice the fairness of the proceedings.

It is possible that the prosecution would be permitted to adduce evidence of the circumstances of the previous offence under the common law because of the defence raised on that occasion. It could be argued with some force that the jury ought to know about the earlier defence which failed because it makes it most unlikely that, remembering his earlier experience, this defendant would have accepted a very similar story had he indeed been told it. If this evidence were to be admitted, it would, of course, be relevant only on count 1. The judge would have to make this clear to the jury and tell them to consider each count separately.

It appears that if the previous conviction is put to Hector he will insist that it is a wrongful one. The ordinary rule, provided by s 74(3) of the Police and Criminal Evidence Act 1984, is that where it is proved that the accused has been convicted, he shall be taken to have committed the offence in question unless he proves the contrary. However, s 74(3) applies only 'in so far as that evidence [that is, of the commission of another offence] is relevant to any matter in issue in the proceedings for a reason other than a tendency to show in the accused a disposition to commit the kind of offence with which he is charged ...'. But, the prosecution will be able to counter a defence argument that s 74(3) is inapplicable because of the proviso by pointing out that the similar fact evidence in this case is not adduced to show disposition to commit handling. It is adduced to prove guilty knowledge on the occasion referred to in the indictment, and this will be so whether the prosecution relies on the Theft Act provision or the common law.

Question 35

Steven, aged 18, has been charged with murder. The case for the prosecution is that on 3 May he raped and strangled Lynne, a classmate, after taking her in his car to an area known as Coppett's Wood where her body was afterwards found. Steven told the police that at Lynne's request he had given her a lift to a nearby railway station, had left her there, and had never seen her again. The prosecution have a statement from Jocelyne, another classmate of the accused. She said that she and Steven had made an arrangement to go bird watching on 3 May in Coppett's Wood. Jocelyne said that Steven had asked her to keep the arrangement secret. On the day in question, Jocelyne had changed her mind and had decided to go shopping with some other classmates instead. There is also police evidence that when they searched Steven's locker at school they found a collection of heterosexual pornographic magazines. Two weeks before the murder, Steven had been arrested for indecently exposing himself to two women in Coppett's Wood.

Advise the prosecution on the evidential issues that arise.

Answer plan

This question requires consideration of three items of evidence:

- Jocelyne's statement. You need to discuss its relevance. Remember the need to determine what probative job the disputed evidence is expected to do. Note the discussion of the generalisation on which the prosecution would need to rely. *Rodley* (1913) is a useful case to bring in by way of illustration. Don't forget to reach a conclusion, with reasons, for admissibility or inadmissibility.
- The magazines. Note the importance of the initial assumption that they had no special bearing on what had been done to Lynne. In practice, you would need to know the exact nature of these magazines, and you should indicate this to the examiner. Again, relevance is all important, and finding an appropriate generalisation which would establish this forms a significant part of the discussion.
- The earlier arrest. Note the *Maxwell* (1935) point, but go on to consider the possibility that the prosecution might wish to adduce the evidence of the earlier witnesses as similar fact evidence.

The final paragraph is an important one. Thinking in general is 'not to be conceived to "form a chain which is no stronger than its weakest link"', but as 'a cable whose fibres may be ever so slender provided they are sufficiently numerous and intimately connected'. (Peirce, CS, *Collected Papers* 5, p 265.) Much defence advocacy works on the assumption that this is *not* the case.

Answer

With regard to Jocelyne's statement, the main problem is one of relevance. Does the arrangement with Jocelyne tend to show that the accused was not telling the truth to the police about his encounter with Lynne? It might do so if it indicated that Steven had determined to take *some* girl, regardless of who it was, to Coppett's Wood that day for the purpose of sexual intercourse, to be obtained by force if necessary. It would then appear that when Jocelyne dropped out, Lynne was substituted as the victim.

It is useful to consider whether Jocelyne's statement would be thought to have significance if she had said nothing about a request for secrecy. Almost certainly it would not. But a person who asks another to keep an assignation secret usually does so because he does not wish others to know about it. One reason, but only one, why he might wish this is because he intends to do something unlawful, or at least improper, with his companion. But there might be innocent reasons for not wanting to be disturbed by others. Thus, if a bird watching exercise were planned, stillness and silence would be wanted.

On the assumption that Steven said nothing else to throw light on his request, the position would be that if Jocelyne were to testify, the jury would have before them a piece of evidence with very little probative value but which might easily mislead because of its tendency to invite speculation. Perhaps a similar problem arose in *Rodley* (1913). The appellant was charged with housebreaking with intent to rape. The prosecution called evidence to show that he had entered a house by climbing down the chimney and had been met by the father of his supposed victim. The appellant said that he had indeed intended to have intercourse with the daughter, but only with her consent. The prosecution also called evidence to show that later that night he had climbed down the chimney of another house and had had consensual intercourse with a woman living there. It was held that this evidence should have been excluded. It proved nothing at all about the real issue of the appellant's willingness to commit rape. On the other hand, it certainly showed a lustful disposition which may well have prejudiced the appellant in the eyes of the jury.

So here, Jocelyne's testimony would prove nothing about Steven's willingness to commit rape and murder, but it might prejudice him because it would leave the jury guessing and without the means to advance beyond that stage to a reasoned conclusion. It is likely, therefore, that her evidence would be excluded.[1]

In considering the pornographic magazines, it is assumed that the pornography has no marked resemblance to what was done to Lynne. Apart from this, the finding of these magazines will be relevant if, and only if, an appropriate generalisation can be found about the way things are in the world that makes them so. We must discard at once something like 'Most persons who rape and murder girls take an interest in pornography'. (This generalisation will be referred to as 'G1'.) While it might be the case that most persons who rape and murder girls do in fact take an interest in pornography, it is not the case that most persons who take an interest in pornography rape and murder girls. If G1 is used to establish relevance, you attain it only by assuming the truth of the very thing that the pornography is meant to prove – that Steven is a rapist and murderer.

Might a more useful generalisation be that people who take an interest in pornography are more likely to rape and murder girls than those who do not ('G2')? In the first place, although this *may* be true, it is not obviously so, and if the prosecution is going to rely on its truth to establish guilt they must be prepared to adduce expert evidence on the matter, for it would almost certainly be challenged by the defence.

But, supposing that G2 can be established, what is the probative value of the discovery? It must be almost nothing. The police evidence will have put Steven in a class of persons who are more likely to rape and murder girls than those not in that class. However, that class will certainly be a large one, and the question in relation to any individual in it will be how much greater his membership makes the likelihood of his having raped and murdered a particular victim. The possession of pornography is unlikely to increase significantly the probability that Steven committed this crime. Unless there is a resemblance between what appears in the magazines and what was done to Lynne, its discovery, even if relevant, is likely to be far more prejudicial than probative, and it will be excluded.

Steven's arrest for indecent exposure by itself proves nothing. Even assuming that Steven was subsequently charged, the mere fact that a man has been charged with an offence is no proof that he committed the offence. Such a fact is therefore irrelevant, and ought to be excluded.[2]

If the prosecution wants to establish as part of its case that Steven did indecently expose himself in Coppett's Wood, it will have to apply to call evidence from those who say they observed him do so. But relevance would again be in question. Is there any evidence to show that persons who indecently expose themselves are more likely than others who do not to commit rape and murder?

In relation to all three items of evidence – Jocelyne's statement, the pornographic magazines, and whatever may be the evidence of indecent exposure – the prosecution might argue that all are items of circumstantial evidence and that they operate cumulatively. Like the strands in a cord, one might be insufficient to sustain the weight of the prosecution case, but three woven together may be of sufficient strength.[3] The answer to this is that circumstantial evidence must be evidence of relevant facts, and the objection in all three cases has been that the evidence in question is of irrelevant facts. Something that you have already decided to be irrelevant will not be made relevant by being added to something else that is irrelevant, although it is sometimes the case that what initially appears to be irrelevant may later be seen to be relevant in the light of some later discovery of relevant matter. Suppose, for example, that the magazines, contrary to the supposition in this answer, contained material that resembled what had been done to Lynne. They would then acquire more significance and would stand a greater chance of being considered relevant, and so admissible. The position would also change if it were discovered that Steven had no interest in bird watching, so that he would appear to have been lying to Jocelyne and to have had some hidden purpose in persuading her to accompany him to Coppett's Wood.

Notes

1   Cf the Canadian case *Reference re R v Truscott* (1967); Le Bordais, I, *The Trial of Steven Truscott*, 1966.

2   See *per* Viscount Sankey LC in *Maxwell v DPP* (1935).

3   Cf Pollock CB in *Exall* (1866).

CHAPTER 9

THE CHARACTER OF THE ACCUSED

Introduction

Most of the problems which arise in the questions in this chapter concern cross-examination of the accused under the Criminal Evidence Act 1898, but other circumstances in which the accused's character may be revealed are also considered. You should note that some minor amendments have been made to the 1898 Act by Sched 4 to the Youth Justice and Criminal Evidence Act 1999. The most significant, and irritating, of these is that by para 1(7), 'paras (a), (e), (f), and (g) of the proviso shall be respectively numbered as sub-ss (1), (2), (3) and (4) of the section'. So, for example, what was formerly known as s 1(f)(i) is now to be referred to as s 1(3)(i).

The golden rule is to distinguish between cases where the accused gives evidence and those where he does not. Section 1(3) of the 1898 Act applies only to 'a person charged *and called as a witness*'. If the defendant does not give evidence, his position is governed by the common law as set out in *Butterwasser* (1948); s 1(3) will not apply at all.

Another basic point to remember is that the section applies *to defendants only* and not to any other witnesses. Subject to the rules of professional conduct and to the provisions of the Rehabilitation of Offenders Act 1974, it is open to defence counsel to attack the credibility of any prosecution witness by asking in cross-examination about that witness's previous convictions, and the same is true for prosecuting counsel in relation to defence witnesses other than the defendant.

This area of law tends to be covered by problem questions rather than essays, although subjects for the latter might be the relation between s 1(2) and s 1(3), or the reform of s 1(3) by making it either easier or more difficult to reveal to the jury any previous convictions of the accused. In problem questions, the emphasis tends to be on s 1(3)(ii) and (iii). Section 1(3)(i) would normally give rise to no difficulties because the question of the admissibility of similar fact evidence would have been determined at an earlier stage in the trial when the prosecution applied to adduce it as part of their case. Occasionally, as in *Jones v DPP* (1962) and *Anderson* (1988), an application may be made under s 1(3)(i) as a result of evidence given by the defendant, but this is rare. It is likely to be even more rare now that the defence has an obligation of advance disclosure under s 5 of the Criminal Procedure and Investigations Act 1996. In practical terms, defences are likely to be revealed during police interviews, at which, because of s 34 of the Criminal Justice and Public Order Act 1994, very few defendants now exercise their right to silence.

In relation to s 1(3)(ii), it may be useful to see how an application works in practice, because this is likely to make more sense of the cases you read.

Assume that you are acting for Bill Buggins who has several recent convictions for burglary. He is being prosecuted for another burglary, and part of the prosecution evidence comes from Buggins's ex-girlfriend. She says that, shortly after the burglary took place, Buggins admitted his part in it to her. Buggins says that this is a complete fabrication which has been made from jealousy because she found out that he was sleeping with someone else. You will have to put this allegation to her in cross-examination, and doubtless it will be denied. Nothing will happen if Buggins chooses not to give evidence. According to common law, he has not put *his* character in issue by suggesting that a prosecution witness is committing perjury. No question of cross-examining Buggins can possibly arise because he never goes into the witness box, and the prosecution will not be entitled to call evidence to prove his previous convictions.

If Buggins does give evidence, the position is different. He will deny the account given by his ex-girlfriend and will describe her jealousy on discovering that he had another girlfriend. Before beginning his cross-examination, counsel for the prosecution will say: 'Your Honour, at this stage there is a matter of law that arises.' This is coded language for 'I want to ask leave to cross-examine this defendant about his previous convictions'. It's coded because, of course, the jury must not know yet that the defendant has previous convictions, and the defence will probably have some submissions to make to dissuade the judge from allowing such questions. The judge will send the jury out. Now, the prosecution must establish that a s 1(3)(ii) situation has arisen. In this example, there is no doubt about that, but in other cases, the answer may not be so easy. There may be problems, for example, about whether something said by the defendant while giving evidence-in-chief has amounted to giving evidence of his good character, or about whether something does involve an imputation on the character of a prosecution witness.

Once it has been established that a s 1(3)(ii) situation has arisen, all is not entirely lost for the defence; the judge has a discretion to disallow cross-examination under this provision (*Selvey v DPP* (1970)). At this stage, you will make submissions in an attempt to persuade the judge to exercise his discretion in your favour. No doubt you will say what you can about the almost impossible task the jury will have in doing justice when they learn that not only does your client have previous convictions, but also that they are convictions for burglary (see *Powell* (1985)). The judge then makes his decision, the jury returns, and the cross-examination begins.

It is useful to have this picture in mind when answering a problem which contains a s 1(3)(ii) point because it should serve as a reminder of the arguments that you should be presenting:

- is this a s 1(3)(ii) situation at all?;
- if it is, what arguments are available to each side about the way in which the discretion should be exercised? In particular, are any of the previous convictions spent? This would not automatically exclude them, but it would make the exercise of discretion in the defendant's favour more likely.

If you wish to take advantage of s 1(3)(iii) in your cross-examination of a co-accused, you must get the judge to decide whether, as a matter of law, a s 1(3)(iii) situation has arisen. After that, however, you are entitled to cross-examine on the co-accused's previous convictions. There is no judicial discretion to disallow such cross-examination as there is under s 1(3)(ii) (*Murdoch v Taylor* (1965)). In *Corelli* (2001), the Court of Appeal held that this is so even if a conviction is spent.

A good account of cross-examination of the accused as to character can be found in May, R, *Criminal Evidence*, 4th edn, 1999, pp 132–55. The author was a circuit judge and is particularly helpful on procedure and the exercise of discretion.

Checklist

Students should be familiar with the following areas:

- limitations on the way in which character evidence can be given;
- the difference between cases where the defendant testifies and where he does not;
- the interplay of s 1(2) and s 1(3) of the 1898 Act;
- circumstances in which a s 1(3)(ii) situation arises;
- matters which may be taken into account when exercising discretion under s 1(3)(ii);
- spent convictions under the Rehabilitation of Offenders Act 1974;
- circumstances in which a s 1(3)(iii) situation arises.

Question 36

Edna and Mavis are being tried in the Crown Court for theft. The case for the prosecution is that they are both guilty of shoplifting in the Ealing branch of Bromides, the well known chain of chemists. A store detective gives evidence and states that Edna and Mavis were together in the store. She says that Mavis was carrying a holdall and that she opened it to allow Edna to conceal in it a bottle of shampoo and a tin of talcum powder, the property of Bromides, for which neither defendant paid. Edna gives no evidence, but her counsel cross-examines the manager of the store, who is one of the prosecution witnesses, about a conviction which he had for indecent exposure when he was a student at university. Mavis gives evidence in her own defence and states that she was with Edna in the store, but was not herself involved in any shoplifting. She admits that when stopped outside the store she was carrying the holdall, but says that it belonged to Edna, who alone had been carrying it in the store. She said that Edna had given it to her to hold outside the store so that she, Edna, could more easily look for her season ticket, which she thought she had lost. Edna has a number of recent convictions for theft and for offences involving prostitution. Mavis has several recent convictions for theft. They all involved similar items stolen from other branches of Bromides.

Edna and Mavis are separately represented. Discuss the evidential issues that arise.

Answer plan

The following points need to be considered:

- the comments that can be made on Edna's failure to testify;
- the cross-examination of the manager: spent convictions; *Hobbs v Tinling* (1929); *Butterwasser* (1948);
- whether Mavis has brought s 1(3)(ii) into play by denying the store detective's account of who was carrying the bag in the store;
- whether Mavis has brought s 1(3)(iii) into play by the account which she gives in the witness box;
- if Mavis can be cross-examined under s 1(3)(iii), can she be asked about the details of her previous offences?

Answer

Edna has chosen not to give evidence, and the first question that arises concerns the extent to which comment can be made upon this. By s 35(3) of the Criminal Justice and Public Order Act 1994, the court or jury, in determining whether the accused is guilty of the offence charged, may draw such inferences as appear proper from the failure of the accused to give evidence. Further, under the pre-1994 law, counsel for a co-defendant always had a right to comment on a defendant's failure to give evidence, and the judge had no discretion to prevent this (*Wickham* (1971)). The 1994 Act has not altered this. Thus, Edna's failure to testify is likely to be the subject of comment by both the judge and counsel for Mavis.

The Court of Appeal emphasised in *Napper* (1996) the general rule that it should be open to a jury to draw adverse inferences when a defendant fails to testify, and said that attempts to marginalise the section are contrary to the spirit of its provisions. The judge, in any direction under the section, must tell the jury that: (1) the defendant is entitled to remain silent; (2) an inference from silence cannot prove guilt on its own; and (3) they must be satisfied that there is a case to answer before drawing any inferences from silence. (The judge must have thought there was, or the case would have already been stopped. But the jury may not believe the witnesses whose evidence was considered by the judge to raise a *prima facie* case.) The judge must also tell the jury that if they conclude that the silence can only sensibly be attributed to the defendant's having no answer, or none that would stand up to cross-examination, they may draw an adverse inference. The effect of this appears to be that the jury must not draw such an inference unless sure that there is no other explanation, consistent with innocence, to account for it. However, the defence will not be able to suggest innocent reasons for the defendant's silence that are unsupported by evidence at trial (*Cowan* (1996)).

The cross-examination of the manager by Edna's counsel may well have been improper. If the conviction was spent, it should not have been referred to without leave of the judge, who should not have given leave unless he was satisfied that the interests of justice required that this matter be put.[1] It is difficult to see how the interests of justice could require this. In *Hobbs v Tinling & Co Ltd* (1929), it was said in the Court of Appeal that cross-examination about the character of a witness on matters relating to credibility ought to be limited to questions where the answers would seriously impair the credibility of the witness, and that questions would be improper if they related to matters so remote in time, or were of such a character, that if true they could not seriously impair the credibility of the witness. Questions would also be improper if there was a substantial disproportion between the importance of the imputation against the witness's character and the importance of his evidence to the issue to be decided.

If Edna had testified, the cross-examination of the manager would have activated s 1(3)(ii) of the Criminal Evidence Act 1898 because the nature or conduct of her defence would have been such as to involve an imputation on a witness for the prosecution. But because she has chosen not to give evidence, the common law and not the statute governs the situation. Had she put her character in issue, for example, by calling evidence to the effect that she had a good character, the prosecution could have adduced evidence of her previous convictions. But the accused does not at common law put his character in issue merely by making imputations on prosecution witnesses (*Butterwasser* (1948)). Evidence of Edna's previous convictions may not therefore be given merely because of the line taken in cross-examining the manager.

Mavis's evidence that she held the holdall only outside the store contradicts the evidence of the store detective, but it is most unlikely that for this reason it would be held to have involved an imputation on the store detective. Indeed, it would only do so if the inevitable inference from Mavis's testimony was that the store detective was committing perjury. It is much more likely that this part of the defence has been put on the basis that the store detective made an honest mistake, and such an explanation is likely to be regarded by the judge as at least plausible. Accordingly, Mavis will not have exposed herself to cross-examination under s 1(3)(ii).

She may, however, be held to have given evidence against her co-accused and so have exposed herself to the risk of cross-examination under s 1(3)(iii). Evidence against a co-accused is evidence that either supports the prosecution case against that person or undermines that person's defence. It may be given in examination-in-chief or in cross-examination (*Murdoch v Taylor* (1965)). Mavis has not said anything directly against Edna. However, what the prosecution alleges in effect is that Edna and Mavis were engaged in a joint venture, and while the mere denial of participation by one member of a joint venture does not by itself amount to evidence against the other, it will do so if the effect of the denial is to make it more likely that it was the other who committed the offence (*Varley* (1982)). It does seem that the effect of Mavis's evidence is to make it more likely that Edna was guilty of theft. It remains uncontested that neither Edna nor Mavis paid for the goods, and that these items were later found in the holdall. If the holdall belonged to Edna, and she had possession of it throughout the time that the defendants were in the store, it is more likely that she stole the goods than that Mavis did.[2]

The judge has no discretion to disallow s 1(3)(iii) cross-examination, which is relevant only to credibility and not to guilt (*Murdoch v Taylor* (1965)).

Because of its limited relevance, cross-examination under s 1(3)(iii) should go into the details of previous offences only when these are relevant to credibility. In *Reid* (1989), for example, cross-examination about the details of a defence which had been run in a trial for another offence was permitted because it tended to show that the defendant in question was disposed to lie in order to incriminate others. The fact that Mavis's previous offences were committed in relation to similar articles in other branches of Bromides does not appear to affect her credibility, as opposed to her guilt, in this case and questions about these matters would therefore be prohibited.

Notes

1   Rehabilitation of Offenders Act 1974; *Practice Direction (Crime: Spent Convictions)* (1975); *Paraskeva* (1982).

2   See also *Bruce* (1975); *Kirkpatrick* (1998); cf *Crawford* (1998).

Question 37

Ian and Jason are both aged 26 and are charged with committing an act of gross indecency in a public place, the case for the prosecution being that they were seen engaging in fellatio on Hampstead Heath by PC Plod. Both plead not guilty. Ian wishes to call Katie as a defence witness. She is prepared to say that she has known Ian since they were at university together seven years ago, and that during that period she and Ian have had regular, normal sexual intercourse. Ian plays football most weekends and he also wishes to call Larry, a fellow member of his football club, to say that Ian is well known among members for his dislike of homosexuals. Ian has a letter from his local vicar which states that Ian has sung in the church choir for the last five years. The vicar also writes that from his knowledge of Ian he is sure the allegation must be false. Ian has no previous convictions of any kind, but Jason has two recent convictions for persistently importuning for immoral purposes.

(a) Discuss the evidential issues that arise in relation to admissibility.

(b) On the assumption that Ian and Jason both testify in their own defence, how should the judge direct the jury about their characters?

Answer plan

The first part of this question requires you to consider what is admissible as evidence of good character. You should refer to the restriction imposed by

Rowton (1865) and point out that the sort of evidence permitted in *Redgrave* (1982) is heard because of a concession only.

You should then consider generally the impact of Jason's previous convictions and conclude by referring to the ruling of the Court of Appeal in the case of *Vye* (1993).

Answer

The defence may call witnesses to testify as to the accused's good character. However, the right to adduce such evidence is restricted by the rule in *Rowton* (1865) that evidence of specific acts, or of the opinions of specific persons, is inadmissible to establish either good or bad character. In strictness, the only way in which character evidence can be given is by getting a witness to speak of the reputation of the accused among those who know him. In practice, this rule tends to be loosely applied.

However, so far as Katie's evidence is concerned, the court would have to take into account the decision of the Court of Appeal in *Redgrave* (1982). In that case, the appellant had been charged with persistently importuning for immoral purposes in a public lavatory. The trial judge refused to allow him to call evidence of his relationships with a number of girlfriends which would, the defence hoped, establish that the accused had heterosexual rather than homosexual inclinations. The Court of Appeal acknowledged that in that sort of case, indulgence was sometimes shown to accused persons, but said that it was only an indulgence and not a right. Failure to extend it to any particular defendant could not form the basis of a successful appeal.

Lawton LJ said that the court was not trying to stop defence counsel from putting questions designed to show that the accused was happily married and had a normal sexual relationship with his wife. He went on to suggest that evidence of a sexual relationship with one woman, even though she was not married to the defendant, might be unobjectionable. But he emphasised that questions on such matters could be asked only with the indulgence of the court. Katie's evidence will not, therefore, be heard as of right, but only with the goodwill of the judge. It should be added that it is not clear on the facts that the relationship with Katie has the substantial quality that Lawton LJ seems to presuppose. If, when the facts were more fully investigated, it turned out, for example, that she was merely one regular sexual partner among several and that Ian had no special emotional ties to her, it is doubtful whether her evidence would be admitted.

By contrast, Larry's evidence does appear to be evidence of reputation and so is admissible under the rule in *Rowton*.

It seems clear that the evidence of the vicar, even if he were willing to attend court and give oral testimony, would be inadmissible under *Rowton* (1865). The fact that Ian sings in the church choir is today likely to be thought irrelevant to any question of character. In any case, testimony to this effect would not be testimony of Ian's reputation. The vicar's own opinion of Ian's innocence would certainly not be admitted.

Ian's counsel will, of course, be able to bring out the fact that his client is of previous good character in the sense of having no previous convictions recorded against him.

Jason's previous convictions will not be admissible for the prosecution. They establish no more than homosexual promiscuity and are as inadmissible to prove this offence as would be the previous convictions for burglary of someone being currently tried for another such offence. They establish a propensity, but not a sufficiently idiosyncratic one to be admissible as similar fact evidence. Jason will, however, have to take care that he does not in the conduct of his case bring himself within the provisions of s 1(3)(ii) or (iii) of the Criminal Evidence Act 1898.

Rules for the proper direction of the jury where good character is relevant were laid down by Lord Taylor CJ in the judgment of the Court of Appeal in the case of *Vye* (1993). They are as follows:

- A direction as to the relevance of good character to a defendant's credibility should be given where he has testified or made pre-trial answers or statements. Such a direction will clearly be appropriate in Ian's case, assuming that he testifies or has at least made some admissible pre-trial statement.

- A direction as to the relevance of good character to the likelihood of the defendant's having committed the offence charged is to be given, regardless of whether he has testified or made any pre-trial answers or statements. Again, such a direction will obviously be appropriate in Ian's case.

- Where there are two defendants, one of good character and the other not, the first two principles still apply. The trial judge should either say nothing at all about the character of the defendant with previous convictions, or he should direct the jury that they have heard nothing about this and should not speculate.

Ian's position is therefore unaffected by the fact that Jason has previous convictions, and Jason's counsel will have to decide which course he wishes the judge to take so as to do as little damage as possible to his client in these circumstances.

Question 38

Alex and Bess are charged with the robbery of Philip. Philip testifies that he was attacked in a car park one evening by Alex and Bess, one of whom grabbed a gold watch from his wrist. Alex, wearing the uniform of a security company, testifies in his defence that Philip attacked him and Bess without warning, and that he hit back to defend himself and Bess. He says that the strap of Philip's watch probably broke in the struggle, and denies stealing it. Bess subsequently testifies in her defence that she was some distance from Alex in the car park, and that she did not see what happened when Alex and Philip met. After her arrest, she made a statement to the police in which she admitted that she alone robbed Philip. The trial judge has already refused to allow the prosecution to adduce evidence-in-chief of this statement, because it was made in response to a promise by the police that she would get bail if she confessed. Alex has a recent conviction for robbery of a man whom he attacked in a car park. Bess has no previous convictions.

Discuss the cross-examination of Alex and Bess.

Answer plan

It is important to *answer the question asked*, so do not waste time telling the examiner about s 76 of the Police and Criminal Evidence Act (PACE) 1984. The following problems arise:

Alex

Possible grounds for cross-examination under s 1(3)(ii):

- his evidence that he hit back to defend himself and Bess;
- the uniform;
- the suggestion that the watch strap broke in the struggle;
- evidence that Philip attacked them;
- judge's exercise of his discretion.

Possible ground for cross-examination under s 1(3)(iii):

- his defence contradicts Bess's account.

Bess

- Can Alex cross-examine about the excluded confession?

Answer

There appear to be several opportunities for cross-examination of Alex under s 1(3)(ii) of the 1898 Act. First, it may be argued that he has given evidence of his own good character, either by his testimony that he hit back to defend himself *and Bess*, or by appearing in the witness box in the uniform of a security company.

It may be difficult to tell whether a defendant who denies a charge and gives evidence has, in doing so, given evidence of his own good character. The essential test appears to be the nature of the connection between the assertion, express or implied, of good character, and the prosecution's allegations. The defendant will have to counter the prosecution's version of events. In doing so, he may give evidence that has the incidental effect of showing his character in a good light. That will not come within the proviso. But if the defendant goes beyond his need to meet the prosecution case about the facts in issue, so as to raise the issue of his good character independently, the proviso will apply. For example, in *Malindi v R* (1967), the defendant was charged with conspiracy involving the use of violence against property. He gave evidence that at a meeting in his house at which violence was discussed, and which the prosecution relied on as part of its case, he had disapproved of violent action and advised against it. It was held by the Privy Council that this should not have brought s 1(3)(ii) into play: the defendant had restricted his evidence to his own account of an incident relied on by the prosecution. He had not asserted his own good character as an independent reason for making it unlikely that he had done what the prosecution alleged.

On this basis, Alex's evidence that he hit back to defend Bess, as well as himself, will not amount to giving evidence of his own good character. However, it may be that his wearing the security company's uniform would be so regarded. The Law Commission remarked that the law where good character was impliedly asserted was uncertain,[1] but favoured the view that the proviso should apply. Thus, a person wearing 'a Securicor-style uniform' could impliedly assert his character as a man of integrity. There is some support in case law for this proposition, although, in *Hamilton* (1969), the Court of Appeal took the view that wearing a regimental blazer did not amount to an assertion of good character, the uniform of a security company could be differently regarded, because it suggests that his employers currently regard him as a man of integrity. Even before the 1898 Act, the appearance of the accused was regarded as something the jury could take into account and so, presumably, as evidence in the case. In *AG for New South Wales v Bertrand* (1867), the Privy Council assumed that the jury could consider the accused's manner when something of particular significance was said in evidence by a witness.

Alex's suggestion that the watch strap broke in the struggle does not, in itself, suggest that Philip was lying, as opposed to merely being mistaken in his testimony, and alone would not bring s 1(3)(ii) into play. But the evidence that Philip was the aggressor is a clear imputation on a witness for the prosecution.

Bess might argue that Philip's defence to some extent contradicts her account of events, and thus undermines her defence. It is unclear whether this argument would succeed. In *Bruce* (1975), the Court of Appeal allowed an appeal where the trial judge had held that one defendant's account had differed from that of another, and so brought him within s 1(3)(iii). The court said that the different account had made the co-defendant's acquittal not less, but more likely, because it had provided the jury with an additional doubt about the accuracy of the prosecution's case. But, if *Crawford* (1998) were to be followed, the result might well be different. In that case, the Court of Appeal said that it was enough for s 1(3)(iii) to apply that the evidence of one defendant should jeopardise the credibility of the other, and so make the prosecution case against the other more likely to be true.

Given that the judge rules cross-examination admissible under s 1(3)(ii), how is his discretion to disallow it likely to be exercised? Alex's recent conviction is for robbery in a similar location. In *McLeod* (1995), the Court of Appeal said that the 'primary' purpose of cross-examination under s 1(3)(ii) is to show that the accused is not worthy of belief, not to show that he has a disposition to commit the type of offence charged. Unless the earlier offences are relied on as similar fact evidence, prosecuting counsel should not try to bring out similarities between the underlying facts of previous offences and that currently charged. But the mere fact that that the previous offence is of a similar type to that charged will not make cross-examination improper: see, for example, *Owen* (1985); *McLeod* (1995). In these circumstances, cross-examination is likely to be permitted, but not to the extent of bringing out the location of the earlier offence.

Can Alex cross-examine Bess about her excluded confession? Where a defendant's confession has been excluded under s 76 or 78(1), it is no longer available to the prosecution, but in *Myers* (1997), the House of Lords held that it may still be available to a co-defendant. Myers and her co-defendant were charged with murder. At trial, they ran 'cut throat' defences. Myers gave evidence, and the judge allowed her to be cross-examined on behalf of her co-defendant about confessions she had made to the police, which had been excluded by the prosecution from the case because of breaches of the relevant Code of Practice. Her appeals against conviction were unsuccessful. The House of Lords held that a defendant in a joint trial has the right to ask about a *voluntary* statement made by a co-accused outside court, even though it is not relied on by the prosecution. The only requirement is that the statement should be relevant to the defence of the party who wishes to refer to it. The judge has no discretion to refuse to allow reference to relevant evidence by a co-accused. But, it is important to note that there was no suggestion in *Myers* that the confessions had been made in the sort of circumstances referred to in s 76(2) of PACE, and the Law Lords were careful to refer to the admissibility of 'voluntary' statements of a co-defendant. They acknowledged that there might be a distinction between confessions inadmissible on grounds of oppression or unreliability, and confessions inadmissible on other grounds. That *may* serve to distinguish the facts of this case, where the confession appears to have been obtained as the result of an inducement held out by the police. It might, therefore, be argued that it was unreliable or not voluntary. Under the pre-PACE law, a confession made in such circumstances would not have been held 'voluntary': see *Thompson* (1893). If that were the case, Alex would not be permitted to refer to Bess's confession.

In *Corelli* (2001), however, the Court of Appeal held, distinguishing *Myers*, that a defendant always has a right to cross-examine a co-defendant about a confession that was inadmissible, for whatever reason, as part of the prosecution case. But where this happens, the jury must be warned that the confession is relevant only to the credibility of its maker, and the judge must explain why the prosecution was not allowed to refer to it. Alex can therefore cross-examine Bess if she gives evidence about her confession, but the judge must direct the jury on the basis set out in *Corelli*.

Note

1   Law Commission, Consultation Paper No 141, paras 11.28–11.31.

Question 39

Liza, Mabel and Nellie are charged with committing burglary in a block of flats. Liza chooses not to give evidence in her own defence, but her counsel in cross-examination puts to one of the prosecution witnesses that her evidence against Liza is concocted out of spite because Liza has been having an affair with the witness's husband. Liza has three previous convictions for burglary.

Mabel gives evidence in her own defence and claims to have been elsewhere at the time the burglary was committed. When prosecuting counsel puts it to her in cross-examination that this is a lie, Mabel bursts into tears and shouts, 'I'm an honest woman! I've never told a lie in my life!'. Last year, Mabel was convicted of obtaining property by deception and of assisting in the management of a brothel.

Nellie gives evidence in her own defence. She admits having entered the building and climbed the stairs, but says that she did so because she loves animals and wanted to rescue a kitten which she had seen stranded on a window ledge. Nellie has two spent convictions for burglary.

Discuss the evidential issues that arise.

Answer plan

Take the defendants in turn.

Liza

- The examiner is looking to see if you realise that the common law, and not the 1898 Act, applies.
- Something should be said about comments on failure to testify.

Mabel

- Has a s 1(3)(ii) situation arisen?
- How is the discretion likely to be exercised?

Nellie

- Has a s 1(3)(ii) situation arisen?
- How is the discretion likely to be exercised?

Answer

Liza is not a person charged *and called as a witness* in pursuance of the Criminal Evidence Act 1898. Accordingly, s 1(3) of the Act does not apply to her. Instead, the common law applies. This was explained by the Court of Criminal Appeal in *Butterwasser* (1948). In that case, the accused was charged with wounding with intent to do grievous bodily harm. The victim and his wife gave evidence and were cross-examined by defence counsel about their previous convictions. In the Court of Criminal Appeal, Lord Goddard CJ said that where the accused did not take advantage of the 1898 Act, there was no authority which would permit evidence of his bad character to be given merely because through his counsel he had attacked the witnesses for the prosecution. By doing this, he was not putting his own character in issue, but theirs. It would have been otherwise had the accused put his own character in issue, for example, by calling character witnesses. The prosecution therefore cannot call evidence of Liza's previous convictions.

By s 35(3) of the Criminal Justice and Public Order Act 1994, the court or jury, in determining whether the accused is guilty of the offence charged, may draw such inferences as appear proper from the failure of the accused to give evidence. In any direction under s 35, the judge must follow the guidelines laid down in *Cowan* (1996). He must tell the jury that: (1) the defendant is entitled to remain silent; (2) an inference from silence cannot prove guilt on its own; and (3) they must be satisfied that there is a case to answer before drawing any inferences from silence. The judge must also tell the jury that if they conclude that the silence can only sensibly be attributed to the defendant's having no answer, or none that would stand up to cross-examination, they may draw an adverse inference. The effect of this appears to be that the jury must not draw such an inference unless they are sure that there is no other explanation, consistent with innocence, to account for the defendant's silence. However, the defence cannot suggest reasons for silence that are unsupported by evidence.[1]

The question in Mabel's case is whether she has brought herself within s 1(3)(ii) by claiming to be an honest woman and never to have told a lie in her life. Strictly speaking, she has, for by making these claims she has given evidence of her good character. However, the judge retains a discretion to disallow cross-examination under s 1(3)(ii) which is exercised in accordance with the guidance given in *Britzman* (1983) and *Burke* (1985). This guidance is given mainly in the context of cases where an imputation has been made on a witness for the prosecution, but there are factors mentioned in that context which should be relevant here. These are whether the cross-examination would have a prejudicial effect far outweighing any use it might have in assessing credibility, and whether allowance should be made for the strain imposed by cross-examination on the accused.

Since evidence obtained by cross-examination under s 1(3)(ii) is not relevant to guilt, but only to credibility (*Inder* (1977)), the fact that one of the convictions that might be revealed is for an offence unlike that charged is no reason for disallowing cross-examination. However, the judge in this case might take the view that the conviction for assisting in the management of a brothel is so prejudicial that it ought to be kept from the jury. Further, Mabel's weeping suggests that she was under special strain at this point and the judge might feel justified in refusing to allow cross-examination at all under s 1(3)(ii). On the other hand, it could be argued that it would be equally unfair to the prosecution to allow the jury to assess Mabel's evidence while under an erroneous impression as to her character. The judge might also take into account the ease with which an appearance of stress may be simulated.

In relation to Nellie, the first question is whether she has brought herself within the scope of s 1(3)(ii) at all. *Selvey v DPP* (1970) establishes that 'character' when used in the 1898 Act means disposition as well as reputation. However, the protection against cross-examination is not lost simply because the defendant testifies to matters which are relevant and which, if believed, will show her in a good light. This was the basis of the decision in *Malindi v R* (1967) where the accused, charged with a conspiracy involving the use of violence against property, testified that, at a meeting in his house at which violence was discussed, he had disapproved and had advised against it. It was held that this did not bring s 1(3)(ii) into play because the accused had restricted his testimony to an account of what had taken place, and had not independently asserted that he was a man of good character. Nellie's story about the kitten should not by itself bring s 1(3)(ii) into play. Further, it may be doubted whether her allegation that she was an animal lover amounts to evidence of good character, for there seems to be no reason why an animal lover should not also be criminally inclined.

If, however, the judge were to decide the contrary, her spent convictions would have to be considered. Although the Rehabilitation of Offenders Act 1974 does not apply to evidence given in criminal proceedings, the *Practice Direction* (1975) provided that no one should refer in open court to a spent conviction without the authority of the judge, which authority was not to be given unless required by the interests of justice. Although the judge might not think it proper in the circumstances for the defence to put Nellie forward as a woman of good character, he might decide that it would be within the spirit of the Rehabilitation of Offenders Act to exclude cross-examination under s 1(3)(ii) if he thought that her testimony had brought Nellie within its scope.[2]

Notes

1   On the propriety of putting an allegation of dishonesty to a witness without calling evidence to substantiate it, see May, R, *Criminal Evidence*, 4th edn, 1999, pp 535–36. See also Question 36.

2   The Rehabilitation of Offenders Act 1974 does not confer on a rehabilitated person the right to be called a person of good character. If the defence wanted to put Nellie forward as such, they would have to apply to the judge and it would be a matter for his discretion whether this should be done or not. A ruling of this kind should be asked for at the beginning of the trial (*Nye* (1982); *Bailey* (1989)).

Question 40

Oscar is charged with burglary of Penelope's flat. He gives evidence in his defence and admits being in the flat on the day when the burglary took place. But he says he was there because Penelope had given him a key as they were lovers, and he had called in that evening on his way home in the hope of having sexual intercourse with her. In cross-examination, it is put to him by the prosecution that he entered by a window, not the door. Oscar replies: 'Anyone who says that is a liar.' Oscar has three previous convictions for domestic burglaries. In each case, he gave evidence that he was on the premises at the invitation of the owner, with whom he alleged that he was having a sexual relationship. The trial judge has ruled at the start of this trial that this information is not admissible as similar fact evidence.

Discuss the evidential issues that arise.

Answer plan

You should deal with the following points:

- has a s 1(3)(ii) situation arisen? (Note: there are two possible reasons);
- what is the extent of cross-examination under s 1(3)(ii)?;
- how is the discretion likely to be exercised?

Answer

The first question that arises is whether the nature or conduct of Oscar's defence is such as to involve an imputation on a witness for the prosecution so as to expose Oscar to cross-examination under s 1(3)(ii). One reason why this might be the case is that Oscar's testimony involves an allegation that Penelope was having a sexual relationship with someone to whom she was not married. Not all the facts are given and there might be additional circumstances that would make it fairly clear that there had been an imputation on Penelope; for example, she might be a married woman, or in holy orders. In the absence of such circumstances, the question would be whether the allegation of an extra-marital sexual relationship involved of itself an imputation for the purposes of s 1(3)(ii). This is uncertain. One thing, however, is clear: the fact that the allegation is a necessary part of the defence does not exclude the operation of this provision. In *Selvey v DPP* (1970), the defendant was charged with buggery. The alleged victim gave evidence for the prosecution. The defendant testified that the prosecution witness had offered to go to bed with him for £1 and had already been buggered by another man that afternoon for money. It was a necessary part of the defence to make these imputations, but the House of Lords held that they nevertheless brought the defendant within the scope of s 1(3)(ii).

But the prosecution need not rely on the allegation of a sexual relationship to support its contention that it is entitled to cross-examine on Oscar's previous convictions. This allegation must have been put to Penelope in cross-examination by Oscar's counsel and have been denied by her. When Oscar testified, he must have made it plain that his case rested on Penelope's denial being untrue. Even if the defence has not explicitly alleged that Penelope is committing perjury, they must have done so in effect, for that is an inevitable inference from what Oscar is saying. It is not conceivable that Penelope should have made an honest mistake about whether or not she had been having a sexual relationship with Oscar, or whether she had given him the key of her flat to facilitate it. One of the guidelines given by the court in *Britzman* (1983) is that cross-examination under s 1(3)(ii) should be allowed only if the judge is sure that there is no possibility of mistake, misunderstanding or confusion, and that the jury will inevitably have to decide whether the prosecution witnesses have fabricated evidence. For the reasons given above, those conditions appear to be satisfied in this case.

Oscar having brought himself within s 1(3)(ii), it has to be considered whether the convictions alone may be put to him, or whether he can be asked about the circumstances surrounding the previous offences – namely, that they involved burglary of domestic premises and that on each occasion he had provided the same sort of defence as has been provided in the present case. The prosecution has not been allowed to use this information as similar fact evidence, and these details cannot now be brought out merely because the defendant has happened to open himself to cross-examination under s 1(3)(ii). Such cross-examination is relevant only to credit, but the details of the circumstances of previous offences, including defences raised, may be relevant to credit, and so become the subject of cross-examination under s 1(3)(ii). In *Khan* (1991), the Court of Appeal emphasised that under s 1(3)(ii) evidence which goes beyond credit and is relevant solely to disposition is inadmissible. In that case, the accused's convictions for affray and assault were quashed after cross-examination under s 1(3)(ii) had been allowed by the trial judge to extend to details of previous offences so as to show their similarity to the offences for which the defendant was being tried. But, in *McLeod* (1995), the Court of Appeal acknowledged that the rejection of similar defences by juries on previous occasions may be a legitimate subject of cross-examination under s 1(3)(ii). The reason stated was that such matters do not show a disposition to commit the offence in question, but are clearly relevant to credibility. Such cross-examination is therefore particularly likely to be relevant to credibility where the defence in question is a rather unusual one such as that employed here.

But, apart from the details, three previous convictions for burglary may make it difficult for the jury to use the information solely in relation to credibility. Would this be a ground for the exercise of the judge's discretion to exclude such cross-examination? The courts have not always been consistent on this. In *Maxwell v DPP* (1935), Viscount Sankey suggested *obiter* that the discretion should be exercised in favour of the accused where the offences that would be revealed were of a similar nature to the offence charged. This *dictum* was applied in *Watts* (1983), but in the later decision of *Powell* (1985), the Court of Appeal recognised that there was no absolute rule to this effect. It is therefore far from certain that the discretion would be exercised in Oscar's favour. The Court of Appeal recently emphasised in *McLeod* (1995) that the mere fact that the earlier offences are of a similar type to that charged, or that because of their number and type they have the incidental effect of suggesting a tendency or disposition to commit the offence charged, will not make them improper. We are not told whether Oscar's previous convictions are spent. This is a relevant consideration because in *Lawrence* (1995), the Court of Appeal indicated that judges should more readily exercise their discretion in favour of a defendant where a conviction is spent.

Another reason to bring Oscar within the scope of s 1(3)(ii) is the answer 'Anyone who says that is a liar', which he gives in cross-examination. If there are prosecution witnesses who have testified to this effect, it might be argued that this is an imputation on them. But such an argument would be unlikely to succeed. In *Selvey v DPP* (1970), Viscount Dilhorne acknowledged the existence of a rule whereby if what is said amounts in reality to no more than a denial of the charge, expressed in emphatic language, it should not be regarded as coming within the section.[1] Even if what was said were to be regarded as bringing Oscar within the section, the judge would still have to consider the *Britzman* (1983) guidelines. The first of these states that the discretion to exclude should be used if there is nothing more than a denial, however emphatic or offensively made, of an act or a short series of acts amounting to one incident, or of the contents of a short interview.[2]

Oscar is likely to be cross-examined upon his previous convictions, assuming that they are not spent, and the details of his unsuccessful defences, because he alleges, in effect, that Penelope is committing perjury.

Notes

1   The rule is derived from *Rouse* (1904), in which the accused said in cross-examination that a prosecution witness's evidence was a lie and the witness a liar. Lord Alverstone refused to regard this as an imputation, saying that it was 'nothing more than a traverse of the truth of an allegation'. In practice, the word 'lie' is used very loosely by some people; thus, some will use the expression 'I tell a lie' when they merely wish to correct something they have said. As so often in evidence, the key to understanding the problem is to see how the words are used. Compare with *Rouse* (1904) the case of *Rappolt* (1911) where what was said was that the prosecution witness was such a horrible liar that even his own brother would not speak to him. Here it can be inferred that the words were used to paint a picture of a man with a firmly established habit of lying. This goes well beyond a mere vigorous denial and accounts for the fact that in *Rappolt*, the defendant was held to have brought himself within s 1(3)(ii).

2   The point being made is that where the defendant makes a denial of something that could be wrong because of an honest mistake, he will be safe. It will be otherwise where his denials, even if politely made, amount in effect to allegations that evidence has been fabricated against him; for example, where he denies that a particular lengthy conversation ever took place. By contrast, he could safely deny the accuracy of a witness's recollection of exactly what was said during a small part of it.

Question 41

Rufus, Steve and Terry are charged with committing a robbery at the premises of Western Bank plc in Bedford Row, London. Rufus does not give evidence. Steve does give evidence and says that he was in Exeter when the robbery was committed. But later, under the pressure of cross-examination by counsel for the prosecution, Steve admits that on the day in question he was with Terry in London, although he denies taking part in the robbery. When Terry gives evidence, he denies being with either of his co-accused on that day, saying that, at the time, he was on holiday with an aunt in Edinburgh. He says that Rufus and Steve had earlier invited him to take part in the robbery, but he had told them that he wanted nothing to do with it. Both Steve and Terry are cross-examined by counsel for Rufus, who puts to them that they had invited Rufus to take part in the robbery, but that he had declined vigorously. Counsel for both Steve and Terry intend to comment in their closing speeches on Rufus's failure to testify.

Rufus has seven previous convictions for robbery. Counsel for Terry wishes to adduce evidence of these in an attempt to diminish the credibility of the suggestion made in cross-examination by Rufus's counsel. This is opposed not only by Rufus's counsel, but by counsel for Steve, who thinks that such evidence will do his own client more harm than good. Steve has a spent conviction as a result of pleading guilty 20 years ago to causing death by dangerous driving. Three weeks ago, he was committed for trial in a different matter on a charge of burglary. Terry has been tried for robbery on three previous occasions, but each time he has been acquitted. In evidence, he claims to be of good character.

Discuss the evidential issues that arise.

Answer plan

Probably the best plan is to take the defendants in turn.

Rufus

- Does the 1898 Act or the common law apply?
- The test of admissibility at common law: relevance. No judicial discretion to exclude.
- Note the detailed consideration of the facts and possible arguments in relation to them which is called for by any discussion of relevance.
- Comments on failure to testify.

Steve

- The effect of his evidence on Terry.
- Section 1(3)(iii).
- Has a s 1(3)(iii) situation arisen?
- The significance of the fact that the conviction is spent.
- The pending charge.
- *Lucas* direction.

Terry

- Past acquittals are never relevant to prove bad character.
- *Vye* direction.
- Burden of proof where an alibi is raised.

Answer

Rufus is not a person 'charged and called as a witness' and, accordingly, the provisions of s 1(3) of the Criminal Evidence Act 1898 do not apply to him. The question whether his co-accused, Terry, may adduce evidence of Rufus's convictions for robbery will be governed by the common law. The fact that Steve's counsel does not wish this line to be pursued is immaterial; although the trial judge has a discretion to exclude relevant prosecution evidence, he has none in relation to relevant defence evidence (*Neale* (1977)).

The key to the admissibility of evidence of Rufus's previous convictions is its relevance. For example, in *Miller* (1952), the co-accused were charged with offences in connection with the evasion of customs duties. The defence of one of them was that he had had no part in what was going on and that all the offences had been committed by another accused. To support that defence, his counsel wished to ask a prosecution witness to confirm that the offences had stopped when that co-accused had been sent to prison and had started again only after his release. Devlin J allowed this because the evidence was relevant to the defence case being put forward. The importance of relevance also appears in *Neale* (1977). The defence of one of the defendants to charges of arson and manslaughter arising from a fire at an institution was that he had been absent when the fire broke out. This defendant wished to adduce evidence that his co-accused had on two previous and two subsequent occasions started fires alone. The Court of Appeal said that the only question to be considered was whether this evidence was relevant to the defence raised, and went on to hold that it was not. Even if accepted, it was said, it could not support an inference that on this occasion the co-accused had been acting alone.

On the facts given, Terry's defence is an alibi. He also says that he rejected an offer to take part in the robbery from Rufus and Steve. Are Rufus's previous convictions for robbery relevant to his defence? They do not support the alibi. But, do they make Terry's version of an invitation more probable than the one suggested to him in cross-examination by Rufus's counsel? On one view, they make Terry's account neither more nor less likely. A person with previous convictions for robbery is as likely to be asked to participate in another one as to issue the invitation himself. On the other hand, it might be argued that the more experienced man would be likely to act as instigator. Of the two arguments, the latter seems weaker. It ignores the fact that a man can participate regularly in robberies but always in a subsidiary role; someone can be experienced in a particular line of business without having qualities of leadership. It is likely, therefore, that evidence of Rufus's previous convictions will be held to be irrelevant and therefore inadmissible. A remaining possibility, however, is that the suggestion made on Rufus's behalf in cross-examination might be thought to have put Rufus's own character in issue. In that case, *Butterwasser* (1948) would permit evidence of his previous convictions to be adduced in rebuttal.

By s 35(3) of the Criminal Justice and Public Order Act 1994, the court or jury, in determining whether the accused is guilty of the offence charged, may draw such inferences as appear proper from the accused's failure to give evidence. The trial judge will tell the jury this in his summing up. He may go further and add that it is surprising, if the suggestion put by Rufus's counsel in cross-examination is true, that Rufus himself did not go into the witness box to support it. Even if the judge does not say something like this, he cannot prevent similar criticism from counsel for Steve and Terry. Under the pre-1994 law, counsel for a co-defendant always had a right to comment on a defendant's failure to testify, and the judge had no discretion to prevent this (*Wickham* (1971)). The position is unaltered by the 1994 Act.

In any direction under s 35, the judge must follow the guidelines laid down in *Cowan* (1996). He must tell the jury that: (1) the defendant is entitled to remain silent; (2) an inference from silence cannot prove guilt on its own; and (3) they must be satisfied that there is a case to answer before drawing any inferences from silence. The judge must also tell the jury that if they conclude that the silence can only sensibly be attributed to the defendant's having no answer, or none that would stand up to cross-examination, they *may* draw an adverse inference. The effect of this appears to be that the jury must not draw such an inference unless they are sure that there is no other explanation, consistent with innocence, to account for the defendant's silence. However, the defence cannot suggest reasons for silence that are unsupported by evidence.

With regard to Steve, where a defendant gives evidence, that evidence is evidence for all the purposes of the case, including the purpose of being evidence against a co-defendant (*Rudd* (1948)). Steve's admission under cross-examination that he was with Terry in London on the day of the robbery is therefore evidence in the case against both himself and Terry.[1] He has given evidence against someone charged in the same proceedings. He may have had no hostile intent towards Terry; that is not necessary. Lord Morris in *Murdoch v Taylor* (1965) stated that the 1898 Act does not call for any investigation as to the motives or wishes which may have prompted the giving of evidence against the co-accused.[2] It is the nature of the evidence that must be considered. *Murdoch v Taylor* established that 'evidence against' means evidence which supports the prosecution's case in a material respect, or which undermines the evidence of the co-accused. Steve has clearly undermined Terry's alibi and brought himself within the provisions of s 1(3)(iii).

In *Corelli* (2001), the Court of Appeal held that the judge has no discretion to exclude cross-examination under s 1(3)(iii) even though the conviction is spent. Steve has admitted lying about an alibi and the judge must give a *Lucas* (1981) warning to the effect that the mere fact of a lie is not in itself evidence of guilt, and that sometimes, innocent defendants lie to bolster up an apparently weak case. Only if the jury is sure that the defendant did not lie for an innocent reason can a lie support the prosecution case.

What the judge might well decide is that he cannot stop Terry's counsel from asking about the spent conviction, but that he will direct the jury to ignore it when considering Steve's credibility and to treat him effectively as a man of good character. An approach on similar lines was approved by the Court of Appeal in *Timson and Hales* (1993). In that case, the defendants were charged with conspiracy to obtain property by deception. Timson gave evidence of good character in his defence, admitting also that five years before he had been fined and disqualified for driving with excess alcohol. The Court of Appeal was of the opinion that the trial judge ought to have invited the jury to treat this conviction as irrelevant to the issue of dishonesty and to have treated Timson effectively as a man of good character.

Steve cannot be asked about pending charges. In *Smith* (1989), the Court of Appeal quashed the conviction of a defendant in a case of affray who had been cross-examined under s 1(3)(ii) about the fact that she was awaiting trial on another offence of violence. The court said that when a defendant had other charges hanging over him, it was wrong to ask questions about them. To do otherwise would circumvent safeguards to prevent a defendant's being questioned on matters about which he had the right to remain silent. In any case, an unproved charge could not affect credibility, though it might have done if, for example, Steve had sworn that he had never been accused of any offence of dishonesty.[3]

Terry's allegation that Rufus and Steve invited him to take part in the robbery shows an intention on their part to commit it, and when one finds that a particular robbery has been committed, it is more likely to have been committed by persons who intended to commit it than by others. His evidence therefore supports the prosecution case against his co-defendants. If Terry had had any previous convictions, he would have laid himself open to cross-examination under s 1(3)(iii). However, Terry has a history only of acquittals. These are most unlikely to be relevant to his credibility as a witness (*Maxwell v DPP* (1935)).

Since Terry has no previous convictions, he will be entitled to a *Vye* (1993) direction on good character, to the effect that it is relevant to his credibility and to the question whether he is likely to have behaved as alleged by the prosecution.

Finally, in relation to Terry's alibi, the judge should direct the jury on the lines indicated in *Popat (No 2)* (2000): it is for the prosecution to disprove the alibi beyond reasonable doubt before there can be a conviction.

Notes

1 Compare the position where one co-defendant implicates another in a statement made outside court: see *Gunewardene* (1951). Note that Code C of the Codes of Conduct made under PACE does not apply to a defendant giving evidence in the witness box. I should have thought this an unnecessary warning had I not read so many scripts where candidates have thought that an admission made in these circumstances should somehow be 'excluded' because of the absence of a caution.

2 'Its character does not change according as to whether it is the product of pained reluctance or malevolent eagerness.'

3 See *Stirland v DPP* (1944).

Question 42

What is the relationship between s 1(2) and s 1(3) of the Criminal Evidence Act 1898?

Answer plan

The best way of dealing with this question is to begin by explaining the compromises that s 1 was designed to achieve. Then deal with the theory that the sub-sections are designed to cover different situations, but point out the possibility of conflict. This leads to the solution proposed in *Jones v DPP*, with some criticism of the distinction that seems to have emerged between direct and indirect relevance to an issue.

In summary, therefore, the essay is constructed as follows:

• the purpose of s 1 of the 1898 Act, and earlier attempts to protect defendants who gave evidence;

• the compromise achieved by s 1;

• the scope of sub-ss (2) and (3): *Maxwell v DPP* (1935); *Jones v DPP* (1962);

• the potential for conflict, and how it was resolved in *Jones v DPP*;

• criticism of *Jones v DPP*.

Answer

Section 1 of the Criminal Evidence Act 1898 made the accused a competent witness for the defence in all criminal cases. The question of the accused's competence had been debated intermittently during the 40 preceding years, and inevitably some consideration had been given to the special position in which an accused person would be placed as a witness. In 1876, for example, a Private Member's Bill was introduced which extended competence to accused persons generally and attempted to give them some measure of protection in the witness box by providing that no accused person should be cross-examined as to any previous convictions, or as to his character. There was a fear that without such protection innocent persons might be deterred from giving evidence because of their past history.[1] Another suggestion was that the court should be given a wide discretion to limit cross-examination as to credit.[2] There were other attempts to strike a balance. For example, a Bill introduced in 1888 forbade cross-examination on previous convictions unless proof of the previous conviction was admissible evidence to show that the accused was guilty of the offence with which he was currently charged, or the accused had given evidence of his own good character.[3]

Section 1 of the 1898 Act is a compromise of this kind. Sub-sections (2) and (3) ensure that the accused is not treated exactly as any other witness. Section 1(2) removes the privilege against self-incrimination on which a witness could ordinarily rely. Section 1(3) provides a protection which a witness would not ordinarily have against cross-examination about past misconduct and bad character generally.

The two sub-sections have been interpreted as dealing with different situations. Sub-section (2) permits cross-examination on the present charges. Sub-section (3) is a general prohibition, subject to exceptions, on cross-examination about other offences, previous convictions or bad character (*Maxwell v DPP* (1935), *per* Viscount Sankey). Sub-section (2) has been said by Lord Morris to refer to 'questions or matters directly relevant to the charge' (*Jones v DPP* (1962)). But questions about previous convictions or bad character may be matters from which guilt of the present offence can be inferred, or by means of which the accused's credibility can be attacked. If 'tend to criminate' in sub-s (2) were to mean 'tend to convince or persuade the jury that the accused is guilty', a conflict could arise because a line of questioning might be permitted under sub-s (2) but forbidden under sub-s (3). In *Jones v DPP* (1962), Lord Reid suggested that such a conflict could be avoided if the words in what is now sub-s (2) were given a narrower meaning: '... tend to connect him with the commission of the crime charged.'

But sub-ss (2) and (3) may still appear to conflict where the prosecution is not trying to prove previous offences for the purpose of showing bad character or disposition, but where evidence that is relevant to guilt tends incidentally to reveal that the defendant has been guilty of other offences also.

This problem arose in *Jones v DPP* (1962). The defendant was charged with the murder of a Girl Guide. During the investigation, he gave a false alibi to the police. At his trial, he gave evidence and explained the false alibi by admitting that he had previously been in trouble with the police. He then put forward another alibi, saying that he had been in London with a prostitute at the time when the murder had been committed. To support this, he told of his return home and of a conversation that he had had with his wife about where he had been. The prosecution was allowed to cross-examine him about an identical conversation that he had had with his wife on a previous occasion. The purpose of this was to discredit the alibi by showing the improbability of identical conversations having taken place on different occasions. However, this line of questioning also showed that the accused had been suspected of a serious crime on the earlier occasion. A majority of the House of Lords held that the cross-examination was not admissible under what is now sub-s (2) because it was not directly relevant to the offence charged.[4] They went on to hold that cross-examination was not prohibited by what is now sub-s (3) because the defendant had already revealed that he had been in trouble with the police, so that cross-examination had not tended to show *for the first time* the commission of another offence.[5] They held further that what is now sub-s (3) always prevails over what is now sub-s (2), so that if cross-examination tends to show for the first time that the accused has committed other offences, it can be permitted only in the circumstances set out in provisos (i), (ii) or (iii).

This approach has been criticised for adding to 'the notorious distinction between relevance to the issue and relevance to credibility' another distinction between direct and indirect relevance to the issue.[6] One way of perceiving the unsatisfactory nature of this further distinction is to try to explain why showing the second alibi in *Jones v DPP* (1962) to be false was not directly relevant to the issue of guilt. It might be said to be only indirectly relevant because, to make sense at all, we have to accept the truth of some generalisation, such as 'Persons who lie on oath when charged with an offence frequently do so in order to conceal guilt'. But, to accept such apparently directly relevant evidence as that of observation or fingerprints, we need to adopt at least tacitly some generalisation about the way things are in the world.

Perhaps the real distinction between evidence of a false alibi and evidence, say, of observation or of fingerprints is that evidence of a false alibi is more ambiguous and so does not point so 'directly' to guilt.[7] It is tempting to conclude that despite the talk of a distinction between direct and indirect relevance, what we are often looking at is a distinction between evidence of more or less weight. In an area of law so close to that relating to similar fact evidence, a development which also took probative worth as the test for admissibility would be particularly appropriate.

Notes

1   *Parl Deb,* 3rd series, 229 cols 1182–84 (24 May 1876); 230 cols 1925–39 (26 July 1876).

2   Clause 523 of the Criminal Code (Indictable Offences) Bill 1879; cl 106 of the Criminal Law Amendment Bill 1882.

3   *House of Commons Parliamentary Papers* 1888 (132) II 407.

4   The minority thought it was relevant because it disproved the alibi.

5   See also *Anderson* (1988).

6   Zuckerman, AAS, *The Principles of Criminal Evidence,* 1989, p 253.

7   See *Lucas* (1981); *Goodway* (1993); *Burge and Pegg* (1996).

CHAPTER 10

THE COURSE OF TESTIMONY

Introduction

You are likely to find the sort of problems in this chapter inserted as part of questions dealing with more central topics such as hearsay or similar fact evidence.

Most topics concerning the course of testimony are well explained in textbooks, but a warning is needed about the finality of answers to collateral questions. The rule is sometimes expressed in this way, and sometimes by saying that when a witness in cross-examination answers questions on collateral matters, his answers are conclusive. There is quite a common misunderstanding that the effect of this is that once counsel in cross-examination gets a denial of the collateral matter that is being put, he may ask no further questions about it. This is not the case. Counsel may continue to question the witness about the collateral matter if he thinks he is likely to obtain any advantage in doing so. What he cannot do is call evidence in rebuttal if the witness persists in his denial. It is only in this sense that the witness's answers are 'final' or 'conclusive'.

You should note that the provisions of the Sexual Offences (Amendment) Act 1976 dealing with cross-examination of complainants in cases where a 'rape offence' was alleged have been repealed and replaced by far more stringent provisions, which are to be found in ss 41–43 of the Youth Justice and Criminal Evidence Act 1999. In *A* (2001), the House of Lords held that these restrictions are to be interpreted in the light of Art 6 of the European Convention on Human Rights.

Checklist

Students should be familiar with the following areas:

- refreshing memory;
- unfavourable and hostile witnesses;
- previous consistent statements;
- cross-examination of the parties as to credit;
- *Edwards* (1991) and subsequent decisions;
- ss 41–43 of the Youth Justice and Criminal Evidence Act 1999 and *A* (2001);

- previous inconsistent statements;
- finality of answers to collateral questions.

Question 43

Len is being prosecuted for assaulting Mick, who had identified Len to the police in a nearby street shortly after the attack and subsequently on an identification parade. At his trial, Len claims that he has been wrongly identified. Mick has a recent conviction for handling stolen goods.

(a) Mick identifies Len in court as the person who attacked him. May he also give evidence of his previous identifications of Len in the street and on the identification parade?

(b) Len tells his counsel that Mick is a heavy drinker and that he can produce a witness, Olive, who will support this and who can say that she saw Mick drinking whisky in a public house on the evening when Mick alleged that he was assaulted by Len, but at a time before that attack took place. In cross-examination, Mick denies being a heavy drinker and says that he had nothing at all to drink that evening. May Len's counsel call Olive to rebut these denials?

(c) Len also tells his counsel that a month before the alleged assault, he had quarrelled with Mick about a woman and Mick had threatened that he would 'get even' with Len some day. Len says that his cousin Percy was present at the time and can confirm this. What use, if any, can Len's counsel make of this information?

(d) Should Len's counsel put Mick's previous conviction to him? If he does so, and Mick denies it, what is likely to happen?

Answer plan

The question raises the following points:

- evidence of previous identification;
- whether the evidence about Mick's drinking is collateral to the main issue;
- the rule concerning the finality of answers on collateral matters and the exceptions to it;
- cross-examination of prosecution witnesses as to character.

Answer

(a) Despite the general rule which excludes evidence of previous consistent statements (see *Roberts* (1942)), evidence of an earlier identification is admissible to show that the witness was able to identify the accused at the time and to exclude the idea that any later identification in court was an afterthought or a mistake (*Christie* (1914)). Mick can therefore give evidence of his earlier identifications of Len as his attacker.

(b) The purpose of establishing that Mick is a heavy drinker and that he had been drinking before the attack is to suggest that his identification of Len could well have been wrong as his faculties were impaired, at least to some extent, by the alcohol that he had consumed. The identification is the central issue in the case and questions designed to show that it might have been impaired by alcohol will therefore not be regarded as dealing with collateral matters. Olive can be called to rebut Mick's denial that he had had anything to drink that evening. She may also give evidence of his heavy drinking if that is a matter within her own knowledge, or of his reputation as a heavy drinker under the rule in *Rowton* (1865). The question whether Mick is a heavy drinker is probably not a collateral matter. If true, it tends to make it more probable that he was drinking on the evening in question, and also that he drank enough to impair his ordinary powers to make an accurate identification.

(c) The quarrel with Mick is a collateral matter, but if Mick denies that it took place or that he threatened Len on that occasion, evidence may nevertheless be called in rebuttal because the effect of such evidence will be to show bias on the part of Mick against Len. Facts showing that a witness is biased against a party may be elicited in cross-examination and if they are denied, rebutting evidence can be called. Thus, in *Shaw* (1888), evidence was held admissible to show that on a previous occasion a witness had threatened the defendant (see also *Phillips* (1936)). Both Len and Percy can therefore be called to give an account of the incident during which Mick threatened Len.

(d) Two matters have to be taken into account when deciding whether to put this conviction to Mick. The first is whether Len will thereby be laid open to cross-examination under s 1(3)(ii) of the Criminal Evidence Act 1898 if he has any previous convictions. But the nature or conduct of his defence may well already have involved an imputation on the witness for the prosecution. There has been an allegation that Mick is a heavy drinker and a person whose testimony is affected by a grudge which he bears towards Len. If this is regarded as sufficient to bring s 1(3)(ii) into operation, there will be nothing to lose by going further and putting Mick's conviction for handling to him.

The second question is whether this conviction ought to be put, bearing in mind the restraints referred to in *Hobbs v Tinling & Co Ltd* (1929). Would knowledge of this conviction seriously affect the jury's opinion of Mick's credibility? It is an offence of dishonesty, so it might do so. Is there a great disproportion between the importance of the imputation made against the witness's character and the importance of his evidence? Almost certainly not; the offence may not be very serious and Mick's evidence is crucial to the prosecution case.

If the conviction is put and Mick denies it, it may be proved against him by virtue of s 6 of the Criminal Procedure Act 1865. Proof would be made by producing a certificate of the conviction under s 73 of the Police and Criminal Evidence Act 1984. But it is likely that counsel for the prosecution would forestall the need for this by making a formal admission of the fact, since the information will have come from him in the first place.[1]

Note

1   The prosecution has a duty to disclose to the defence any previous convictions recorded against their witnesses. See *Paraskeva* (1983).

Question 44

Amy is prosecuted in the Crown Court for assaulting Bella, her neighbour. She pleads not guilty. The case for the prosecution is that Amy punched Bella during a quarrel in the street, causing Bella to fall and break her leg. When Amy was interviewed by the police, she told them that Bella's allegation was untrue and that on the occasion in question Bella had been about to hit her, but fell after tripping over a paving stone.

Consider the evidential issues that arise in each of the following circumstances:

(a) Amy gives evidence in her defence. During cross-examination, she states for the first time that at the time of the fall Bella was drunk. Counsel for the prosecution says: 'You've just made that up a moment ago, haven't you?' Amy replies: 'No, I haven't. The truth is, that woman needed half a bottle of gin before she could get up in the morning.' Defence counsel later wants to call Amy's cousin, Eddie, to give evidence that shortly after the incident, Amy spoke to him about it and said: 'It was that bitch Bella's own fault. She was out of her mind with drink as usual.'

(b) Amy calls her husband, Charlie. He wants to refresh his memory about the incident, which he observed, from a diary that Amy keeps. As well as a record of these events, the diary contains entries in which Amy has described fantasies of sexual encounters between herself and several pop singers.

(c) After Charlie has given evidence, Amy's brother, Dan, is called. He is asked about the incident, which he observed, but says: 'I'm sorry. I'm trying hard to remember, but it's just gone out of my head.'

Answer plan

Part (a) involves an allegation of recent fabrication; you should refer to *Oyesiku* (1971). It also raises the possibility that the prosecution might want to rely on s 34 of the Criminal Justice and Public Order Act 1994. Don't forget to set out the *Gill* direction. Part (b) is a straightforward question about the use of memory-refreshing documents. Part (c) raises a number of possibilities. You should discuss the law relating to hostile and unfavourable witnesses, refreshing memory during the course of giving evidence, and the possibility of using s 23 of the Criminal Justice Act 1988.

Answer

(a) The general rule is that evidence of a statement previously made by a witness which is consistent with his present testimony is inadmissible. Thus, in *Roberts* (1942), a trial for murder where the defence was that a gun had gone off by accident, the accused was not allowed to call evidence to show that two days after the incident he had told his father that the death had resulted from an accident.

Exceptionally, however, evidence of such a statement can be adduced in order to rebut an allegation of recent fabrication. In *Oyesiku* (1971), for example, counsel for the prosecution challenged the evidence of the accused's wife on the basis that she had concocted a story with her husband after his arrest. It was held that the defence should have been allowed to show that she had made a previous consistent statement about the events to her solicitor at a time when she had had no opportunity to discuss matters with her husband because he was then still in custody. But testimony of the previous statement will not be evidence of the truth of its contents; it will be evidence only of the witness's consistency.

Amy was presumably interviewed by the police and failed to mention Bella's drunkenness at that stage. The prosecution could therefore ask the judge to give a direction under s 34 of the Criminal Justice and Public Order Act 1994. If he does so, he must give directions on the lines set out in *Gill* (2001), that is to say, he must identify the fact on which the defendant relies and which was not mentioned on questioning. He must direct the jury that it is for them to decide whether in the circumstances, that fact was something that the defendant could reasonably have been expected to mention. He should tell them that if they think it was, they are not obliged to draw any inferences, but that they may do so. Further, he must tell the jury that a suspected person is not bound to answer police questions, that an inference from silence cannot on its own prove guilt, and that the jury must be satisfied that there is a case to answer before they can draw any adverse inferences from silence. Finally, he should tell the jury that they can draw an adverse inference only if they are sure that the defendant was silent because he had no answers, or none that would stand up to investigation.

(b) A witness may refer to a document to refresh his memory while giving evidence if it was made as soon as possible after the events to which it refers, and the events were then still fresh in the maker's memory (*Richardson* (1971)). Where a witness wants to refer to a note made by someone else, it is necessary to establish that the person using the note had checked it with the maker when the matters were still fresh in the user's memory (*Kelsey* (1982)). Unless both these conditions are satisfied, Charlie will be unable to use the entry in Amy's diary to refresh his memory. If they are satisfied, another problem arises. A witness who has used such a document must produce it for the inspection of the opposing party, who can cross-examine on it. Counsel for the prosecution may well want to argue that the diary entry is fictitious, and that this is supported by the references to the pop singers, which prove the general unreliability of the contents of the diary. It seems clear from *Senat v Senat* (1965) that counsel inspecting a document that has been used to refresh a witness's memory is not confined in cross-examination to those parts which were used for memory-refreshing purposes, provided it is relevant to go beyond them. But if counsel for the prosecution does go beyond them, either party can apply to have the diary made an exhibit in the trial so that in due course the jury can take it into account as a whole when assessing the evidence. If the diary is made an exhibit, the judge should warn the jury that it is not evidence of the truth of the facts stated in it, but is evidence only of a witness's credibility (*Virgo* (1978)).

(c) If Dan is simply suffering from a lapse of memory, his evidence can be interrupted while he reads his statement to refresh his memory. (It is assumed that he has already acknowledged the written statement as his by signing it.) In *Da Silva* (1990), the Court of Appeal held that this procedure was available where a witness had not read over his statement before testifying, and in *South Ribble Magistrates ex p Cochrane* (1996), the Divisional Court held that a witness could do the same even where he had done so. If Dan is not suffering from a lapse of memory, he may be a hostile witness, that is to say, a person who is not desirous of telling the truth to the court at the instance of the party calling him. A witness ruled hostile by the judge can be cross-examined by the party calling him with a view to showing what he said in his written statement on an earlier occasion. The power is provided by both statute and common law. By s 3 of the Criminal Procedure Act 1865, the advocate calling the witness may, by leave of the judge, 'prove that he has made at other times a statement inconsistent with his present testimony'. If the witness, as seems to be the case here, does not provide enough 'present testimony' to be inconsistent with the previous statement, he can still be treated as hostile and cross-examined on the statement by virtue of common law (*Thompson* (1976)). It is possible that Dan is 'hostile' because he is afraid to testify on Amy's behalf. If that could be proved, it would be possible to apply to have the statement put in as a piece of documentary hearsay under s 23(3)(b) of the Criminal Justice Act 1988. In *Waters* (1997), the Court of Appeal held that this sub-section can be relied on even though a witness has already begun to give evidence. Admissibility would, however, depend on the exercise of the judge's discretion under s 26 of the Act because Dan's statement was almost certainly a document prepared for the purpose of criminal proceedings.

Question 45

Irma is being prosecuted for living on immoral earnings. Consider the evidential issues that arise in each of the following circumstances:

(a) Jacqueline, a prostitute who also has convictions for theft, made a statement to the police in which she said that she used to bring clients to Irma's house and that she gave Irma half of what she earned from them. When called by the prosecution, Jacqueline appears to be very frightened and says no more than that she stayed at Irma's house overnight with a boyfriend on one or two occasions.

(b) When Irma was told the reason for her arrest she exclaimed: 'I've only ever been inside for tax fraud. As God is my judge, I am not guilty of this.'

(c) DI Dalgliesh says in his statement that Irma confessed her guilt to him while being driven, under arrest, to the police station. Irma's defence is that no such confession was made. Her counsel would like this evidence to be excluded if possible. Alternatively, he would like to cross-examine Dalgliesh about two previous trials not involving Irma in the course of which he gave evidence that the defendants had confessed to him in the back of a motor car while on the way to a police station. In the first of these trials, the defendant was acquitted by the jury; in the second, the defendant was convicted but the conviction was subsequently quashed by the Court of Appeal as being unsafe and unsatisfactory.

Answer plan

The question requires you to consider the following points:
• the definition and treatment of a hostile witness;
• the admissibility of previous consistent statements;
• editing prejudicial passages in otherwise admissible statements;
• the admissibility of self-serving statements;
• the limits of cross-examination under *Edwards* (1991).

Answer

(a) The question is whether Jacqueline is merely an unfavourable witness or a hostile one. The former is a witness who desires to tell the truth, but who does not 'come up to proof'. The latter is a witness who is not desirous of telling the truth at the instance of the party calling him.[1] It seems clear that Jacqueline is in fact a hostile, and not merely an unfavourable, witness. The normal procedure when counsel has a statement which contradicts the witness's testimony to such a degree is to show it at once to the judge and apply for the witness to be treated as hostile (*Fraser* (1956)). In *Darby* (1989), the Court of Appeal said that such an application should be made in the presence of the jury.[2] If the judge rules that Jacqueline is a hostile witness, counsel for the prosecution may cross-examine her about her previous statement to the police. By s 3 of the Criminal Procedure Act 1865, before proving that she has made an inconsistent statement, Jacqueline must be reminded of the circumstances in which it was made and asked whether or not she made such a statement. Section 3 also provides, however, that counsel who has called a hostile witness cannot impeach her credit by adducing evidence of her bad character. Thus, Jacqueline cannot be asked about any of her previous convictions.

If Jacqueline admits the truth of her previous statement, it will become evidence of the facts contained in it. But if she continues to deny its truth, its only value lies in the doubt it casts on the credibility of her evidence in court, and the jury will have to be warned that the previous statement is not evidence in the case (*Golder* (1960); *Oliva* (1965)).

Since Jacqueline appears to be frightened, it might be possible to avoid treating her as a hostile witness and, instead, have her statement to the police admitted as documentary hearsay evidence under s 23 of the Criminal Justice Act 1988. The argument would be that she does not give evidence through fear and so comes within s 23(3). The sub-section can be used even though a witness has already begun to give evidence. In *Waters* (1997), the Court of Appeal said that it is available so long as there remains any relevant evidence that the witness is still expected to give.

(b) This is a statement made by Irma in response to an allegation of crime. In relation to the offence for which she is being prosecuted, it is wholly exculpatory. It is nevertheless admissible as evidence of her reaction at the time. In *Storey* (1968), the accused was present when police searched her flat and discovered cannabis. She told them that it belonged to a man who had brought it there contrary to her wishes. The Court of Appeal held that her statement was not evidence of the facts stated in it, but was admissible as evidence of her reaction when confronted by incriminating facts.[3]

However, it would be unfortunate if the jury were to learn of Irma's previous convictions for tax frauds, and her reaction will therefore be edited so as to exclude the first sentence. In *Weaver* (1968), Sachs LJ said that a statement by an accused person ought to be edited at trial to avoid prejudice and to eliminate matters which it would be better that the jury should not know. And, in *Pearce* (1979), it was said that the rule of practice whereby the courts admit in evidence all unwritten and most written statements made by an accused person to the police, whether they contain admissions or denials, was subject to the limitation that any admission of a previous conviction would be excluded.

(c) The alleged confession in the car counts as a 'significant statement', which should have been put to Irma in her interview under para 11.2A of PACE Code C. Further, Dalgliesh should have followed the requirement of para 11.13, requiring that a written record be made of any comments made by a suspected person, including unsolicited comments, which are made outside the context of an interview, but which might be relevant to the offence. The paragraph also requires that the suspect be given the opportunity to read and check the record. If Dalgliesh failed to comply with both these provisions, an application to exclude the evidence under s 78(1) of the Police and Criminal Evidence Act 1984 is likely to succeed, on the basis that Dalgliesh has failed to secure its reliability in either of the ways envisaged by the Code. Although exclusion will not be automatic, the Court of Appeal in *Keenan* (1989) said that in cases where there had been significant and substantial breaches of the 'verballing' provisions of the Code, evidence would frequently be excluded.

Any cross-examination that was permitted could be relevant only to the credit of DI Dalgliesh, and not to the issue, because Irma was not involved in the earlier cases. In *Edwards* (1991), the Court of Appeal rejected a submission that the behaviour of police in other unrelated cases could be relevant to the issue because it established a consistent course of conduct, or system of a strikingly similar pattern, over a certain period.

In *Edwards*, the Court of Appeal said that it may be possible to cross-examine a police officer about another unrelated case in which he gave evidence of an accused's confession, and in which the jury had nevertheless acquitted. But it was said that the acquittal must have demonstrated that his evidence in the earlier case was disbelieved. Where an acquittal did not 'necessarily' indicate that the jury disbelieved the officer, such cross-examination should not be allowed. A verdict of not guilty may mean only that the jury had some doubt about the prosecution case, not that they believed a particular witness was lying. But in the absence of reasons for a jury's verdict, this is an impossible test to satisfy. The Court of Appeal acknowledged as much in *Meads* (1996). In that case, counsel for the appellant and for the prosecution agreed that where the circumstances of an earlier acquittal 'pointed to' fabrication of evidence by a police officer, cross-examination should be permitted. The court remarked that it might be necessary on another occasion for an appellate court to consider whether an acquittal could ever demonstrate that the evidence of a prosecution witness had been disbelieved. However, in *Guney* (1998), the Court of Appeal followed *Edwards* (1991). *Meads* (1996) appears not to have been cited to the court.

It would be even more difficult to establish the right to cross-examine about the case where the verdict was quashed in the Court of Appeal. In *Edwards* (1991), it was said that the fact that the Court of Appeal was not satisfied about aspects of the police evidence provided no proper foundation for cross-examination of individual officers about their veracity in general or their truthfulness in the case currently being tried. It appears that there could be cross-examination about a quashed conviction only if the Court of Appeal expressly or by necessary implication had indicated that it disbelieved the police officer in question.[4]

On the facts given, it is not clear on what basis the Court of Appeal found the earlier conviction unsafe and unsatisfactory, but it seems unlikely that the circumstances will prove to be such as to allow cross-examination about this case.

Notes

1 Stephen, JF, *Digest of the Law of Evidence*, 12th edn, 1948, Art 147, quoted in Tapper, C, *Cross & Tapper on Evidence*, 9th edn, 1999, p 284.

2 See the note on this case in [1989] Crim LR 818.

3 See also *Pearce* (1979).

4 See Pattenden, R, 'Evidence of previous malpractice by police witnesses and *R v Edwards*' [1992] Crim LR 549, pp 549–57. See also *Guney* (1998).

Question 46

David is charged with raping Ellen in his flat after meeting her for the first time earlier in the evening in a public house. Ellen says that sex was never mentioned while they were in the public house. According to her, David invited her back to his flat to listen to a CD, but while this was being played, he raped her. Ellen says that she left David's flat shortly after she had been raped, and that when she arrived at her mother's house, where she lived, she told her mother that she had been raped. Her mother died before she could make a statement to the police or be interviewed by them. David's defence is that Ellen consented to sexual intercourse. He says that he met her in the public house at about 9 pm. He had never seen her before, but she came up to him and said: 'You look the sort of man I could end up in bed with. Why don't we go to your place?' David wishes to call Fergus, who was drinking in the same public house earlier that evening. Fergus says that Ellen, whom he knew only by sight, had approached him and said: 'I wouldn't mind a night with you. Let's go to your place.' Fergus says that he made an excuse and left the public house alone. David also wishes to call Gerald, who says that he had sex with Ellen at her invitation after meeting her for the first time in a different public house a week before the alleged rape by David.

Discuss the evidential matters arising. To what extent, if at all, would your advice be different if during cross-examination counsel for David put it to Ellen that she consented, and in reply she, for the first time, volunteered the information that she was a virgin before being raped by David?

Answer plan

The following matters need consideration:

- Ellen's report of the rape to her mother;
- David's account of the meeting;
- David's claim that Ellen consented;
- Fergus's evidence;
- Gerald's evidence;
- Ellen's claim to have been a virgin.

Answer

If a complaint of rape is made at the first reasonable opportunity after the offence, it may be proved in evidence to show the complainant's consistency and to negative consent (*Lillyman* (1896); *Osborne* (1905)). But, for this purpose, it is necessary not only that the complainant should testify to the making of the complaint, but also that its terms should be proved by the person to whom it was made (*White v R* (1998)). In this case, the recipient of the complaint has died without leaving a written statement that could have been adduced under s 23 of the Criminal Justice Act 1988, and without even being interviewed by the police. It follows that Ellen's own evidence of making the complaint will be inadmissible.

David can give evidence of what Ellen said to him without infringing the rule against hearsay. The words uttered were an expression of her contemporaneous state of mind, and so fall within one of the categories of *res gestae* (*Moghal* (1977)). Alternatively, David's purpose in proving what Ellen said would be to show the effect the words had on his mind, and not the truth of what was said. In this case, the rule against hearsay would not apply (*Subramaniam v Public Prosecutor* (1956)).

The effect of s 41 of the Youth Justice and Criminal Evidence Act 1999 is that where a person is charged with a sexual offence, no evidence may be adduced by the accused about any sexual behaviour of the complainant, save in very restricted circumstances. David's evidence relates to an issue of consent, and the sexual behaviour of the complainant to which the evidence relates is alleged to have taken place at or about the same time as the event that is the subject matter of the charge against the accused. It falls within the exception contained in s 41(3)(b). A refusal of leave to adduce such evidence would clearly render the jury's verdict unsafe. Thus, both conditions referred to in s 41(2) for adducing evidence of sexual behaviour are satisfied. David's evidence is admissible.

Fergus's evidence is also evidence of Ellen's sexual behaviour and is subject to the restrictions of s 41, but it is likely to be admissible under s 41(3)(c)(ii). This allows the court to hear about other sexual behaviour of the complainant 'at or about the same time' as the alleged event which is the subject of the charge, if that behaviour is in any respect so similar to the behaviour of the complainant that took place as part of the event that is the subject matter of the charge that the similarity cannot reasonably be explained as a coincidence. It is likely that a broad view would be taken of 'the event which is the subject matter of the charge' so that it would include the circumstances in which David and Ellen met each other. The evidence of Ellen's encounter with Fergus is strikingly similar to David's evidence of her encounter with him. It shows Ellen's intention to have consensual sexual intercourse on that evening and should be admissible under s 41(2). (In fact, striking similarity may not be needed. In *A* (2001), Lord Hutton observed that s 43(3)(c) contained less stringent words.) If this argument is rejected, the defence could argue that the principle of interpretation in *A* should be applied. Section 41(3)(c) is to be construed by applying s 3 of the Human Rights Act 1998. The evidence should not be excluded if it is so relevant to the issue of consent that to exclude it would endanger the fairness of the trial provided for by Art 6 of the European Convention on Human Rights.

Gerald's evidence is likely to be inadmissible because of the requirement, under s 41(3)(c)(ii), that the evidence should be of sexual behaviour taking place 'at or about the same time' as the event which is the subject matter of the charge. In *A*, Lord Hope said that these words will generally be interpreted no more widely than 24 hours before or after the alleged offence.

Section 41(5) allows a question, or evidence, about other sexual behaviour of a complainant to be admitted if it relates to any evidence adduced by the prosecution about any sexual behaviour of the complainant, and would go no further than is necessary to rebut or explain that evidence. The condition in sub-s (2)(b) must also be satisfied. In one sense, this evidence has not been adduced by the prosecution; it has been adduced by the defence during cross-examination. On the other hand, it has been volunteered by a prosecution witness, and it would be extraordinary if such a restricted construction were to be allowed to mislead the jury, especially in view of the decision in *A*. On that basis, Gerald's evidence might well be admitted.

CHAPTER 11

OPINION EVIDENCE

Introduction

From the standpoint of the examination candidate, opinion evidence is a tricky subject to prepare. Your examiners may show little or no interest in it, so that an opinion point comes in, if at all, only as a minor part of a question dealing largely with other matters. On the other hand, it would be possible to devote a whole problem to the subject. It would even be possible – though surely not very interesting – to invite candidates to write an essay on some aspect of opinion evidence, for example, the current state of the so called 'ultimate issue rule'. But let's assume that you have ruled out the possibility of an essay question, or at least of doing it should one turn up. How should you cope with opinion evidence as part of a problem?

In the first place, you should be careful in analysing exactly what it is that the expert is prepared to say. Break it down into a number of separate propositions if need be, because some may be more readily admissible than others.[1]

Next, you need to clarify the basis on which the opinion has been formed. For example, how much is a psychiatrist relying on what a defendant has told him? If he relies too much, he may find himself simply repeating what the defendant has said; that, obviously, would be open to the objection that it infringed the rule against hearsay.

Very often, the examiner will be vague about both these matters – exactly what the expert *is* saying and the basis for his opinion – and it will be for you to point out the difficulties.

Where you are dealing with the expert opinion of a psychiatrist or psychologist you should look at the issue to which it is directed. The reason is that evidence from either which does not amount to evidence of mental abnormality may be admitted to show, for example, the reliability of a confession. But where the issue in question is that of *mens rea*, it is most unlikely to be admitted. See *Coles* (1995). Presumably, it is felt that to allow such evidence to be given would lead to experts deciding the issue which should properly be left to the jury. Alternatively, there may be a fear that a stage would soon be reached where experts were called on each side, the jury would be left no wiser, and the expense and length of proceedings would have been increased for nothing.

Although your problem is likely to involve experts who make a living from their expertise, you may have to advise in relation to a layman who appears to be giving an opinion. Don't forget that an amateur may be an expert, or that an opinion can be given by a non-expert if it is simply a short way of describing facts: see s 3(2) of the Civil Evidence Act 1972 and *Davies* (1962).

Note

1   For an example of close analysis leading to rejection of psychiatric testimony, see *Hurst* (1995).

Checklist

Students should be familiar with the following areas:

- opinion used as a way of conveying the sense of facts perceived;
- when expert psychiatric testimony is needed;
- who may give expert testimony;
- expert opinion on ultimate issues;
- expert evidence and the rule against hearsay – *Abadom* (1983); s 30 of the Criminal Justice Act (CJA) 1988; s 1(1) of the Civil Evidence Act (CEA) 1972;
- advance notice procedures in civil and criminal cases.

Question 47

David and Jonathan are charged with murdering Salome, a prostitute. The prosecution case is that she was beaten and kicked to death by both accused.

(a) David's defence is diminished responsibility. He says that he was one of Salome's regular clients and he acted as he did immediately after Salome said that if he did not give her £500,000 she would tell his wife of their relationship. David wishes to call Goliath, a psychiatrist. Goliath has prepared a report in which he says that he has examined David, that David described his horror at the blackmail attempt and became very emotional when speaking of his wife; in Goliath's opinion, David loved his wife dearly and would have been devastated by the break up of their marriage. Goliath adds that in two other cases in his experience, the sudden shock of a blackmail threat led to violent physical retaliation. He states that this observation has been explained in several privately circulated papers by psychiatrists who have described experiments in which they observed patterns of bodily chemical reactions which appeared to be peculiar to blackmail victims. Goliath concludes his report by saying that in his professional opinion David is not insane within the M'Naghten Rules, but was suffering at the relevant time from diminished responsibility within s 2 of the Homicide Act 1957. May Goliath testify as to all or any of these matters?

(b) Jonathan's case is that he had been with David and Salome on the occasion in question, but that he had had nothing to do with the attack. He says that when he saw what David was doing, he went into a state of shock and ran to the house of his girlfriend, Jezebel, a short distance away. Jezebel is a member of the police force. May Jonathan call her to say that when he arrived at her house, he was in a state of shock? He also wishes to call Zadok, a psychiatrist, who has examined him and who is prepared to state that in his opinion, Jonathan is a truthful man who has a peculiar horror of any sort of violence as a result of having been bullied at school. Will Zadok's evidence be admissible?

Answer plan

(a) Since the expert's evidence is directed towards providing a defence of diminished responsibility for David, it is a good idea to outline briefly what this defence requires. The first paragraph does this, and shows that this is a case where expert evidence will be admissible in principle. But now you have to point out that there may be difficulties about the admissibility of what this expert is prepared to say. To do so effectively, you must break up what Goliath wants to say into separate heads, as follows:

- David's reaction to the blackmail attempt;
- David's reactions when speaking of his wife;
- Goliath's opinion that David loved her dearly;
- Goliath's opinion about the effect on David of the break up of his marriage;
- Goliath's description of his own experience of similar cases;
- his reference to the psychiatric experiments reported in privately circulated papers;
- his opinion as to David's sanity;
- his opinion that David was suffering from diminished responsibility.

(b) The first matter to be considered is whether Jezebel's evidence is expert testimony at all. You then need to break up Zadok's opinion thus:

- his opinion that Jonathan was truthful;
- his opinion about Jonathan's capacity for violence.

Answer

(a) By s 2 of the Homicide Act 1957, a person who kills another shall not be convicted of murder if he was suffering from such abnormality of mind as substantially impaired his mental responsibility for his acts. It is for the defendant to prove that he comes within the section. The requirement that some abnormality of mind be established makes it clear that this is the sort of case where expert opinion evidence is receivable. As was said in *Turner* (1975), the purpose of such evidence is to provide the court with information which is outside the experience and knowledge of a judge or jury. In *Dix* (1982), Shaw LJ said that while s 2 of the Homicide Act did not in terms require that medical evidence be adduced in support of a defence of diminished responsibility, it made it a practical necessity if that defence was to begin to run at all. The question of admissibility in this case will therefore turn on the nature of the testimony that it is proposed that Goliath should give.

It appears that the first thing that Goliath wishes to do is to report the reactions of David when speaking of his wife, and to give his own opinion that David loved her dearly. He adds that David would have been devastated by the break up of his marriage, but whether this is an opinion formed as a result of what David told him directly, or as a result of what Goliath inferred from other things said by David, is unclear.

So far, it seems that nearly all this evidence would be inadmissible. To the extent that Goliath was repeating what David said to him, the evidence would be excluded by the rule against hearsay, although the fact that David became emotional when speaking of his wife would be admissible.[1] The questions of whether David loved his wife and what would have been his reaction to the break up of their marriage are not ones where the jury would require the special assistance of a psychiatrist. Thus, in *Turner* (1975), the Court of Appeal held that the trial judge had rightly excluded psychiatric evidence that the defendant had had a deep emotional relationship with his girlfriend which was likely to have caused a blind explosion of rage after her confession of infidelity. As Lawton LJ said, the fact that an expert witness has impressive scientific qualifications does not by that fact alone make his opinion on matters of human nature and behaviour within the limits of normality any more helpful than that of the jurors themselves.

Then Goliath wishes to say that in two other cases in his experience the sudden shock of a blackmail threat led to violent physical retaliation, and he refers to the experiments of other psychiatrists by way of explanation. The basic question here is the same: does the jury need the assistance of this scientific evidence to determine the particular matter under consideration? At this stage, Goliath's evidence is directed to the issue whether it is more likely than not that when David killed Salome he was suffering from such abnormality of mind as substantially to impair his mental responsibility.

Is Goliath prepared to adopt the explanation of his colleagues as his own? Unless he is, there is not much point in referring to their opinions. Assuming that he does, the argument for admissibility is stronger than in relation to his earlier opinions because this is something that would not be within the ordinary knowledge of jurors. In *Abadom* (1983), the Court of Appeal decided that an expert is entitled to draw on the work of others as part of the process of arriving at his conclusions. The fact that the work is unpublished is immaterial. Goliath may therefore rely on the privately circulated papers in forming his opinion and, as the court pointed out in *Abadom*, he ought to identify them so that the quality of his opinion may be assessed.

However, it remains necessary to be cautious about admissibility. If the judge took the view that the scientists had merely been describing ordinary human reactions in scientific terms, he would very probably conclude that their discoveries would not assist the jury. The evidence would then be excluded.

Lastly, Goliath wishes to say that David was not insane, but was suffering from diminished responsibility. The question of David's sanity is not in issue, so the first part of this opinion would be irrelevant, and therefore inadmissible. Although experts may sometimes give opinions on the ultimate issue in a case, this is not one of them. The defence provided by s 2 of the Homicide Act 1957 involves more than a simple medical issue concerning the accused's state of mind. There is also the question of substantial impairment of responsibility and this is essentially for the jury to decide (*Byrne* (1960)).

However, in *DPP v A and BC Chewing Gum Ltd* (1968), Lord Parker acknowledged that although the question 'Do you think he was suffering from diminished responsibility?' was strictly inadmissible, it was allowed time and again without objection. Thus, on the assumption that there is some admissible evidence that Goliath can give, it is likely that he would also be allowed to say that in his opinion, David was suffering from diminished responsibility.

(b) Jezebel may certainly give evidence of Jonathan's physical and emotional condition when he arrived at her house; no special expertise is required to do this. If she wishes to give evidence that he was in a specific medical condition known as 'a state of shock', the fact that she is not medically qualified need not prevent her from doing so. It would be enough that she had acquired the necessary medical knowledge as part of her police training and experience. *Silverlock* (1894) is authority for the proposition that an appropriate professional qualification is not essential for an expert witness. In that case a solicitor who had studied handwriting as a hobby was allowed to give evidence as a handwriting expert.

Zadok will not be able to give his opinion that Jonathan is a truthful man. *Toohey v Commissioner for Metropolitan Police* (1965) establishes that medical evidence will be admissible to show that a witness suffers from some disease, or defect or abnormality of mind that affects the reliability of his evidence. But subject to this, it appears that only in the most exceptional cases will psychiatric testimony be admissible concerning the truthfulness of the accused.[2]

Two problems arise in connection with Zadok's opinion about Jonathan's capacity for violence. The first is whether it is in principle admissible at all. There is little to suggest that English courts are likely to follow the example set by the Supreme Court of Canada in *Lupien* (1970), which held admissible evidence showing that the defendant had a temperament which would have made his participation in a particular form of conduct very unlikely. In *Reynolds* (1989), the Court of Appeal took the view that psychiatric evidence about personal traits, such as the habit of fantasising, was inadmissible because the jury could use its common sense about such matters. It is likely that a court would regard an aversion to violence in the same light.

Even if this basic problem can be overcome, a second one remains: on what basis was Zadok's conclusion reached? If it was merely on what Jonathan said to him during a consultation it would be likely to fall foul of the rule against hearsay. At least in *Lupien* (1970), the defendant had been subjected to psychiatric tests for the purpose of determining the issue in question.

Notes

1   What is relevant is David's state of mind at the time of the offence. Light can be thrown on this by David's emotional reaction when talking to Goliath about his wife, but not, according to English law at any rate, by his account to Goliath of

what was his state of mind at the time when he killed Salome. If David wants this to go before the jury, he will have to testify.

2   One such case was *Lowery v R* (1974), where two co-accused blamed each other for a murder and the Privy Council held that the trial judge had properly admitted the evidence of a psychologist, who had carried out tests on both defendants, to show that the testimony of one was more likely to be true than that of the other. Nothing of the kind arises here; David accepts that he killed Salome and has not tried to implicate Jonathan.

CHAPTER 12

PRIVILEGE AND PUBLIC POLICY

Introduction

The first thing to get straight is the difference between these two concepts. A *privilege* is a right which the law gives to a person allowing him to refuse to testify about a certain matter, or to refuse to produce a document or piece of real evidence. *Public policy* (often now referred to as 'public interest immunity') comes into the picture where it is thought that the disclosure of evidence would be damaging in some way to the general good. The most obvious example is where national security would be compromised if the evidence in question had to be given, or the disclosure made.

There are four privileges which you ought to study. The first is the privilege against self-incrimination. One theoretical topic that could come up as an essay question is whether such a privilege should exist at all. You should note that this is not the same question as whether the accused should have a right to silence. Some writers do refer to 'the privilege against self-incrimination' in the broad sense of a 'right to silence', but this is confusing and it will be better if you keep the two ideas distinct.

The classic context for the operation of the privilege against self-incrimination is a *civil* action where one of the witnesses is being cross-examined about conduct which would amount to a criminal offence. For example, suppose I sue a storage company for the loss of my valuable furniture which was in store with them, and it is my case that the furniture was destroyed when the company deliberately set fire to the premises to collect on an insurance policy. In those circumstances, the privilege might well be invoked at some stage of the hearing by a witness for the company who was being cross-examined.

You should note the increasing number of statutory exceptions to this privilege.

Legal professional privilege is also of considerable importance. Note the various circumstances in which this applies, especially those cases where the communications are not directly between lawyer and client, but between lawyer and third parties on behalf of the client.

This privilege can be 'waived' by accident. What happens is that, in any large action, the task of preparing documents for disclosure is so great that quite often one side shows the other privileged documents by mistake. By r 31.20 of the Civil Procedure Rules 1998, inadvertently disclosed privileged documents may only be used with the consent of the court. Some knowledge of the former law that governed the granting of injunctions to restrain the use of such documents is likely to be helpful in judging whether consent will be given.

Two more privileges ought to be studied. One is the limited privilege that has been given in respect of a journalist's sources. (See s 10 of the Contempt of Court Act 1981.) The other is the privilege that attaches to 'without prejudice' statements. With the latter, remember that if the negotiations result in agreement there is no longer any need for 'without prejudice' protection. It follows that, if there is any subsequent litigation concerning that agreement, you are free to use the documents marked 'without prejudice' as evidence of the agreement and its terms (*Tomlin v Standard Telephones and Cables Ltd* (1969)). But note also *Rush and Tomkins Ltd v GLC* (1989), which makes evidence of negotiations inadmissible in any subsequent litigation connected with the same subject matter. This is particularly likely to affect a situation where a main contractor reaches a settlement with one of several subcontractors.

Public policy questions are not ones which many candidates answer well, and unless you have also studied public law it is, perhaps, better to avoid the topic in the examination. I have nevertheless suggested in the checklist some areas with which you might make yourself familiar. The subject of police informers is interesting, topical and not too difficult to master. It is also a subject that might feature as part of a wider question.

Checklist

Students should be familiar with the following areas:

- the privilege against self-incrimination;
- legal professional privilege;
- s 10 of the Contempt of Court Act 1981;
- 'without prejudice' statements;
- public policy considerations involving national security, affairs of state, and the proper functioning of government and its services;
- public policy considerations in respect of information in the possession of the police relating to the investigation of crime;
- public policy considerations in respect of confidential or personal statements made in official reports or inquiries.

Question 48

'The fact that evidence which is relevant and otherwise admissible may be excluded by public policy or privilege gives to the two subjects an appearance of similarity which is misleading. The rules and their operation are quite distinct, and any superficial identity of result is more than outweighed by substantial and far reaching differences.'

Discuss.

Answer plan

Sometimes, the examiner sets quite a lengthy quotation as the subject for an essay. To write an effective essay, it is of course vital that you should read the quotation carefully, probably at least twice, in order to determine exactly what it means. All too often I have read scripts where it seemed as if the candidate had glanced at the quotation, had seen that it had something to do with public policy, and had assumed he would pass if he regurgitated his lecture notes on *Conway v Rimmer* (1968) and all that. I emphasise again that the examiner is looking for an argument, not an exposition of basic law. If you fail to provide an appropriate response, you will fail the question.

What is this particular quotation about? First, the writer refers to the fact that the rules of both privilege and public policy have the effect of excluding evidence that would otherwise be relevant and admissible. To that extent, the two sets of rules appear to be alike, but, he goes on, the fact that the rules have the same *result* does not mean that there are any other similarities. Similarity of result need not involve similarity in the way the result is reached. This is certainly true in some matters; is it true in this case? In other words, what are the differences and similarities between the rules relating to privilege and those relating to public policy?

It probably strikes you that the idea contained in the quotation is basically correct. But it is not very interesting to say so at once, and the key to producing a really competent answer is to argue a little *against* the idea contained in the quotation. This is done here by arguing that there is not only a similarity in outcome, but a similarity in the way the rules are operated.

You can then move on to make obvious points about waiver, use of secondary evidence and persons entitled to make the claim. You conclude by agreeing with the proposition contained in the quotation. But you do so with reservations, and have shown some independent thought on the subject.

In summary, therefore, the essay is constructed as follows:

- difference between outcomes and the means of achieving them;
- argument for similarity of means based on the balancing of potential harms;
- place of balancing interests in privilege and public policy;
- potential differences between privilege and public policy: waiver and use of secondary evidence;
- persons who can claim privilege and raise issues of public policy;
- concluding remarks on the quotation.

Answer

Similarity of outcomes does not necessarily involve similarity in the way the outcomes under consideration were achieved. Dr Crippen died by hanging and Louis XVI lost his life by means of the guillotine. The outcome in each case was the same: death. However, the procedures preceding those outcomes and the methods by which death was achieved were vastly different. It does not, therefore, appear to be a very impressive argument for similarity between the rules relating to privilege and those relating to public policy that they achieve the same outcome.

But it can be argued that there is more than identity of outcome, and that in fact there is similarity in the way the rules are operated. If a claim to privilege succeeds, it does so because when you balance the harm that will follow if the privilege is upheld against the harm that will follow if it is not, the latter is found to be greater. Yet this is the very same principle that operates in the sphere of public interest immunity.

When privilege is being considered, this balancing exercise operates in a way about which it is difficult to generalise, but which may best be described as 'oiling the wheels of the administration of justice'. For example, for each party to have his case presented as well as possible within our adversarial context, it is necessary that the lawyers on each side be fully acquainted with all the relevant facts. To achieve this, it is vital that the client should be able to trust the lawyer. This could not be the case if what he said to his own lawyer could be used against him, and this gives rise to rules about legal professional privilege.

The fact that justice can be done by disputants themselves, and not only by courts, is recognised by rules which encourage parties to settle their quarrels without recourse to litigation. So, for example, we find that there are rules which say that admissions made by parties while trying to reach a settlement cannot afterwards be proved against them if negotiations break down and the matter has to go to court.

On another level, there may be public interests which conflict with the doing of justice in a particular case. Thus, the public interest in the detection of crime or in the maintenance of national security may require non-disclosure of certain matters, even though this may harm an individual litigant by depriving him of vital evidence.

In both types of case, there is a balancing of interests. Is the interest in rectitude of decision outweighed by the interest in keeping the administration of justice working as well as possible, both inside and outside the courts? Is the interest in doing justice to the parties in a particular case outweighed by some wider public interest? So far, it seems that although the situations giving rise to such problems of balancing may be very different, the principle that is operating in each case is essentially the same. Have we found a common feature other than outcome that would disprove the contention expressed in the passage quoted?

Closer examination suggests that although the balancing of interests is indeed a feature common to both the law of privilege and the law relating to exclusion on grounds of public policy, this does not disprove the contention. The reason for this is that it is too common a feature of evidence law, for it can be used to account for all the ordinary rules of exclusion, such as those governing hearsay evidence or evidence of the accused's criminal propensity. The public may be said to have an interest in the full disclosure of relevant information in a criminal trial, but it also has an interest in rectitude of decision. This latter interest may be served better by concealing some information, because, if it were disclosed, its capacity to mislead the jury would increase the chances of misdecision. Thus, it may be said that a balancing exercise takes place in which greater weight is given to one interest rather than the other, depending on the amount of harm likely to result.

On the other hand, there appear to be quite strong arguments to justify the contention expressed in the passage quoted.

Matters covered by public policy are those where the safety or well being of citizens generally is concerned. Privilege, by contrast, covers matters that directly affect only the particular litigant or witness. This gives rise to differences in the way in which the law deals with two subjects: waiver, and the use of secondary evidence.

A party or witness who has a privilege may always waive it voluntarily, and, in such a case, the once privileged document or testimony will be treated in the same way as any other evidence in the case. But, because public policy objections exist, in theory, for the benefit of citizens generally there is some difficulty with the idea that objections of this type can be waived. Thus, in *Rogers v Home Secretary* (1973), Lord Simon said that once the public interest which demands that evidence be withheld has been found weightier than the public interest requiring courts to have access to all relevant material, the evidence cannot in any circumstances be admitted. It is not a privilege which may be waived, either by the Crown or by anyone else.

However, in *Alfred Crompton Amusement Machines Ltd v Customs and Excise Commissioners (No 2)* (1974), Lord Cross thought that waiver could be allowed if a person or party, such as an informer, for whose benefit the objection was made volunteered to testify or disclose the evidence. One way of analysing such an odd situation would be to say that it was not a case of waiver at all, but one where the public interest had just disappeared, because the interest in question is that of protecting a person from having to disclose certain information *against his will*.[1] This approach was adopted by the Court of Appeal in *Savage v Chief Constable of the Hampshire Constabulary* (1997), where it was held that a police informer could waive his anonymity in order to sue the defendant on an alleged contract to make payments to the claimant in return for information.

The courts have recently brought the operation of public interest immunity more closely into line with that of privilege in respect of waiver. An important distinction used to be that, while a privilege could be waived, a claim to public interest immunity could not. As Lord Scarman said in *Air Canada v Secretary of State for Trade* (1983), when the Crown puts forward a public interest immunity objection, it is not claiming a privilege but discharging a duty. Similarly, in *Makanjuola v Commissioner of Metropolitan Police* (1992), Bingham LJ said that public interest immunity 'is not a trump card vouchsafed to certain privileged players to play as and when they wish'. He added that it could not, in any ordinary sense, be waived, because although rights can be waived, duties cannot. On that approach, it followed that where a litigant held documents in a class that was *prima facie* immune, he should (save in a very exceptional case) assert that they are immune and decline to disclose them. The ultimate decision about where the public interest lay was not for him, but for the court.

However, this approach, coupled with a claim to immunity based on the class into which a document fell, rather than on its specific contents, led to undesirably wide public interest immunity claims by ministers. The practice was criticised in the Scott Report,[2] and the central government has now effectively abandoned class claims.

Further, in *R v Chief Constable of West Midlands Police ex p Wiley* (1995), the House of Lords held that a class claim cannot be made in respect of documents compiled as part of the investigation of a complaint against the police, and it seems likely that class claims generally will be reduced in future. After *ex p Wiley*, it is clear that if a minister believes that the overriding public interest requires government documents to be disclosed, he is not obliged to request immunity for them. It appears that ministers must now consider, before making a claim for public interest immunity, whether the public interest is better served by disclosure than by concealment. It looks very much as if they are expected to exercise a discretion in deciding whether or not to waive public interest immunity.

The second main difference between information affected by privilege and information affected by public policy is in relation to the use of secondary evidence. When public policy requires that information be concealed, the documents which are the immediate subject of the exclusion are obviously affected but, in addition, it is not possible to prove their contents by secondary means. Privilege, however, attaches only to an original document or communication. Subject to the possibility of protection under the law relating to confidentiality, secondary evidence is in principle admissible. Thus, an opponent may be able to prove facts contained in a privileged document by producing a copy, or by calling a witness to give oral evidence of its contents.

A final point of distinction between claims based on privilege and claims based on public policy is that in the case of privilege the claim must be made by the person who is entitled to the privilege, but an objection made on grounds of public policy may be made by someone who is not even a party to the proceedings. The court may even do so of its own motion.

Thus, it can be seen that, despite superficial similarities in both effect and operation, there are significant differences between the rules relating to privilege and public policy and between the ways in which those rules operate.

Notes

1   Lord Denning has on several occasions said that there could be waiver of objections based on public policy. In *Campbell v Tameside Metropolitan Borough Council* (1982), he proposed a distinction between claims affecting documents which must be kept secret on such grounds as those of national security or the preservation of diplomatic relations, and documents in a lower category which are kept confidential in order that persons should be candid in their reports or for other good reasons. In these latter cases, he suggested, immunity should be capable of being waived either by the maker or by the recipient of the document.

2   *Report of the Inquiry into the Export of Defence Equipment and Dual-Use Goods to Iraq and Related Prosecutions*, 1996, HC 115, 15 February.

Question 49

Answer BOTH parts of this question.

(a) Francis is being prosecuted for possession of cannabis which has been found at his house. When the police raided the premises, they discovered a small quantity of the drug wrapped in silver paper at the bottom of a pile of underclothes which lay on the floor. Francis denies the charge. He says that he is an asthmatic and unable to smoke, but that writers, artists and students are frequent callers at his house and that any one of them could have dropped the package. He suspects that the police were tipped off by George. George has been employed by Francis as a general handyman for the last eight years. In the past, he has been sentenced to terms of imprisonment; he is now an alcoholic and has often made false allegations against Francis when drunk.

May the defence require the police to disclose the name of their informer?

(b) Harry is being prosecuted for supplying drugs. The only evidence against him is that of four police officers. Two officers, Ian and John, give evidence that while keeping watch in private premises, they observed Harry selling drugs. Two others, Kate and Larry, give evidence that while keeping watch in an unmarked police vehicle, they also observed Harry selling drugs.

May the defence cross-examine Ian and John to discover the exact location of their observation point in order to test the quality of their observations?

May they cross-examine Kate and Larry to discover the colour, make and model of their vehicle and the times of their alleged surveillance?

Answer plan

This is a straightforward question involving cases on the public interest in non-disclosure of information concerning police investigations.

Part (a) deals with the traditional problem of the informer. The basic rule stated in *Marks v Beyfus* (1890) must be your starting point; it will be useful to refer to what Lawton LJ said in *Hennessey* (1978) about the reason for that rule. Don't rush things; deal with the basic rule first and turn to the exception only after that. Then comes the factual problem: is disclosure necessary to show the accused's innocence? The point is best made here by a comparison of *Agar* (1989) and *Slowcombe* (1991). Don't forget though to provide your own conclusion on the facts of this question; the cases you have cited are useful illustrations of a principle, but no more.

Part (b) is even more straightforward and is designed to test the candidate's knowledge of *Rankine* (1986), *Brown* (1987) and *Johnson* (1988).

Answer

(a) The basic rule is that in public prosecutions witnesses may not be asked, and will not be allowed to disclose, the names of informers or the nature of the information given. Thus, in *Marks v Beyfus* (1890), an action for malicious prosecution, the Director of Public Prosecutions, who had been called as a witness, refused on grounds of public policy to give the names of his informants or to produce the statement on which he had acted in directing the earlier unsuccessful prosecution of the plaintiff. His objection was upheld by the trial judge, and the plaintiff was unsuccessful in his appeal. Lawton LJ stated in *Hennessey* (1978) that the rationale of the rule is that informers need to be protected, both for their own safety and to ensure that the supply of information about criminal activities does not dry up.

However, in *Marks v Beyfus* (1890), Lord Esher qualified this basic rule by stating that it could be departed from if the disclosure of the name of the informant was necessary or right in order to show the prisoner's innocence. In such a case, one public policy would be in conflict with another, and the policy which said that an innocent man should not be condemned when his innocence could be proved had to prevail. However, it is for the accused to show that there is a good reason for disclosure (*Hennessey* (1978)).

An example of a case where disclosure was considered appropriate is *Agar* (1989). In that case, a prosecution for possession of drugs, the Court of Appeal said that the trial judge should have ordered the informer's disclosure because it was necessary for the support of the accused's defence that the informer and the police had acted together to frame him.

But it may well be the case that knowledge of the informer will not affect the defence, and then disclosure will not be ordered. An example is *Slowcombe* (1991). Following a tip off, the defendant had been arrested in possession of a shotgun outside a sub-post office. He claimed to have been recruited by V, and to have been told by him that there was an accomplice working in the post office who would hand over the money, but that the gun was necessary for the sake of appearances. The defendant argued accordingly that he was not guilty of conspiracy to rob, but only of conspiracy to steal. The judge refused a defence application to ask a police officer whether their informer had been V. The Court of Appeal upheld this decision. If V had not been the informer, the defendant's story could still have been true. If it had been V, that would not establish that the defendant had been told that only a theft was planned. V could have conspired with the defendant to commit robbery, but then have turned informer. Disclosing the name of the informer could contribute little or nothing to the issue the jury had to consider: might the defendant's explanation have been true?

The issue in the case of Francis is whether his explanation for the presence of the cannabis might be true. Knowing that George was the informer can contribute nothing to the resolution of this question. If Francis were to suggest that George planted the cannabis and then tipped off the police, the position would be different, but that does not appear to be his case.

It is unlikely, therefore, that the defence application would succeed.[1]

(b) It was held in *Rankine* (1986) that the rule in *Marks v Beyfus* (1890) also protects the identity of persons who have allowed their premises to be used for police observation, and the identity of the premises. Even if the accused argues that identification of the premises is necessary to establish his innocence (as it surely would be in this case), the judge may still refuse to allow the question to be put. For example, in *Johnson* (1988), where the accused was charged with supplying drugs, the only evidence against him was supplied by police officers who had kept observation from private premises. The defence applied to cross-examine about the exact location in order to test whether the officers could have seen what they said they did. The trial judge nevertheless ruled that the exact location should not be revealed, and the Court of Appeal upheld this decision.

But the prosecution must have first provided a proper evidential basis to support their claim for protection of identity. In *Johnson* (1988), Watkins LJ stated the following as minimum requirements:

- the police officer in charge of the observations must testify that he had visited all the observation places to be used and ascertained the attitude of their occupiers, both as to the use to be made of them and to possible subsequent disclosure;

- a police officer of at least the rank of chief inspector must testify that immediately prior to the trial he visited the places used for observation and ascertained whether the occupiers were the same as when the observation took place and, whether they are or not, the attitude of those occupiers to possible disclosure of their use as observation points.

In *Johnson* (1988), the prosecution called evidence as to the difficulty of obtaining assistance from the public and the desire of the occupiers, who had been occupiers throughout, that their names and addresses should not be disclosed because of fear for their safety. Assuming that similar evidence is available in this case, the defence will not be permitted to cross-examine Ian and John about the exact location of the premises which they used.

But the object of keeping the identity of the premises secret is to protect the owner or occupier. Where this consideration does not apply, cross-examination may be permitted on detailed aspects of surveillance. Thus, in *Brown* (1987), where officers gave evidence that they had kept observation from an unmarked police vehicle, it was held that the defence was entitled to information relating to the surveillance and to the colour, make and model of the vehicle.

The defence will therefore be entitled to ask Kate and Larry about these matters.

Note

1   But for what happened in the case on which this question is based, see Farson, D, *The Gilded Gutter Life of Francis Bacon*, 1993, Chapter 12.

Question 50

Cedric was employed by AB Ltd, a company engaged in the manufacture of meat pies. One day, his hand was caught in a mincing machine and he suffered grave injuries, because of which he decided to sue AB Ltd for compensation. When AB Ltd learned of the accident, they obtained a report from an independent safety expert in accordance with their usual practice when accidents occurred on their premises. Copies of this report were sent to the board of directors and to the legal department of the company.

Cedric wrote a letter to Derek, his solicitor, setting out his account of the accident in which he admitted that he had not complied with safety regulations when operating the mincing machine because he had been 'chatting someone up' at the time. Enid, Derek's secretary, took a photocopy of this letter and gave it to her lover Fabian, who is a director of AB Ltd.

Cedric wishes to obtain a copy of the safety expert's report. He suspects that his employers may have obtained a copy of his letter to Derek and is afraid that they may use it against him. Advise Cedric.

Answer plan

A relatively straightforward question about privilege. You need to discuss the following points:

- the safety expert's report – legal professional privilege in relation to third party communications;
- is Cedric's admission privileged?;
- will AB Ltd be allowed to use the photocopy of the letter sent by Cedric?

Answer

Communications which are made between a party or his legal advisers and a third party will be privileged provided the dominant purpose in making the communications was to obtain or provide advice in connection with pending or contemplated litigation. The requirement that advice in such a connection be the dominant purpose of the communication was established by *Waugh v British Railways Board* (1980). In that case, the claimant sued the defendants under the Fatal Accidents Act 1976 in respect of the death of her husband which had occurred in a railway collision. Her advisers wished to obtain discovery of an internal report prepared by the defendants for submission to the railway inspectorate and the ministry. Another object of the report was to provide information for the Board's solicitor to enable him to advise the Board. The House of Lords held that the Board was not entitled to claim privilege in respect of this report. To attract such privilege, preparation for the purposes of intended or contemplated litigation had to be 'at least the dominant purpose' for bringing a document into existence. But the report in *Waugh's* case had been prepared not only for the purpose of litigation but for other major purposes in relation to the safe running of railways. Submission to the solicitor had not been shown to be the dominant purpose of making the report; therefore it was not privileged.

Whether such a document is privileged will turn on the facts of each individual case. But, on the facts given, it looks as if assistance in litigation was only one of the objects of AB Ltd in obtaining the safety expert's report, and that the maintenance of safe working practices was equally important. The report is thus unlikely to be privileged.

All communications between solicitor and client made for the purpose of giving or receiving legal advice are privileged (*Waugh v British Railways Board* (1980)). It is clear that the letter which Cedric wrote to Derek was privileged for this reason.

However, privilege attaches only to the original letter sent by Cedric. In principle, secondary evidence of a privileged document is admissible. Thus, in *Calcraft v Guest* (1898), it was held that the defendant was entitled to put in evidence copies which he had made of certain proofs of evidence. By r 31.20 of the Civil Procedure Rules 1998, inadvertently disclosed privileged documents may only be used with the consent of the court. But, this document has not been *inadvertently* disclosed. Use of a document that is an admissible piece of evidence may be restrained on the ground that it contains confidential information. In *Lord Ashburton v Pape* (1913), the claimant opposed the defendant's discharge from bankruptcy. The defendant obtained by trickery a number of relevant documents from a clerk in the employment of the claimant's solicitors. Having obtained them, he took copies. The Court of Appeal held that the claimant was entitled to an injunction requiring the defendant to deliver up all originals and restraining him from making any use of the copies or of the information which he had obtained. Provided the privileged documents or copies of them have not already been used as secondary evidence in the litigation, the party entitled to the privilege will be able to obtain a similar injunction (*Goddard v Nationwide Building Society* (1987)).

Cedric's solicitors will therefore be able to obtain an injunction restraining the use by AB Ltd of the photocopy which was given to Fabian and of the information contained in it.

INDEX